A Hybrid Approach to Teaching Chinese through Digital Humanities, CALL, and Project-Based Learning

A Hybrid Approach to Teaching Chinese through Digital Humanities, CALL, and Project-Based Learning presents an exposition of current thinking, research, and best practices in Computer-Assisted Language Learning (CALL), Digital Humanities (DH), and Project-Based Language Learning (PBLL) in the context of teaching Chinese as a foreign language (TCFL).

It proposes integrating CALL and DH into PBLL to form a Digital Humanities–Augmented Technology-Enhanced Project-Based Language Learning (DATEPBLL) approach to transform student learning. By combining DH pedagogy and CALL technology with PBLL, the approach takes advantage of their synergies, which enables instructors to help students develop linguistic and cultural competency as well as 21st century skills. Case studies and best practices from experienced Chinese language teachers are presented to demonstrate the value of the DATEPBLL approach. This is the first volume that covers all three fields and makes a strong case for the importance of incorporating CALL, DH, and PBLL for effective language learning.

Written for professionals in language education, including educators, curriculum designers and developers, graduate students, publishers, government personnel, and researchers, the book provides theoretical insights and practical applications of CALL, DH, and PBLL.

Dongdong Chen is Professor of Chinese and Director of the Chinese Program in the Department of Languages, Literatures and Cultures at Seton Hall University, USA.

Routledge Studies in Chinese as a Foreign Language
Series Editor: Chris Shei
Swansea University, UK
Der-lin Chao
New York University, USA

The series will strive to produce not only scholarly books investigating aspects of Chinese language learning such as pedagogy, policy, materials and curriculum, assessment, psychology and cognition, aptitude and motivation, culture and society, media and technology and so on, but also textbooks drawing from results of this research and compiled following the pedagogical models suggested by these studies and taking into consideration the individual and social factors related to Chinese language learning uncovered by this series of research. The two strands of books published within this series complement and strengthen each other in their academic achievement and practical implication.

Teaching Chinese by Culture and TV Drama
Lingfen Zhang

Reading in Chinese as an Additional Language
Learners' Development, Instruction, and Assessment
Edited by Liu Li and Dongbo Zhang

Online Chinese Learning
Exploring Effective Language Learning Strategies
Lijuan Chen

Using Chinese Classics for Intercultural Communicative Competence
A Teacher's Guide
Jinai Sun, Xuehua Xiang, and Li Ye

A Hybrid Approach to Teaching Chinese through Digital Humanities, CALL, and Project-Based Learning
Dongdong Chen

For more information about this series, please visit: www.routledge.com/outledge-Studies-in-Chinese-as-a-Foreign-Language/book-series/RSCFL

'Exciting to know that such innovations are occurring in the Chinese-language teaching world! This volume contributes significantly to the professional language-teaching literature.'

Fredricka L. Stoller, *Emerita Professor, Applied Linguistics/TESL, Northern Arizona University, Flagstaff, AZ*

'This book stands out for its solidity and meticulous attention to detail. Dr. Chen skillfully weaves together theoretical insights and practical applications, providing a valuable resource that is both comprehensive and accessible to language educators and researchers alike.'

Yong Ho, *author of* Aspects of Discourse Structure in Mandarin Chinese, *Former Head of Chinese Program, UN*

'By seamlessly blending the latest research in Computer-Assisted Language Learning (CALL) and Digital Humanities (DH), this book serves as a comprehensive guide for educators seeking to enhance the Project-based Learning (PBL) approach when teaching foreign languages in general and Chinese in particular.'

Artem Kalyanov, *CALL Researcher, DLIFLC, Monterey, CA*

A Hybrid Approach to Teaching Chinese through Digital Humanities, CALL, and Project-Based Learning

Dongdong Chen

LONDON AND NEW YORK

Designed cover image: gremlin via Getty Images

First published 2025
by Routledge
4 Park Square, Milton Park, Abingdon, Oxon OX14 4RN

and by Routledge
605 Third Avenue, New York, NY 10158

Routledge is an imprint of the Taylor & Francis Group, an informa business

© 2025 Dongdong Chen

The right of Dongdong Chen to be identified as author of this work has been asserted in accordance with sections 77 and 78 of the Copyright, Designs and Patents Act 1988.

All rights reserved. No part of this book may be reprinted or reproduced or utilised in any form or by any electronic, mechanical, or other means, now known or hereafter invented, including photocopying and recording, or in any information storage or retrieval system, without permission in writing from the publishers.

Trademark notice: Product or corporate names may be trademarks or registered trademarks, and are used only for identification and explanation without intent to infringe.

British Library Cataloguing-in-Publication Data
A catalogue record for this book is available from the British Library

Library of Congress Cataloging-in-Publication Data
Names: Chen, Dongdong (Linguist), author.
Title: A hybrid approach to teaching Chinese through digital humanities, CALL, and project-based learning / Dongdong Chen.
Description: Abingdon, Oxon ; New York, NY : Routledge, 2024. | Series: Routledge studies in Chinese as a foreign language | Includes bibliographical references and index.
Identifiers: LCCN 2024016734 (print) | LCCN 2024016735 (ebook) | ISBN 9781032272764 (hardback) | ISBN 9781032272757 (paperback) | ISBN 9781003292081 (ebook)
Subjects: LCSH: Chinese language—Study and teaching—Foreign speakers. | Chinese language—Study and teaching—Computer-assisted instruction for foreign speakers. | Digital humanities. | Project method in teaching.
Classification: LCC PL1065 .C5624 2024 (print) | LCC PL1065 (ebook) | DDC 495.180078/5—dc23/eng/20240525
LC record available at https://lccn.loc.gov/2024016734
LC ebook record available at https://lccn.loc.gov/2024016735

ISBN: 978-1-032-27276-4 (hbk)
ISBN: 978-1-032-27275-7 (pbk)
ISBN: 978-1-003-29208-1 (ebk)

DOI: 10.4324/9781003292081

Typeset in Times New Roman
by Apex CoVantage, LLC

To My Students

Contents

List of Figures and Tables   *xii*
Acknowledgments   *xiii*
List of Acronyms and Abbreviations   *xv*

1 Introduction   1

    1.1 Introduction 1
    1.2 Background to CALL and DH 1
    1.3 Learning Theories and Theoretical Accounts of Second Language Acquisition 6
    1.4 Major Players in Language Learning 8
    1.5 Research Focus 12
    1.6 Overview and Significance of the Book 12

2 Computer-Assisted Language Learning   19

    2.1 Introduction 19
    2.2 What Is CALL? 20
    2.3 The CALL Development 21
    2.4 The History of Chinese CALL 24
    2.5 Different Stages of CALL 27
    2.6 Benefits of CALL 29
    2.7 Issues Associated With CALL 34
    2.8 Conclusion 36

3 Digital Humanities   43

    3.1 Introduction 43
    3.2 What Is DH? 45
    3.3 What Do Digital Humanists Do? 48
    3.4 The Historical Developments of DH 51

   3.5 *The Accomplishments of DH* *58*
   3.6 *Conclusion* *65*

4 Project-Based Learning   71

   4.1 *Introduction* *71*
   4.2 *What Is PBL?* *71*
   4.3 *Development From PBL to PBLL* *73*
   4.4 *Literature Review of PBLL and Its Benefits* *76*
   4.5 *Standards for Foreign Language Learning and 21st Century Skills* *81*
   4.6 *Integrating CALL and DH via PBL to Address Standards* *84*
   4.7 *Conclusion* *87*

5 Case Studies   92

   5.1 *Introduction* *92*
   5.2 *Project Framework* *93*
   5.3 *Case 1: Gaming Project* *97*
          5.3.1 Background *98*
          5.3.2 Developing a Game for the Chinese Language Classroom *100*
          5.3.3 Engaging Students to Create Matching Games *104*
          5.3.4 Summary *108*
   5.4 *Case 2: Podcast Project* *108*
          5.4.1 Background *109*
          5.4.2 Engaging Students to Develop Podcasts *110*
          5.4.3 Summary *116*
   5.5 *Case 3: e-Portfolio Project* *117*
          5.5.1 Background *118*
          5.5.2 Engaging Preservice Teachers to Produce e-Portfolios *120*
          5.5.3 Summary *130*
   5.6 *Conclusion* *131*

6 Best Practices in PBLL From Other Chinese Language Teachers   141

   6.1 *Introduction* *141*
   6.2 *Exemplary Projects in K–12 Settings* *141*
   6.3 *Exemplary Projects in University Contexts* *144*
          6.3.1 Calligraphy Project *144*

      6.3.2 Website Development Project 149
      6.3.3 Music and Culture Project 156
  6.4 Conclusion 160

7   **DATEPBLL: From Here to Where?**   165

  7.1 Introduction 165
  7.2 Generative AI Tools: Risks and Opportunities 166
  7.3 Implications of the DATEPBLL Approach 170
  7.4 Future Directions of the DATEPBLL Approach 175

Author Index   *183*
Subject Index   *185*

Figures and Tables

Figures

3.1	Cirrus of the Frequent Words Used in Chapter 2	61
3.2	Cirrus of the Frequent Words Used in Chapter 3	61
4.1	Relationship Between DH and CALL	85
4.2	The DATEPBLL Approach	86
5.1	Interface of the Matching Game with Four Modules	103
5.2	Interface of Matching Character to English	103
6.1	Students' Calligraphy Created with Unusual Materials	148
6.2	Home Page of a Website Created by Two Students	153

Tables

2.1	Outline of CALL Development	24
3.1	Information about Chapter 2 and Chapter 3 Generated by Voyant Tools	61
5.1	PBL Five-Stage Framework (Stoller and Myers, 2019)	97
5.2	Eight Matching Pairs	102
5.3	Student Reflections on the Matching Game Project	107
5.4	Scores of Preservice Teachers' e-Portfolios	123
5.5	Perceptions of Preservice Teachers on Learning and Viewpoints About Benefits	125
5.6	Perceptions of Preservice Teachers About Accomplishments Obtained	127
5.7	A Summary of Three Projects	131
6.1	PROJECT (Meng, 2022)	142
6.2	Language Requirements for Four Topics (Lee et al., 2023a)	151
6.3	Final Project Grading Rubric (Lee et al., 2023b)	152
6.4	Class Survey (Xu, 2023)	157
6.5	Students' Work (Xu, 2023)	158
7.1	Selected Benefits of LLMs for Students (MLA-CCCC, 2023)	169
7.2	Selected Benefits of LLMs for Teachers (MLA-CCCC, 2023)	169

Acknowledgments

Many people have contributed in different ways to my completion of this project. Let me start with Mary Balkun and Marta Deyrup because they aroused my interest in Digital Humanities by including me in Seton Hall's DH Faculty Learning Group that they initiated. Participating in numerous group discussions of various issues over the years cultivated my understanding of DH, resulting in my journey to search for the relationship between DH and CALL for language teaching. I extremely appreciate Mary's leadership as well as her constant and strong support throughout the entire process. Rachael Warmington, who is enthusiastic in running the DH Faculty Learning Group, reinforces my interest in DH. I thank her for her DH expertise and willingness to share.

The Teaching, Learning, and Technology Center of Seton Hall University awarded me two Faculty Innovation Grants, a SHUmobile Grant, and a SHU DH Faculty Fellowship, which offered me the fortune to work on a number of technology projects with an excellent team of administrators, instructional designers, and developers, including Shayle Adrian, Lisa Bond, Renee M. Cicchino, Paul E. Fisher, Thomas McGee, Kate Sierra, Michael Soupios, and a few no longer working there.

I want to deeply acknowledge Fredricka Stoller whose project framework (developed with CeAnn Myers) is adopted in the current book. Not only has she profoundly inspired my work, but she has also kindly read my chapters, offering many constructive comments and thought-provoking questions. Furthermore, she corrected my mistakes, including the one in the book title.

I wholeheartedly thank Michael Hegedus, Melvin Chih-Jen Lee, Liping Meng, Jenny Yan Qin, Peisong Xu, and Kang Zhou for their generosity in allowing me to include their best practices in Project-Based Language Learning. Their expertise in teaching Chinese has benefitted me a great deal.

The following colleagues read some of my writings in different stages: Mary Balkun, Jun Da, Michael Hegedus, Yong Ho, Artem Kalyanov, Melvin Chih-Jen Lee, Robyn Lemanski, Victor Mair, Liping Meng, Jenny Yan Qin, Kate Sierra, Peisong Xu, and Kang Zhou. Their feedback tremendously helped me refine my thinking and writing.

My colleagues at the Department deserve special thanks for intellectual conversations: Diana Alvarez-Amell, David Beneteau, Frederick J. Booth, Deborah

A. Brown, Jorge Lopez-Cortina, Matthew R. Escobar, Cynthia W. Fellows, Anne Giblin Gedacht, Charles A. George, Anna Kuchta, Pak-Wah E. Leung, Michael C. Mascio, Anne Mullen-Hohl, Eric W. Pennington, Jose M. Prieto, Victoria Rivera-Cordero, Shigeru Osuka, Jeffrey Rice, Carlos Rodriguez, Gabriella Romani, Peter Shoemaker, Michael Stone, Jessica Wilson, Youssef Yacoubi, and Daniel Zalacain. I am grateful to the Interlibrary Loan Service, Walsh Library, which delivered my requested articles and books faster than I expected. I am indebted to the Provost's Office for granting me a sabbatical leave and one course release for conducting research and writing the book.

I must thank Andrea Hartill, senior publisher, Iola Ashby, editorial assistant, and Christina McGinn, copyeditor, at Routledge, who have guided me from submission of the book proposal to the completion of the manuscript. Without their support, this project would not have been possible.

Finally, my deepest gratitude goes to my family and friends, whose unfailing love is the backbone that I can always count on. I am thankful for their patience and tolerance with me.

Acronyms and Abbreviations

AAPI	Asian Americans and Pacific Islanders
ACTFL	American Council on the Teaching of Foreign Languages
ACH	Association for Computers and the Humanities
ADHO	Alliance of Digital Humanities Organization
AI	Artificial Intelligence
ALLC	Association for Literary and Linguistic Computing
BIE	Buck Institute for Education
CAI	Computer-Assisted Instruction
CALI	Computer-Accelerated Language Instruction
CALL	Computer-Assisted Language Learning
CALICO	Computer-Assisted Language Instruction Consortium
CCCC	Conference on College Composition and Communication
CCSS	Common Core State Standards
ChatGPT	Chat Generative Pre-Trained Transformer
CBI	Content-Based Instruction
CBLT	Competency-Based Language Teaching
CD-ROM	Compact Disc Read-Only Memory
CEFR	Common European Framework of Reference for Languages
CHum	*Computers and the Humanities*
CLASS	Chinese Language Association of Secondary-Elementary Schools
CLIL	Content and Language Integrated Learning
CLT	Communicative Language Teaching
CLTA-GNY	Chinese Language Teachers Association of Greater New York
CMC	Computer-Mediated Communication
CPLL	Computer-Participated Language Learning
DATEPBLL	Digital Humanities–Augmented Technology-Enhanced Project-Based Language Learning; DH–Augmented Technology-Enhanced PBLL DH-Augmented Technology-Enhanced Project-Based Language Learning
DH	Digital Humanities
DHML	Digital Humanities Modern Languages
DHQ	*Digital Humanities Quarterly*
DSH	*Digital Scholarship in the Humanities*

EADH	European Association for Digital Humanities
EAP	English for Academic Purposes
EFL	English as a foreign language
ENIAC	Electronic Numerical Integrator and Computer
ESL	English as a Second language
EUROCALL	European Association of Computer-Assisted Language Learning
GDP	Gross Domestic Product
GIS	Geographic Information System
HTML	HyperText Markup Language
ICT	Information and Communication Technology
ISO	International Organization for Standardization
JITP	*Journal of Interactive Technology and Pedagogy*
JTCLT	*Journal of Technology and Chinese Language Teaching*
LLCC	Literary and Linguistic Computing Center
LLC	*Literary and Linguistic Computing*
L1	First Language
L2	Second Language
LLM	Large Language Model
MALL	Mobile-Assisted Language Learning
MIT	Massachusetts Institute of Technology
MLA	Modern Language Association
Mphil	Master of Philosophy
NITLE	National Institute for Technology and Liberal Education
PBI	Project-Based Instruction
PBL	Project-Based Learning
PBLL	Project-Based Language Learning
PLATO	Program Logic for Automated Teaching Operation
PPT	PowerPoint
SGML	Standard Generalized Markup Language
SLA	Second Language Acquisition
TCFL	Teach Chinese as a Foreign Language
TCHE	*The Chronicle of Higher Education*
TCLT	Technology and Chinese Language Teaching
TEFFPBLL	Technology-Enhanced Form-Function Project-Based Language Learning
TEI	Text Encoding Initiative
TELL	Technology-Enhanced Language Learning
TEPBLL	Technology-Enhanced Project-Based Language Learning
TESOL	Teachers of English to Speakers of Other Languages
THATCamp	The Humanities and Technology Camp
TICCIT	Time-Shared Interactive Computer Controlled Information Television
TBLT	Task-Based Language Teaching
UCLA	University of California, Los Angeles
UG	University Grammar

UIUC	University of Illinois at Urbana-Champaign
WIDA	World-Class Instructional Design and Assessment Consortium
XML	eXtensible Markup Language
ZPD	Zone of Proximal Development

1 Introduction

1.1 Introduction

This book attempts to examine Computer-Assisted Language Learning (CALL), Digital Humanities (DH), and Project-Based Language Learning (PBLL) in the context of teaching Chinese as a foreign language (TCFL). CALL means to empower language learning via the assistance of computer technology, while DH aims to enhance the teaching and research of humanities with digital pedagogy and digital tools. Historically, it was with computer aid that exploration of language teaching or text analysis was initiated and that computing technologies, while developing on their own, drove the exploration forward, ultimately leading to CALL and DH as two separate fields. PBLL is an approach that promotes active learning by engaging students with meaningful real-world projects, which has been widely applied for teaching foreign and second languages. Given that both CALL and DH rely on technology, questions arise naturally. Are there any commonalities between CALL and DH in regard to language education? If yes, what are they? If not, to what extent do they differ from each other? For language instructors, are CALL and DH the same thing, or are they two different approaches? Are both needed for second language instruction, on the whole, and TCFL, in particular? In what way are CALL and DH related to PBLL? What can CALL and DH do to enhance PBLL? These questions have long been puzzling to me, and searching for an answer to them is the objective of this work. In the sections that follow, I will first provide a technological background about CALL and DH and then theoretical accounts of second language acquisition. I next describe characteristics of major players in language learning, including learners, instructors, and teaching pedagogy. I will finally present the research focus of the current work, followed by an overview and significance of the book.

1.2 Background to CALL and DH

CALL has been exploited since the beginning of computing (e.g., Lian, 2008). Reinhardt and Oskoz (2021) attributed the origin of CALL to the post-WWII computer revolution, programmed learning, and applied linguistics to promote language education. Levy (1997) defined CALL as "the search for and study of applications of the computer in language teaching and learning" (p. 1). In Morton et al. (2008), CALL is defined as "an approach in language learning in which a computer presents material to the learner or where the computer is used as a tool to aid language learning" (p. 239). Others referred to CALL as computer applications used for language teaching and learning (e.g., Lewis, 2016) or software designed specifically for teaching English language skills to English-as-a-second language (ESL) students (e.g., Gitsaki, 2009). Along with development of computing technologies and improvement of language education, CALL has evolved from a means to aid language instruction into an independent discipline involving psychology, sociology, natural language processing, linguistics, artificial intelligence, human-computer dialogue, and computing (e.g., Thomas et al., 2012). Different acronyms were used before CALL was adopted (e.g., Davies & Higgins, 1982; Davies et al., 2012; Kalyaniwala & Ciekanski, 2021). There are other terms such as Mobile-Assisted Language Learning (MALL) coined by Chinnery (2006) and used by many other scholars (e.g., Arvanitis & Krystalli, 2021) or Technology-Enhanced Language Learning (TELL) preferred to cover different technologies (e.g., Shrum & Glisan, 2010). Levy and Hubbard (2005) argued for the general label *CALL* because of the unique nature of language learning, the necessity for a global term, and the consistency of the name used for international community or professional organizations. I will, agreeing with Levy and Hubbard (2005) and Hubbard (2021), use *CALL* in this book. Intermittently, words like *computer, computer technology, technology, and information communication technology* may be used interchangeably to include hardware such as network, cables, mobile devices, and software programs and apps, where computers may sometimes not be involved directly.

It is generally recognized that the first computer came into being in the 1940s for military and scientific purposes. Computing technology has since then been upgraded constantly and tremendously, starting in the 1950s with the form of a mainframe as big as a large building. In the late 1970s, microcomputers or personal computers were manufactured, resulting in a microcomputer boom associated with multimedia technologies in the 1980s. Following that development appeared laptops, tablet PCs, and mobile devices one after another. In the current century, smartphones of different brands contain various social media applications that are made easily accessible with the advent of the World Wide Web and Wi-Fi services. Information technology has become omnipresent in our daily lives, from receiving and sending emails to pursuing a bachelor's or master's or even a doctorate degree online, or from booking an airline flight to getting a boarding pass in advance. In terms of technology for language education, thanks to the continuous advance of hardware and software, on the one hand, and the growing demands for more effective ways to empower language learning, on the other hand, there are innumerable CALL programs developed that have played significant roles for both instructors and learners. In fact, computer apps and tools are available for almost anything that a language teacher can imagine or wish for, ranging from instruction to assessment. For more details about the chronological development of the computer, see a brief history of computer science (https://cs.illinois.edu/about/history-timeline), provided by the Department of Computer Science of the University of Illinois at Urban Champaign (UIUC), or the link provided by Computer History Museum, (www.computerhistory.org/timeline). There have been many volumes that introduce CALL or examine how CALL technologies are applied to enhance language studies. Among others, see the collections as edited by Zhang and Barber (2008), Farr and Murray (2016), Chapelle and Sauro (2017), Ducate and Arnold (2019), and Ziegler and González-Lloret (2022). In TCFL, for a recent survey of technologies applied to the teaching of Chinese, see Da and Zheng (2018), Zhang (2019), and Liu and Da (2022). For the latest research on the teaching and learning of Chinese with online technologies, see Tseng and Gao (2021) and Liu (2022a, 2022b).

While CALL was thriving, a buzz word, Digital Humanities, spread with the publication of Schreibman et al.'s (2004) book *A Companion to Digital Humanities*, resulting in an innovative way of teaching and researching humanities. The emergence of DH, its groundbreaking approach, and myriad digital tools necessitated simultaneously understanding what DH is and what DH is not (e.g., Burdick et al., 2012; Carter, 2013; Terras et al., 2013). In fact, defining DH has been challenging since the very beginning. In 2009, the Day of Digital Humanities project was created by Jason Heppler, a historian of modern America and Digital Engagement Librarian, University of Nebraska, to solicit answers to the question "What is Digital Humanities?" By the year 2014, the online platform, (https://whatisdigitalhumanities.com/), prompted over 800 submissions. Following are a few quotes taken randomly from participants in the project (For the printouts, see the chapter "Selected definitions from the Day of Digital Humanities: 2009–2012" of the book *Defining Digital Humanities: A Reader* by Terras et al. (2013, pp. 279–287):

- Digital humanities are an interdisciplinary field working on the relations between humanities and digital technology.

  —Ana Guzman

- Digital Humanities is the use of digital technologies for the pursuit of a greater understanding of the humanities.

  —John Wall

- The use of technology to make teaching, research, and learning better, whether through new tools and ways of asking questions, or innovative new forms of scholarly presentation and communication.

  —Alan G. Pike

- DH stands for a wide variety of disparate practices, methodologies, and ways of communicating that take advantage of technology in order to enable and encourage the act of thinking deeply and critically about life. From this perspective, DH is the name given to the work of the most open-minded and courageous humanists working today.

  —Stewart Varner

The differences in this sampling of how participants answer the question vary depending on the individual's educational goal, need, audience, and the resultant parameters of the DH "field" and/or on which side of the field s/he stands (e.g., Carter, 2013; Terras et al., 2013). Despite the different views of what DH is, there is no doubt that DH aims to teach and make inquiries of subjects that typically belong to the domain of humanities by employing digital technologies in hopes to advance learning and understanding of the subject matter as well as to preserve and present human cultures and heritages for scholarship. What makes DH distinct from traditional humanities is not merely the employment of technologies but, more crucially, its innovative approach towards teaching and research to achieve its unique objectives: building, collaborating, and sharing (e.g., Ramsay, 2013a, 2013b; Davis et al., 2020). By building or making, it emphasizes creation or production rather than consumption of texts or materials while teaching or researching (e.g., Ramsay, 2013b). If building is underscored with a focus on process rather than product, collaborating with others becomes indispensable in order to make a thing or get work done efficiently (e.g., Harris, 2013). The result of building through collaboration—the outcomes or "reproduction of knowledge"—should be disseminated openly with others to benefit the community (Sample, 2011; Davis et al., 2020). These essentials of DH are regarded as part of "digital pedagogy," which also includes the concepts of openness, play, practice, and student agency in the teaching process, as addressed by Davis et al. (2020). Other than the previously mentioned primary traits, DH's potential to transform the way faculty teach and research has been recognized (e.g., Svensson, 2009; Balkun & Deyrup, 2020; Cro, 2020; Chen, 2021).

According to Burdick et al. (2012), the term *Digital Humanities* has evolved from *Humanities Computing*, which originated from a pioneering work that started in 1949. Italian Jesuit scholar Roberto Busa began to compile words used in the writings of St. Thomas Aquinas in hopes that other scholars could conduct text searches for linguistic or literary analysis (e.g., Busa, 1980). Collaborating with IBM computing experts, Busa and his associates worked for around 33 years, eventually producing *Index Thomisticus*, a database containing 179 texts centering around Thomas Aquinas, with "11 million words, each morphologically tagged and lemmatized" (https://itreebank.marginalia.it/view/projet.php). Such a magnificent accomplishment would not have been completed without the involvement of computers. The subsequent success of the innovative approach and its impact drew enormous attention from humanists of different disciplines. "'Digital Humanities' became the prominent name for the field" (Vanhoutte, 2013, p. 120) in 2004 when it was adopted to assure an accurate interpretation of the work being done. Related to the name change, its scope of coverage became much broader, as manifested by the call for proposals for Digital Humanities 2009, a primarily Humanities Computing conference. The call invited submissions of abstracts on "any aspect of digital humanities, broadly defined to encompass the common ground between information technology and problems in humanities research and teaching." The special subjects that fall in the "common ground" include the following (Svensson, 2009, para 12–15):

- text analysis, corpora, corpus linguistics, language processing, language learning

- libraries, archives, and the creation, delivery, management, and preservation of humanities digital resources
- computer-based research and computing applications in all areas of literary, linguistic, cultural, and historical studies, including electronic literature and interdisciplinary aspects of modern scholarship
- use of computation in such areas as the arts, architecture, music, film, theatre, new media, and other areas reflecting our cultural heritage
- research issues such as information design and modelling; the cultural impact of the new media; software studies; Human-Computer interaction
- the role of digital humanities in academic curricula
- digital humanities and diversity

As can be seen, DH is an interdisciplinary field that comprises social sciences like computer science, information science, library science, and traditional humanities disciplines including arts, architecture, film, history, linguistics, literature, music, philosophy, religion, etc. Applied with novel methodologies, digital tools facilitate and enhance the teaching of and research on humanities subjects through various activities such as developing platforms to create and publish humanities scholarship; analyzing digital and non-digital data to disseminate and preserve cultural heritage; and studying social, cultural, and historical contexts. In bringing together scholars and practitioners of different humanities disciplines, DH explores human culture and history, ethical and philosophical issues related to the use of digital technologies, and the impact of these technologies on society and culture more broadly. DH enables teachers to engage students to achieve richer learning-centered, experiential, and collaborative learning experiences.

Putting aside for the time being why "Humanities Computing" became Digital Humanities half a century after its first appearance, two points deserve attention. First, Busa's humanities computing project, which started in the late 1940s, was conducted and completed with the assistance of computer technology. Second, language learning was at the top of the special subject list identified in the call for proposal for a 2009 DH conference. These two are coincidently associated with the two primary aspects of CALL: computer technology and language education. It is technology and language education where CALL and DH intersect that becomes a fascinating theme for the current project.

Although language learning is included as part of DH by the call for proposal for the conference in 2009, that prestigious status seemed to fade away until Oskoz (2020), which shows that with digital pedagogy, instructors can involve students with technology-enabled projects to create products or make things, results of which are shared in a community. In curating digital pedagogy in different language-learning scenarios, Oskoz demonstrated that new digital tools can be utilized to empower teaching methods, enrich receptive and productive capacity, encourage multiple modes to convey meanings, and enhance learner agency, thereby creating a better learning experience. Following Pitman and Taylor's (2017) proposal for a "Critical DHML," Cro (2020) proposed a DH-inflected second language (DHL2) pedagogy, which incorporated DH into the language classroom, with DH's "focus on the pedagogical aspect of second language learning and acquisition" (p. 16). Inspired by the work mentioned, I take a further action by proposing a new model that combines DH and CALL and adds it to PBLL to form a Digital Humanities–Augmented Technology-Enhanced Project-Based Language Learning (DATEPBLL) approach. Through case studies and best practices from other Chinese language teachers, it will be demonstrated that DATEPBLL serves as an effective approach for language education.

1.3 Learning Theories and Theoretical Accounts of Second Language Acquisition

A general learning theory is a prerequisite for understanding how an instructor can help advance student learning of a foreign or second language. This is particularly important as far as CALL is concerned. Oxford (1995) outlined three theories when discussing the design of Intelligent CALL related to natural language parsing, sound and video production, and error analysis. First is the so-called novice-to-expert paradigm, derived from the information-processing model of learning. The theory assumes that a novice must go through an experiential learning process from (i) the novice stage, (ii) the advanced beginner stage, (iii) the competent stage, (iv) the proficient stage, to (v) the expert stage (Dreyfus & Dreyfus, 1986). After passing these different momentums, learners will develop schemata, that is, "connected knowledge structure," to draw upon (Oxford, 1995, p. 360). Second is constructivism, which stipulates that learners will be actively engaged in constructing meanings out of their learning experiences if they have a purpose for learning. This theory emphasizes "the development of rich, complex constructs built on interactions with the world" (p. 365). Thus, a person is said to know something only if s/he can make her/himself understood to others when delivering ideas. Third is individual difference theory (Skehan, 1989), which assumes that humans possess individual differences in personality traits, perceptual understanding, cognitive needs, beliefs, values, attitudes, etc. As such, each person learns in different ways. Since no single methodology will be useful for all, educators must, therefore, create a learning environment that can optimize learners' potential through some activities to provide diverse assistance, such as raising a leading question, offering a pictorial representation of a verbal explanation, conducting a cooperative learning activity, and saying an encouraging word (p. 366).

Ally (2008), on the other hand, suggested four different learning approaches when addressing the design of effective online learning materials: the behaviorist theory; the cognitivist theory; the constructivist theory; and the connectivism theory. Behaviorists consider learning as the formation of habits, in which external stimuli in the environment cause changes in observable behavior (e.g., Skinner, 1974). Language learning, under this view, is through exposure, repetition, and reinforcement. Cognitivists see learning as an internal process that involves the use of memory to think, abstract, reflect on the information, etc. Processing capacity, amount of effort, and existing knowledge structure determine how much one learns (Ally, 2008, p. 4). Constructivists regard learning as interpreting the information and the world and turning that information into personal knowledge. Under this view, learners are active players, constructing knowledge based on their observations while the instructor may only serve as advisor and facilitator rather than lecturer delivering knowledge through instruction. According to Ally, who cited Ertmer and Newby (1993), behaviorists' strategies can be used to teach the what (facts); cognitive strategies to teach the how (processes and principles); and constructivist strategies to teach the why (higher-level thinking). Unlike the previous three schools of thought, which emphasize the role of individuals in the learning process, connectivism, a theory proposed by Siemens (2004) for the digital age, presents a model of learning that acknowledges that in the society where there is an information explosion, "learning is no longer an internal, individualistic activity" (p. 6). As information is changing continually, learning becomes more complicated, with learners sometimes having to unlearn what they already learned and other times learning how to learn and evaluate new information (Ally, 2008, p. 4).

In their study on teaching students to learn to speak Chinese using technology, Shi and Stickler (2019) used three popular learning theories to analyze three types of CALL-enhanced instructional activities to support learners' speaking skills. The first type is the behaviorism-based drill-like websites for learning Chinese sounds targeting beginners or interactive software for improving learners' pronunciation intonation, and tone. The second type is the cognitivism-oriented interactions through *Moodle* (a learning management system). The third type is the socio-constructivism-rooted telecollaboration via social media such as *Skype* or *WeChat* to develop learners' authentic communication skills in the real world. While it is not the purpose of this book to select a theoretical learning framework for a CALL study, I advocate that questions such as what kind of learning theories support CALL should be addressed. I next turn to the theories proposed to explain second language acquisition (SLA).

Four accounts are generally recognized as primary theories to explain how a second language (L2) is acquired: the behaviorist, the innatist, the cognitivist, and the sociocultural (e.g., Lightbown & Spada, 2013). The behaviorist perspective, represented by Nelson Brooks (1960) and Robert Lado (1964), considers the learning of an L2 as a process of forming habits, thus requiring of learners repeated mimicry and memorization of what is being learned. If learning a second language involves establishing new habits, then what about the habits of the first language, which L2 learners already formed? Will the old habits support or oppose the development of new habits? These questions pose challenges for the behaviorist account.

The innatist perspective (e.g., White, 2003; Cook, 2003), in contrast, recognizes the premise that University Grammar (UG), that is, "an innate component of the human mind that yields a particular language through interaction with presented experience" Chomsky (1986), still plays a role for L2 acquisition just as it does for first language (L1) acquisition. Along with the argument first proposed for L1 acquisition (Chomsky, 1965, 1981; Pinker, 1984, 1994), generative language acquisition researchers like Schwartz (1998) argue that L2 learners face a similar "logical problem"—a mismatch between the language input that learners are exposed to and the language attainment that they achieve. The solution to this problem is to lay a heavy burden on a biological endowment for language. Stephen Krashen's comprehensible input hypothesis (Krashen, 1982) is a popular model to reflect this idea in the L2 classroom. Like a baby who picks up a language if s/he is placed in a language environment, adults are also capable of learning an L2 if they are provided with sufficient input in the target language. According to Krashen, acquisition will occur when the input is "i +1," where "i" represents the learner's level of language while "1" is a step beyond the current level.

The cognitivist perspective is represented by several different hypotheses, one of which is the interaction hypothesis (e.g., Long, 1983, 1996; Gass, 1997). Michael Long argued that modified interaction, that is, interacting between learners and native speakers or learners with learners, and negotiation for meaning, that is, learners' negotiating for mutual comprehension through activities such as comprehension checks, clarification requests, and self-representation or paraphrase, are necessary mechanisms for making language comprehensible. Susan Gass (1997) claimed that language develops as a result of the interaction between the internal (general cognitive) characteristics of the child and the external environment, and language learning, like the learning of any other knowledge or skill, is based on the same cognitive processes. On the other hand, Swain (1985, 1988) argued that language output—the language produced by learners—is just as crucial for acquiring an L2 as language input is assumed to be for acquiring an L1. Therefore, to make language learning possible, learners must produce language.

The sociocultural perspective posits that L2 acquisition takes place as a result of social interactions and is facilitated by ongoing social intervention processes for learners (e.g., Aljaafreh & Lantolf, 1994; Lantolf & Pavlenko, 1995; Lantolf, 2012, 2000). This viewpoint is based on Vygotsky's (1978) theory that learning occurs through interactions within the learner's zone of proximal development (ZPD), the optimal environment in which a learner can reach their maximum potential with guidance and support from a more knowledgeable person. In applying ZPD to L2 learning, Aljaafreh and Lantolf (1994) found that learners who received assistance from a more proficient speaker during a task performed better than when working alone, suggesting that the ZPD is crucial in L2 learning. According to Lantolf (2012), the central tenet of the sociocultural theory is that higher forms of thinking, such as problem-solving and critical thinking, emerge from interactions within the social and cultural environment around us (p. 58). L2 learners need to work with others through interaction to jointly co-construct the L2 knowledge and skills.

1.4 Major Players in Language Learning

Technology is regarded as an initiator and catalyst for CALL. However, as noted by scholars, merely being a vehicle to deliver instruction does not influence student achievement (e.g., Clark, 1983, 1994) neither does it make a teacher better (e.g., Thomas et al., 2012). Likewise, technology cannot make scholarship innovative without reasonable research questions or sound and solid methodology. I argue that involved in language teaching and learning are several critical players other than technologies. They are learners, instructors, and language teaching approaches and methods, though there are other additional factors. It is, thus, necessary to review each of the primary stakeholders. I will start with learners.

Contemporary language learners are among the group dubbed as "digital natives" (Prensky, 2001), or "millennials" (anyone born between 1981 and 1996), or "Generation Z" (those born from 1997 to 2012) (Dimock, 2019), who are different from the learners of previous generations in many aspects. Born and bred in the era of information, current students are keen on locating whatever they are interested in by Googling. They are skillful in multitasking, capable of, for example, listening to music or watching TV or *YouTube* videos while doing assignments simultaneously. They are also used to collaborative learning by working in a team with peers or native speakers, either in-person or online via *Skype, FaceTime, Zoom*, or *Teams*. In addition, the easy spread of information and globalization have greatly impacted modern student learning. Thanks to the internet, Wi-Fi service, broadband speed, and smartphones, an incident that has happened in the corner of a town or the rural area of a country can spread out to the entire world immediately through *Facebook, Instagram, Twitter,* or *YouTube*, as well as traditional media outlets like radios and TVs. Online translation tools such as *Google Translate* can make foreign language content comprehensible with just a few clicks. Easy access to language-related cultural information on the internet suggests that students may not need an instructor's help to satisfy their curiosity. In addition to consuming widely available online materials, the contemporary learners are also "creator(s) of digital texts and media" (Otto, 2017, p. 19). However, some observations have been made that while savvy with technology, today's students may not necessarily be competent in recognizing the value of technologies for professional and personal development (e.g., Dudeney & Hockly, 2016; Oskoz, 2020) or skillful at availing technology to their study when it comes to learning a language (e.g., Kuriscak & Luke, 2009; Chen, 2010, 2013, 2021; Cro, 2020).

Gardner (1993) proposed the "multiple intelligences" model, which believes that humans are all intelligent in different aspects and that intelligence can be developed and strengthened through training and practice. Richards and Rodgers (2014), who cite Armstrong's (1999) memory tags for each intelligence (i.e., "word smart," "number/reasoning smart," "picture smart," "body smart," "music smart," "people smart," "self-smart," "nature smart" and "existence smart"), point out that language learners may have "personal intelligence profiles" consisting of different natural human talents (p. 231). Similar to this model is Oxford's (1995) differentiation of six types of learner based on learning styles. They are (i) concrete-sequential learners, who desire for being instructed on what and how to do any work; (ii) intuitive learners, who enjoy figuring out things by themselves; (iii) thinking-oriented learners, who appreciate factual feedback; (iv) feeling-oriented learners, who need emotional support; (v) analytical learners, who search for accurate and detailed information; and (vi) global learners, who crave meaning and breadth (pp. 366–367).

Diverse learners, whether defined in intelligence or learning style, present huge challenges to teachers. In that regard, instructors should be first willing to acknowledge and take into consideration "individual differences" (Skehan, 1989), such as personal traits, perceptual differences, and cognitive tendencies. They should also be ready to offer tailored education accordingly. On this vein, taking advantage of technologies can be an ideal option because digital tools may come to the rescue if they are appropriately utilized based on curricular objectives. To that end, instructors should learn to appreciate the instrumental role of computer technologies and be competent in using them. Fortunately, as predicated by Thomas et al. (2012), "there is little doubt that a new generation of language teachers and educators currently completing their entry-level qualifications and acquiring teaching experience will have grown up using many aspects of digital media in their daily lives" (p. 5).

Yes, language teachers nowadays act differently from those in the last century. Regarding the teaching philosophy, they are more egalitarian or democratic, willing to serve as a facilitator of learning rather than an authoritarian to transmit knowledge only, thereby endeavoring to embrace the learner-centered approach towards teaching. In terms of methodology, they are eager to try new ways to engage students in class so as to meet with their diverse backgrounds and needs. They are also more receptive towards new technology and brave enough to experiment with novel technology that may help learners with higher-order thinking and problem-solving abilities while building their basic linguistic skills. In studying instructors' views on effectiveness of technology for their ESL students, Holbah (2022) found that "teachers are ready to embrace changes and accept the usage of technology-mediated computer and mobile-assisted language learning (C/MALL) in online classes" and "they have encouraged and motivated students to support the usage of CALL and MALL in English language learning" (p. 620).

Over the history of language teaching pedagogy, a wide variety of teaching approaches and methods have been developed for L2 instruction (e.g., Larsen-Freeman & Anderson, 2013; Richards & Rodgers, 2014). Influential methods in the early days include grammar-translation and audio-lingualism. The former was derived from how Latin was taught during the 17th to the 19th centuries, and the latter found its origin in the Second World War when there was a demand for bilingual military personnel. Grammar-translation focuses on the instruction of grammatical structures, rote learning of rules, and training on translating the target language into the native language or vice versa while audio-lingualism, which aims to improve learners' aural and oral skills, assumes that repeated pattern drills will lead to automatic proficiency in the target language. Criticisms of these two methods lie in the fact that both only focus on students' "grammatical competence" (i.e., the ability to master the grammar rules and vocabulary) without developing their "communicative competence" (i.e., the ability to know the structures and meanings and the appropriateness of language use) (Hymes, 1972). It is for the goal of producing communicatively competent language learners "knowing how, when, and why, to say what to whom" (ACTFL, 2015, p. 13) that the communicative language teaching (CLT) approach was developed in the 1980s. CLT focuses on the meaning and the use of the target language. As a teaching approach, CLT has some fundamental principles, three of which are as follows: (i) "Activities that involve real communication are essential for language learning; (ii) Activities in which language is used for carrying out meaningful tasks promote learning; (iii) Language that is meaningful to the learner supports the learning process" (Richards & Rodgers, 2014, p. 174).

The tenets of CLT like the previous three principles became so popular that they have been widely adopted in teaching L2 languages in classrooms. Some CLT principles were subsequently further expanded in different ways, leading to a number of significant teaching approaches. For example, task-based language teaching (TBLT) organizes instruction around "tasks," which require learners to concentrate more on completing authentic tasks in a context rather than to focus on grammar rules. In so doing, learners acquire language forms (e.g., Nunan, 1989; Willis, 1996; Ellis, 2003; Van Den Branden, 2006; Willis &Willis, 2007). Content-Based Instruction (CBI) or Content and Language Integrated Learning (CLIL), a term popular in Europe (Richards & Rodgers, 2014, p. 116), assume that learners can acquire a target language if the content of a special subject matter is taught in that language, with each supporting the development of the other (Lyster, 2007), also known as the "two for one" (Lightbown & Spada, 2013). Other popular approaches include Competency-Based Language Teaching (CBLT), which builds instruction around the development of competency, and Cooperative Learning, which underscores the value of collaboration among peers while learning the language. Currently, TBLT is a more commonly implemented practice in language classes. Scholars like González-Lloret and Ortega (2014) and González-Lloret (2015) have proposed integrating technology in the design and implementation of tasks, leading to technology-mediated TBLT, which has made TBLT more efficient and effective in L2 classrooms.

It is worth pointing out that between the 1940s and 1990s, teaching professionals believed that there was a single, powerful method for teaching languages. This belief led to the development of various methods as educators searched for a "panacea" for language instruction. However, after decades of exploration, teachers realized that there is no one-size-fits-all pedagogy for teaching different languages. Each method has its own pros and cons, and each class is unique, with students having various learning objectives. This aligns with what Bransford et al. (2000) observed:

> Asking which teaching technique is best is analogous to asking which tool is best—a hammer, a screwdriver, a knife, pliers. In teaching as in carpentry, the selection of tools depends on the task at hand and the materials one is working with . . . There is no universal best teaching practice.
>
> (p. 22)

Ultimately, the choice of which pedagogy to incorporate in language instruction depends on the curricular goals, the group of learners, and the specific context. In the context of teaching Chinese as a foreign language with technology, Zhang (1998) considered CALL as a "cooperative enterprise between language pedagogy and computer technology" (p. 56). A similar statement is made in Zhang (2019). However, he suggests that effectiveness of both technology and pedagogy depends on "the integration of the relevant fields" (p. 504).

1.5 Research Focus

As CALL has been integrated in language instruction and learning for several decades, while DH, as an emerging pedagogy made suitable for different areas of humanities, is becoming more influential, I will present an exposition of current thinking, research, and best practices in the two fields with respect to language learning. With TCFL in mind, a cluster of questions related to CALL, DH, and PBLL will be examined; for example, how is CALL or DH or PBLL formed individually? What milestones are there in each of their historical developments? What are their accomplishments? What benefits can each bring to the teaching and learning of the Chinese language? Above all, the following specific questions are of great interest to explore for this book:

- What is the relationship between CALL and DH for language learning?
- What can bring CALL and DH together for language instruction?
- Why is it crucial to integrate CALL and DH in PBLL to enhance student learning?

As a qualitative study in the nature of action research, I will present my exploration of these questions through theoretical studies based on primary sources and classroom teaching practices. Using my case studies along with the projects designed and implemented by other experienced teachers, I will argue that it is time to apply both DH and CALL into language instruction because DH offers pedagogy, while CALL provides technology. A combination of both will bring in pedagogy and technology into a Chinese classroom. I also argue that PBLL, which has been widely applied in the study of foreign and second language, can be utilized to reconcile DH and CALL. I will argue that integrating DH and CALL through PBLL will address language learning standards and cultivate learners' 21st century skills while, at the same time, building their linguistic and cultural competency. Specifically, case studies of gaming development, podcast creation, and portfolio production will be presented to demonstrate the integrated roles of DH and CALL as they are added to PBLL to reinforce the learning of a target language while also fostering other skills critical to student success for the modern world. Other teachers' best practices in PBLL will, furthermore, show the value of this powerful approach. In addressing the preceding questions and presenting case studies and best practices, I will provide readers with an in-depth understanding of CALL, DH, and PBLL, the operation of a joint approach of the three, and the implications of this model for second language learning.

1.6 Overview and Significance of the Book

The organization of this book is as follows. In Chapter 2, I will examine CALL and provide its historical developments, benefits, and related issues. In Chapter 3, I will explore DH and review its historical developments. In Chapter 4, I will delve into details of PBL and describe its development from PBL to PBLL. On top of that, I will propose a Digital Humanities–Augmented Technology-Enhanced

Project-Based Language Learning (DATEPBLL) approach. I will argue why language education needs both CALL and DH and how they can be connected through PBLL. To illustrate this point, I will use case studies in Chapter 5 to demonstrate how the DATEPBLL approach can be applied in different classrooms. The first two cases involve students of an introductory Chinese course engaging in game development and podcast creation projects. The third case details how preservice teachers of Chinese produced e-portfolios about their journey towards a teaching profession. The presentation of case studies shows how the combination of CALL and DH with PBLL can enhance students' linguistic and cultural competence as well as advancing skills of preservice teachers of Chinese. Chapter 6 will describe six projects developed and implemented by other Chinese language instructors to further emphasize the value of the DATEPBLL approach. The final chapter will introduce emerging generative artificial intelligence technologies and discuss implications of the DATEPBLL approach for TCFL. The chapter will conclude with some possible tasks as future directions for promoting the DATEPBLL approach as well as practical suggestions for integrating it in the classroom.

As this book proposes combining CALL and DH with PBLL for teaching Chinese as a foreign language, it opens up a brand-new territory for exploring the roles of CALL, DH, and PBLL in an integrated perspective. By incorporating the three separate fields into one module, their potential synergies, that is, DH pedagogy, CALL technology, and the collaborative project work of PBLL, can be fully utilized for language education, not only reinforcing the strengths of PBLL but also enhancing DH and CALL individually. The case studies and projects from other Chinese language teachers to be presented in this book will demonstrate that this DATEPBLL approach is effective for TCFL and can be applied for teaching other foreign languages.

Representing the first examination of the integration of CALL, DH, and PBLL in TCFL, it will be of great use to a wide audience, including educators, curriculum designers and developers, graduate students, publishers, government personnel, and researchers, whose work or interests are related to any of these fields. In particular, the presentation of historical developments and the latest innovative applications of CALL, DH, or PBLL within the context of language teaching and learning will provide them with rich information and inspiration. The discussion and analysis of the issues in these fields will help them obtain a deeper understanding of each of these areas.

Language teachers who have already applied CALL or PBLL to their classroom may find this book particularly appealing, as it offers an in-depth examination and illustration of connecting CALL with PBLL to engage students with technology-enhanced projects. They will appreciate the case studies and projects executed in the real-world Chinese classrooms. Those who are familiar with CALL but not PBLL may also find the book useful because it will show how to design, plan, and execute technology-enhanced projects. For language teachers, the book will offer insights about the field of DH, particularly, how DH can enhance the potential of CALL and PBLL. The presentation of projects will guide these teachers as they explore ways to integrate both CALL and DH for improved learning outcomes.

14 Introduction

This book will provide a valuable resource for graduate students who are learning how to teach Chinese as a second language. The comprehensive discussion on the subject of CALL, DH, and PBLL, infused in L2 studies through PBLL, will fill a gap in the existing curriculum, which typically only introduces technology in language teaching to some extent. Both students and instructors will benefit from the updated information about the relationship between CALL, DH, PBLL in the context of TCFL. Furthermore, the case studies and presentation of projects will inspire and inform Chinese language teachers as they search for ways to integrate CALL, DH, and PBLL in their instructional practices to achieve better learning outcomes. The book will encourage them to appreciate and explore the value of the DATEPBLL approach by engaging their students with projects in their classrooms.

The book will provide information and inspiration to the administrators or those who are skeptical about the use of either CALL or DH or PBLL in second language classrooms. The chapters present the studies and research findings of the fields of CALL, DH, and PBLL, supported by the evidence from case studies in TCFL. The discussions offer a comprehensive understanding of the history, current state, and future prospects of CALL, DH, and PBLL in language education.

References

ACTFL. (2015). *World-readiness standards for learning languages*. ACTFL.
Aljaafreh, A., & Lantolf, J. P. (1994). Negative feedback as regulation and second language learning in the zone of proximal development. *The Modern Language Journal*, *78*(4), 465–483. https://doi.org/10.1111/j.1540-4781.1994.tb02064.x
Ally, M. (2008). Foundations of educational theory for online learning. In T. Anderson (Ed.), *Theory and practice of online learning* (pp. 15–44). Athabasca University Press. https://read.aupress.ca/read/6891c77c-3fed-4045-8073-60ed13f79712/section/8949f723-6904-454a-9704-6c241fb891ab#author1
Armstrong, T. (1999). *7 kinds of smart: Identifying and developing your multiple intelligences*. Plume Books.
Arvanitis, P., & Krystalli, P. (2021). Mobile assisted language learning (MALL): Trends from 2010 to 2020 using text analysis techniques. *European Journal of Education*, *4*(1), 13–22. https://intapi.sciendo.com/pdf/10.26417/ejls-2019.v5i1-191
Balkun, M. M., & Deyrup, M. M. (Eds.). (2020). *Transformative digital humanities: Challenges and opportunities*. Routledge. https://doi.org/10.4324/9780429399923
Bransford, J., Brown, A., & Cocking, R. (Eds.). (2000). *How people learn: Brain, mind, experience and school*. National Academy Press. https://doi.org/10.17226/9853
Brooks, N. (1960). *Language and language learning*. Harcourt Brace.
Burdick, A., Drucker, J., Lunenfeld, P., Presner, T., & Schnapp, J. (2012). *Digital humanities*. The MIT Press. https://doi.org/10.7551/mitpress/9248.001.0001
Busa, R. (1980). The annals of humanities computing: The index Thomisticus. *Computers and the Humanities*, *14*, 83–90. https://doi.org/10.1007/bf02403798
Carter, B. (2013). *Digital humanities, current perspectives, practices and research*. Emerald Publishing Limited. https://doi.org/10.1108/S2044-9968(2013)0000007006
Chapelle, C. A., & Sauro, S. (Eds.). (2017). *The handbook of technology and second language teaching and learning*. Wiley-Blackwell. https://doi.org/10.1002/9781118914069
Chen, D. (2010). Enhancing the learning of Chinese with Second Life. *Journal of Technology and Chinese Language Teaching*, *1*(1), 14–30. www.tclt.us/journal/2010v1n1/chen.pdf

Chen, D. (2013). What can a smartphone offer to learners of Chinese?. *Journal of Technology and Chinese Language Teaching*, *4*(2), 86–95. www.tclt.us/journal/2013v4n2/cheng.pdf

Chen, D. (2021). To game or not to game, that is not the question. In S. Jiang, N. Liang, J. Da, & S. Liu (Eds.), *Proceedings of the 11th international conference and workshops on technology and Chinese language teaching* (pp. 7–12). TCLT. www.tclt.us/tclt11/TCLT11_Proceedings.pdf

Chinnery, G. M. (2006). Going to the MALL: Mobile assisted language learning. *Language Learning & Technology*, *10*(1), 9–16. https://scholarspace.manoa.hawaii.edu/server/api/core/bitstreams/a5ff6d56-3f22-4d99-812b-fa964430fd4f/content

Chomsky, N. (1965). *Aspects of the theory of syntax*. MIT Press.

Chomsky, N. (1981). Principles and parameters in syntactic theory. In N. Hornstein & D. Lightfoot (Eds.), *Explanation in linguistics: The logical problem of language acquisition* (pp. 32–75). Longman.

Chomsky, N. (1986). *Knowledge of language: Its nature, origin, and use*. Praeger.

Clark, R. E. (1983). Reconsidering research on learning from media. *Review of Educational Research*, *53*(4), 445–459. https://doi.org/10.3102/00346543053004445

Clark, R. E. (1994). Media will never influence learning. *Educational Technology Research and Development*, *42*(2), 21–29. https://doi.org/10.1007/bf02299088

Cook, V. (2003). The poverty-of-the-stimulus argument and structure dependency in L2 users of English. *International Review of Applied Linguistics*, *41*(3), 201–221. https://doi.org/10.1515/iral.2003.009

Cro, M. A. (2020). *Integrating the digital humanities into the second language classroom: A Practical Guide*. Georgetown University Press. https://doi.org/10.2307/j.ctv19vbgjv

Da, J., & Zheng, Y. (2018). Technology and the teaching and learning of Chinese as a foreign language. In C. Ke (Ed.). *The Routledge handbook of Chinese second language acquisition* (pp. 432–447). Routledge.

Davies, G., Otto, S. E., & Rüschoff, B. (2012). Historical perspectives on CALL. In T. Michael, R. Hayo, & W. Mark (Eds.), *Contemporary computer-assisted language learning* (pp. 19–38). Bloomsbury.

Davies, G., & Higgins, J. (1982). *Computers, language and language learning*. Centre for Information on Language Teaching and Research. www.worldcat.org/title/1259496145

Davis, R. F., Gold, M. K., Harris, K. D., & Sayers, J. (Eds.). (2020). *Digital pedagogy in the humanities: Concepts, models, and experiments*. Modern Language Association. https://doi.org/10.1632/nwvf9766

Dimock, M. (2019). Defining generations: Where Millennials end and Generation Z begins. *Pew Research Center*, *17*(1), 1–7. http://www.pewresearch.org/fact-tank/2019/01/17/where-millennials-end-and-generation-z-begins/

Dreyfus, H. L., & Dreyfus, S. E. (1986). *Mind over machine*. The Free Press.

Ducate, L., & Arnold, N. (Eds.). (2019). *Engaging language learners through CALL: From theory and research to new directions in foreign language teaching* (3rd ed.). Equinox.

Dudeney, G., & Hockly, N. (2016). Literacies, technology and language teaching. In F. Farr & L. Murray (Eds.), *The Routledge handbook of language learning and technology* (pp. 141–152). Routledge.

Ellis, R. (2003). *Task-based language learning*. Oxford University Press.

Ertmer, P. A., & Newby, T. J. (1993). Behaviorism, cognitivism, constructivism: Comparing critical features from an instructional design perspective. *Performance Improvement Quarterly*, *6*(4), 50–70. https://doi.org/10.1111/j.1937-8327.1993.tb00605.x

Farr, F., & Murray, L. (Eds.). (2016). *The Routledge handbook of language learning and technology* (1st. ed.). Routledge. https://doi.org/10.4324/9781315657899

Gardner, H. (1993). *Multiple intelligences: The theory and practice*. Basic Books.

Gass, S. (1997). *Input, interaction, and the second language learner*. Lawrence Erlbaum Associates.

Gitsaki, C. (2009). Modification of learning objects for NESB students. In L. Lockyer, S. Bennett, S. Agostinho, & B. Harper (Eds.), *Handbook of research on learning design and learning objects: Issues, applications, and technologies* (pp. 428–447). IGI Global. https://doi.org/10.4018/978-1-59904-861-1.ch021

González-Lloret, M. (2015). *A practical guide to integrating technology into task-based language teaching*. Georgetown University Press.

González-Lloret, M., & Ortega, L. (2014). *Technology-mediated TBLT: Researching technology and tasks*. John Benjamins Publishing Company. https://doi.org/10.1075/tblt.6

Harris, K. D. (2013). Play, collaborate, break, build, share: "Screwing around" in digital pedagogy. *Polymath: An Interdisciplinary Arts and Sciences Journal*, *3*(3).

Holbah, W. A. (2022). Teachers perspectives on foreign language acquisition and mobile or computer assisted language learning: A qualitative study. *Journal of Language Teaching and Research*, *13*(3), 620–626. https://doi.org/10.17507/jltr.1303.18

Hubbard, P. (2021). *An invitation to CALL: Foundations of computer-assisted language learning*. APACALL. www.apacall.org/research/books/6/

Hymes, D. (1972). On communicative competence. In J. B. Pride & J. Holmes (Eds.), *Sociolinguistics* (pp. 269–93). Penguin.

Kalyaniwala, C., & Ciekanski, M. (2021). Autonomy CALLing: A systematic review of 22 years of publications in learner autonomy and CALL. *Language Learning & Technology*, *25*(3), 106–131. www.lltjournal.org/item/10125-73452/

Krashen, S. (1982). *Principles and practice in second language acquisition*. Pergamon Press.

Kuriscak, L. M., & Luke, C. L. (2009). Language learner attitudes toward virtual world: An investigation of Second Life. *CALICO Monograph Series*, *8*, 173–198.

Lado, R. (1964). *Language teaching: A scientific approach*. McGraw-Hill.

Lantolf, J. P. (2012). Sociocultural theory: A dialectical approach to L2 research. In S. M. Gass & A. Mackey (Eds.), *The Routledge handbook of second language acquisition* (pp. 57–72). Taylor & Francis Group.

Lantolf, J. P. (Ed.). (2000). *Sociocultural theory and second language acquisition*. Oxford University Press.

Lantolf, J. P., & Pavlenko, A. (1995). Sociocultural theory and second language acquisition. *Annual Review of Applied Linguistics*, *15*, 108–124. https://doi.org/10.1017/s0267190500002646

Larsen-Freeman, D., & Anderson, M. (2013). *Techniques and principles in language teaching* (3rd ed.). Oxford University Press.

Levy, M. (1997). *Computer-assisted language learning: Context and conceptualization*. Oxford University Press. http://dx.doi.org/10.14705/rpnet.2012.000070

Levy, M., & Hubbard, P. (2005) Why call CALL "CALL"? (editorial). *Computer Assisted Language Learning, 18*(3), 143–149.

Lewis, T. N. (2016). Creating a micro-immersion environment through telecollaboration. In C. Wang & L. Winstead (Eds.), *Handbook of research on foreign language education in the digital age* (pp. 144–169). IGI Global. https://doi.org/10.4018/978-1-5225-0177-0.ch007

Lian, A. (2008). Foreword. In F. Zhang & E. Barber (Eds.), *Handbook of research on computer-enhanced language acquisition and learning* (pp. XVIII–XIX). IGI Global.

Lightbown, L., & Spada, N. (2013). *How languages are learned*. Oxford University Press.

Liu, S. (Ed.). (2022a). *Teaching the Chinese language remotely: Global cases and perspectives*. Springer Nature. https://doi.org/10.1007/978-3-030-87055-3

Liu, S. (Ed.). (2022b). *Online Chinese teaching and learning in 2020 (2020 Use SimSun font: 中文线上教学中文线上教学)*. National Foreign Language Resource Center.

Liu, S., & Da, J. (2022). Technology in Chinese language teaching. In Z. Ye (Ed.), *The Palgrave handbook of Chinese language studies* (pp. 1–41). Palgrave Macmillan. https://doi.org/10.1007/978-981-13-6844-8_3-2

Long, M. (1983). Native speaker/non-native speaker conversation and the negotiation of comprehensible input. *Applied Linguistics*, *4*(2), 126–141. https://doi.org/10.1093/applin/4.2.126

Long, M. (1996). The role of the linguistic environment in second language acquisition. In W. Ritchie & T. Bhatia (Eds.), *Handbook of second language acquisition* (pp. 413–468). Academic Press. https://doi.org/10.1016/b978-012589042-7/50015-3

Lyster, R. (2007). *Learning and teaching languages through content: A counterbalanced approach.* John Benjamins. https://doi.org/10.1075/lllt.18

Morton, H., Davidson, N., & Jack, M. (2008). Evaluation of a speech interactive CALL system. In F. Zhang & B. Barbar (Eds.), *Handbook of research on computer-enhanced language acquisition and learning* (pp. 219–239). IGI Global. https://doi.org/10.4018/978-1-59904-895-6.ch013

Nunan, D. (1989). *Designing tasks for the communicative classroom.* Cambridge University Press.

Oskoz, A. (2020). Language learning. In R. F. Davis, M. K. Gold, K. D. Harris, & J. Sayers (Eds.), *Digital pedagogy in the humanities: Concepts, models, and experiments.* Modern Language Association. https://digitalpedagogy.hcommons.org/keyword/Language-Learning

Otto, S. E. (2017). From past to present: A hundred years of technology for L2 learning. In C. A. Chapelle & S. Sauro (Eds.), *The handbook of technology and second language teaching and learning* (pp. 10–25). Wiley-Blackwell.

Oxford, R. L. (1995). Linking theories of learning with intelligent computer-assisted language learning (ICALL). In V. M. Holland, J. D. Kaplan, & M. R. Sams (Eds.), *Intelligent language tutors: Theory shaping technology* (pp. 359–369). Lawrence Erlbaum Associates, Inc.

Pinker, S. (1984). *Language learnability and language development.* Harvard University Press.

Pinker, S. (1994). *The language instinct.* William Morrow and Co.

Pitman, T., & Taylor, C. (2017). Where's the ML in DH? and where's the DH in ML? The relationship between modern languages and digital humanities, and an argument for a critical DHML. *Digital Humanities Quarterly, 11*(1). https://dhq-static.digitalhumanities.org/pdf/000287.pdf

Prensky, M. (2001). Digital natives, digital immigrants. *On the Horizon, 9*(5), 1–6. https://doi.org/10.1108/10748120110424816

Ramsay. S. (2013a). Who's in and who's out. In M. Terras, J. Nyhan, & E. Vanhoutte (Eds.), *Defining digital humanities: A reader* (pp. 239–241). Routledge.

Ramsay. S. (2013b). On building. In M. Terras, J. Nyhan, J., & E. Vanhoutte (Eds.), *Defining digital humanities: A reader* (pp. 243–245). Routledge.

Reinhardt, J., & Oskoz, A. (2021). Twenty-five years of emerging technologies. *Language Learning & Technology, 25*(3), 1–5. http://hdl.handle.net/10125/73442

Richards, J., & Rodgers, T. (2014). *Approaches and methods in language teaching* (3rd ed.). Cambridge University Press.

Sample, M. [@samplereality]. (2011, May 25). The digital humanities is not about building, it's about sharing. *Samplereality.* https://samplereality.com/2011/05/25/the-digital-humanities-is-not-about-building-its-about-sharing/

Schreibman, S., Siemens, R., & Unsworth, J. (Eds.). (2004). *A companion to digital humanities.* Blackwell.

Schwartz, B. D. (1998). The second language instinct. *Lingua, 106*, 133–160. https://doi.org/10.1016/s0024-3841(98)00032-1

Shi, L., & Stickler, U. (2019). Using technology to learn to speak Chinese. In C. Shei, E. Monica, M. Zikpi, & D. Chao (Eds.), *The Routledge handbook of Chinese language teaching* (pp. 509–525). Routledge. https://doi.org/10.4324/9781315104652-32

Shrum, J. L., & Glisan, E. W. (2010). *Teacher's handbook* (4th ed.). Heinle & Heinle.

Siemens, G. (2004). Connectivism: A learning theory for the digital age. *International Journal of Instructional Technology and Distance Learning, 2*(1), 3–10.

Skehan, P. (1989). *Individual differences in second language learning.* Edward Arnold. https://doi.org/10.4324/9781315831664

Skinner, B. F. (1974). *About behaviorism.* Knopf.

Svensson, P. (2009). Humanities computing as digital humanities. *DHQ: Digital Humanities Quarterly*, *3*(3). https://dhq-static.digitalhumanities.org/pdf/000065.pdf

Swain, M. (1985). Communicative competence: Some roles of comprehensible input and comprehensible output in its development. In S. Gass & C. Madden (Eds.), *Input in second language acquisition* (pp. 235–53). Newbury House.

Swain, M. (1988). Manipulating and complementing content teaching to maximize second language learning. *TESL Canada Journal*, 68–83. https://doi.org/10.18806/tesl.v6i1.542

Terras, M., Nyhan, J., & Vanhoutte, E. (Eds.). (2013). *Defining digital humanities: A reader*. Routledge. https://doi.org/10.4324/9781315576251

Thomas, M., Reinders, H., & Warschauer, M. (2012). The role of digital media and incremental change. In M. Thomas, H. Reinders, & M. Warschauer (Eds.), *Contemporary computer assisted language learning* (pp. 1–12). Bloomberg Academic.Van Den Branden, K. (Ed.). (2006). *Task-based language education: From theory to practice*. Cambridge University Press. https://doi.org/10.1017/cbo9780511667282

Vanhoutte, E. (2013). The gates of hell: History and definition of digital humanities computing. In M. Terras, J. Nyhan, J., & E. Vanhoutte (Eds.), *Defining digital humanities: A reader* (pp. 119–156). Routledge.

Vygotsky, L. S. (1978). Interaction between learning and development. In M. Lopez-Morillas (Trans.) & M. Cole, V. John-Steiner, S. Scribner, & E. Souberman (Eds.), *Mind in society: The development of higher psychological processes* (pp. 79–91). Harvard University Press.

Wang, C., & Winstead, L. (Eds.). (2016). *Handbook of research on foreign language education in the digital age*. IGI Global. https://doi.org/10.4018/978-1-5225-0177-0

White, L. (2003). *Second language acquisition and universal grammar*. Cambridge University Press. https://doi.org/10.1017/cbo9780511815065

Willis, D., & Willis, J. (2007). *Doing task-based teaching*. Oxford University Press.

Willis, J. (1996). *A framework for task-based learning*. Longman.

Zhang, F., & Barber, B. (Eds.). (2008). *Handbook of research on computer-enhanced language acquisition and learning.*. IGI Global. https://doi.org/10.4018/978-1-59904-895-6

Zhang, Z. (1998). CALL for Chinese: Issues and practice. *Journal of Chinese Language Teachers Association*, *33*(1), 51–82.

Zhang, Z. (2019). The current status of CALL for Chinese in the United States. In C. Shei, M. Zikpi, & D. Chao (Eds.), *The Routledge handbook of Chinese language teaching* (pp. 493–508). Routledge. https://doi.org/10.4324/9781315104652-31

Ziegler, N., & González-Lloret, M. (Eds.). (2022). *The Routledge handbook of second language acquisition and technology*. Routledge.

2 Computer-Assisted Language Learning

2.1 Introduction

On July 30, 1967, an article titled "Computers Ready to Teach Chinese: Seton Hall Will Use Machine to Instruct Its Students" appeared in the *New York Times*. Reported by Malcolm W. Browne, the first five paragraphs of the article read as follows:

> American teachers of Chinese may soon be learning their subject from computers instead of Mandarin scholars, thanks to a Federal grant to Seton Hall University.
>
> Seton Hall's Department of Asian Studies and its Computer Center have cooperated in programing an International Business Machines (IBM) computer to tutor students, who themselves will become teachers of Chinese in high schools and colleges.
>
> The machine handles standard punch cards, which feed its memory bank. The student sits down at a keyboard, and the machine types out questions, first asking the student his name and then drilling him in Chinese.
>
> The Chinese words and phrases are written in the Pinyin system, using, Roman letters and numbers to indicate the four tones of the mandarin language.
>
> Prof. Wang Fang-yu of Seton Hall, who developed the system for teaching by computer, said the Seton Hall computer would be the first in the world to teach Chinese. In future developments, Chinese characters and the spoken language also will be taught by computer.
>
> (Browne, 1967, p. 67)

Although what Prof. Wang described in the news article has long been a reality, having a computer write Chinese characters presented daunting challenges until the Unicode standard was introduced in 1991 (e.g., Cheng, 1973; Davies et al., 2012; Otto, 2017; Zhang, 2019).

Using an IBM machine to instruct students is one of the earliest and most formidable efforts to integrate computer technology in education since the first general-purpose Electronic Numerical Integrator and Computer (ENIAC) was developed at the University of Pennsylvania in 1945. In 1959, the Computer-Based Education Research Laboratory at the University of Illinois at Urbana-Champaign (UIUC) launched a mainframe computer instructional system, Program Logic for Automated Teaching Operation (PLATO), to explore educational possibilities (Alpert & Bitzer, 1970). Expanded for language-learning purposes by taking advantage of the repetition that a computer could offer, which was crucial in learning a language, PLATO was employed to interact with students for the latter to practice the language being learned. Through a terminal station connecting with the mainframe computer, students were able to communicate by inputting on the electronic keyset, with the computer, which displayed responses on the student's terminal screen, all controlled by the PLATO system. Other than interacting with the student directly, PLATO provided correct answers to a given question, pointed out errors if any, and even reminded the student of the areas of difficulty. Moreover, PLATO could inform the instructor of each student's performance for further customized assistance. Being interactive and offering self-paced instruction to many learners simultaneously fosters student learning to a great extent. In 1971, Time-Shared Interactive Computer Controlled Information Television (TICCIT) was initiated as a collaborative project between Brigham Young University, the University of Texas, and Mitre Corporation. This system, which combined television technology with computer technology, was designed with a set of educational goals, such as lowering costs, reducing time to complete materials, and increasing enrollments (Bunderson, 1974). A central tenet of this system was the keyboard that contained 15 instructional displays marked as Rule, Example, Practice, Advice, Objective, Easy, Hard, etc., which empowered the student to select what and how to learn depending on his/her needs. As such, students not only gained control over content and learning strategies but also proceeded at their own pace outside the classroom (Jones, 1995). Having the capacity to incorporate text, audio, and video, TICCIT was regarded as the first example of multimedia computer-assisted instruction (Levy, 1997).

The creation of PLATO and TICCIT subsequently inspired developments of many innovative programs to promote language education, eventually resulting in an established field computer-assisted language learning (CALL). Now CALL has been widely integrated for second language instruction. In this chapter, I will examine CALL by addressing the following questions: What is CALL? What is CALL development? Is there a Chinese CALL? What is the analysis of CALL history? What are the benefits of CALL? What are the issues associated with CALL? In addressing these questions, I will provide readers with an in-depth understanding of the field.

2.2 What Is CALL?

The practices offered by PLATO and TICCIT were initially considered as Computer-Assisted Instruction (CAI, e.g., Alpert & Bitzer, 1970; Alderman et al., 1978). Later, language professionals used terms like Computer-Accelerated Language Instruction (CALI, e.g., Yao & Peterson, 1986), or Computer-Aided Language Learning (CALL, e.g., Bourgerie, 2003) to refer to this kind of instruction. Computer

Assisted Language Instruction (CALI) was used when it was incorporated into the name of the association Computer-Assisted Language Instruction Consortium (CALICO). According to Davies et al. (2012), the terminology Computer-Assisted Language Learning (CALL) was first adopted by Graham Davies and David Steel in their paper presented at the CAL 81 Symposium (Davies & Steel, 1981). It soon became widespread, first in the UK and then in the US and elsewhere. As compared to other terms mentioned before, CALL emphasizes "a student-centered focus on learning rather than instruction" (p. 20); therefore, its use has remained dominant in the field (Levy & Hubbard, 2005; Hubbard, 2021).

Because of its rapid and extensive growth, CALL achievements are so numerous both in quantity and quality that they are impossible to list, let alone describe. However, for the purpose of giving a holistic picture, I endeavor to provide a summary of some milestones of computer technology and the corresponding CALL breakthroughs over the past 60 years. For details of historical developments, see Cuban (1986), which studied the use of technology in classroom since 1920; Sanders (1995) and Levy (1997), which examined CALL from the 1960s to the 1990s; Davies et al. (2012), which covered the period from the 1960s to the beginning of 2000; Hubbard (2009), which reviewed the CALL evolution from the beginning to the time before 2009; Otto (2017), which looked at a hundred years of technology for second language (L2) learning; and Reinhardt and Oskoz (2021), which focused on CALL technologies from 1997 to 2021. For the most recent publications on CALL and language learning, see the volumes edited by Farr and Murray (2016), Chapelle and Sauro (2017), Arnold and Ducate (2019), and Ziegler and González-Lloret (2022).

2.3 The CALL Development

Following the models of PLATO and TICCIT, a great number of mainframe-based programs were created during the 1970s, which acted mostly like tutors and drillmasters, offering students feedback on their errors, tracking their performance, and providing individual assistance (Davies et al., 2012; Otto, 2017). The languages that received most attention from CALL developers and/or practitioners in early days were English, French, German, and Spanish because other languages using non-Roman characters required special technologies to display their fonts. One best-known product of the time is German TICCIT. Built out of TICCIT, this program offered tutorials for the learning of German grammar, covering all grammatical concepts in a three-semester college beginner's German curriculum (Jones, 1995). Another is EXERCISE, a package created out of the mainframe ICL1904S computer developed at the University of Hull in the UK. This program could produce large quantities of drill-and-practice activities, also for students of German (Last, 1984). As can be seen, the objectives of these programs are to assist learners to study language rules by repetition and memorization. This kind of instruction matches the then popular teaching methods, such as grammar-translation and audio-lingualism, both emphasizing accurate use of linguistic patterns through repeated practice (Richards & Rodgers, 2014).

The emergence of microcomputer technologies expanded the use of CALL from institutions of higher education to K–12 settings. In the early 1980s, as different types of microcomputers were manufactured, including Apple II and IBM personal computers, each utilizing its own operating system, there appeared an issue of compatibility—software developers or publishers had challenges determining which operating system to target for their products. However, it was during this period that professional associations like Computer-Assisted Language Instruction Consortium (CALICO) and European Association of Computer-Assisted Language Learning (EUROCALL) were founded, the former in the US in 1982 and the latter in Europe in 1986, to seriously promote CALL among language educators. Meanwhile, CALL program designers started to shift their focus from drilling to raising learners' intrinsic learning motivation; improving their listening, speaking, and reading skills; and cultivating their capabilities to use language. Several trends were notable. First, computer games were incorporated in programs to engage learning. For example, *Juegos Comunicativos* is the microcomputer-based artificial intelligence (AI) software for learners of Spanish (Bassein & Underwood, 1985), while *Spion* is a spy game for learners of German (Sanders & Sanders, 1995), both highlighting the use of language in a fun way. Second, data-driven, learning-based concordancing software—a tool that retrieves a particular word or phrase in its immediate context—became an innovative way to expose learners to authentic content. Third, videodisc-based simulations situated the learning of language in a meaningful context. Two successful products that offered learners immersion experiences in the target language included *Montevidisco* and *A la rencontre de Philippe*. *Montevidisco*, designed by Brigham Young University for learning Spanish, takes the student to visit a Mexican town, where the learner encounters several problems in the real-life situation, which are eventually resolved after interacting with native speakers in Spanish. Depending on how the student responds, s/he may end up in a hospital or in jail, thereby making the program interesting to play with (Gale, 1983). Created by Massachusetts Institute of Technology (MIT), *A la rencontre de Philippe* provides French learners with a background about a young freelance journalist, Philippe, who enlists a student to find him a place to stay because he was thrown out by his girlfriend from their apartment. In the process of helping Philippe with this and many other major problems, the student communicates with various native speakers in Paris, hence developing an understanding of authentic spoken French, as well as speaking and reading skills (Gray, 1992; [https://languages.mit.edu/pedagogies/a-la-rencontre-de-philippe/]). These programs, from games to concordancers to simulation packages, reflect principles of communicative language teaching (CLT) and practices of Task-Based Language Learning (TBLT), both of which shaped up in the 1980s and have remained as effective approaches to teaching a second language in the classroom (Richards & Rodgers, 2014).

The 1990s witnessed volumes of publications that seriously examined CALL development over the previous 30 years, for example, Sanders (1995), Jones (1995), Warschauer (1996), Chapelle (1997), Levy (1997), and Warschauer and Healey (1998). The questions that were addressed included the following: What are CALL benefits? How should the CALL development be analyzed? What are the research methods for CALL? What are the future directions of CALL? The inquiry shed light on a better understanding of CALL for further development. During that period of time, among the advances in information technologies were the multimedia technology of the personal computer, which resulted in the programs that made recording and playing back sound available for language teachers and learners, and the arrival of the World Wide Web in 1990, which opened up a "compelling new horizon in technology-based language learning and teaching" (Otto, 2017, p. 17). The streaming audio and video innovations that arose in the late 1990s made physical media like CDs and DVDs obsolete, yet they remain in function nowadays. With the internet, learners can study, practice, and experience the target language anytime and anywhere. Web-based authoring tools like *Hot Potatoes* enabled teachers to create six different types of educational exercises for students (i.e., multiple choice, matching, short answer, scrambled sentences, crosswords, and cloze) (Arneil et al., 1998–2009; Winke & MacGregor, 2001). Regarding language pedagogy, the late 1990s started the post-methods era, when language professionals no longer regarded methods as the only key factor responsible for the success or failure in language teaching because the latter involved . dynamics. In addition, language teachers, by now, have become aware that no single teaching approach or method could be claimed as the best one. Hence, the application of pedagogical approaches, teaching techniques, and strategies became flexible and adaptive to learners' needs and interests, depending on what happened in the classroom (Richards & Rodgers, 2014).

Entering the 21st century, with the advent of fast broadband networks and Web 2.0 technologies and the affordance of laptops, mobile devices, cloud services, and various social media apps, the ubiquitous technologies made computer-mediated communication (CMC) possible and popular, including both synchronous CMC supported by, for example, *Skype*, and asynchronous CMC such as e-mail. The impact of the internet becomes omnipotent in language instruction. For example, regarded as the second generation of internet, Web 2.0 technologies offer a social platform supported by wiki for creating, sharing, critiquing, networking, and collaborating, which provides a valuable opportunity to give students a voice. Students can express ideas in the target language through writing blogs or speaking by *VoiceThread*. With *YouTube*, a resource that offers many opportunities for language learning, students can post their work involving photos or videos onto *Blackboard or Canvas* (course management systems) for others to view. *Google* search and online dictionaries enable learners to retrieve information immediately at a single click, while multiuser three-dimensional virtual environments like *Second Life* empower learners to communicate with peers or native speakers easily and interestingly. *Google Classroom* tools make online teaching and learning in one place seamless. User-friendly apps such as *Quizlet* and *Kahoot!* facilitate learners to study and review in an engaging and fun fashion. The abrupt shift to the online mode from the traditional in-person teaching in 2020 due to the breakout of COVID-19 has made online learning via *Zoom* or *Teams* a part of the new normal instruction. All these align with what is postulated in the sociocultural theory of language learning that has become more prominent since the 1990s, promoting knowledge co-construction and authenticity and task orientation through collaborative learning, Content-Based Instruction (CBI) and Content and Language Integrated Learning (CLIL), Competency-Based Learning, as well as CLT, TBLT, and Project-Based Learning (PBL). Table 2.1 summarizes the past 60 years of CALL development.

2.4 The History of Chinese CALL

As the focus of the book involves teaching Chinese as a foreign language (TCFL), it is necessary to briefly review what has happened in the field regarding the use of CALL. As observed by Xu (2015), "Chinese CALL" was initiated in early 1970s and has steadily developed ever since (p. 1–2). After Fang-Yu Wang's pioneering attempt, Chin-Chuan Cheng of UIUC created a program, based on the PLATO system, containing separate lessons on character writing, reading comprehension, and pronunciation (Cheng, 1973). In 1970, Cheng and his colleagues succeeded in making the computer write in Chinese, a breakthrough in battling the challenges for the Chinese computing world. To help with character writing, the stroke order lessons demonstrated on the computer how a character was composed one stroke after another. Students were then invited to practice writing themselves on the computer. To enhance reading comprehension, after reading a short passage of around 100 characters displayed on the terminal, students were engaged to complete a comprehension quiz about the passage. Students could look up a given vocabulary word by pressing a designated key. The details of how well students studied for each item were recorded for the instructor so that s/he could contact each student for improvement. For pronunciation practice, students could listen to a narrative

Table 2.1 Outline of CALL Development

Technology Milestones	Time & Program Examples	Pedagogy	Instructional Activities	Goal
Mainframe	1960s–1970s PLATO TICCIT	Grammar-translation Audio-lingualism	drills	providing feedback
Microcomputers videodiscs	1980s *Montevidisco*	CLT TBLT	simulation	making authenticity tasks in contexts
World Wide Web CD/DVD media streaming	1990s *Hot Potatoes*	Approaches flexible & adaptive	e-learning	creating immersion
Web 2.0 social networking mobile devices smartphones	2000s *Second Life Blackboard Skype, YouTube*	Content & competency-based learning CLT, TBLT	collaborative learning	integrating skills

describing Chinese sounds and transcribe them using pinyin—the romanization method used to capture Chinese sounds. All these lessons availed the interactive nature of the PLATO system (Cheng, 1973; Levy, 1997).

Ten years later came two similar learning applications. One was created by Kim Smith of Birmingham University in 1981 (Yao, 1996), running on Apple II to teach Chinese characters, and the other, called *Chinese Character Tutor*, was developed by Tao-Chung Yao and Mark Peterson of Mount Holyoke College in 1986, running on an IBM computer (Yao & Peterson, 1986). It is not surprising that both programs took Chinese characters as the primary instructional target because writing characters, as well as identifying and recalling characters, which is crucial for studying Chinese, constitutes many challenges for learners. Since then, tremendous efforts have been made, resulting in numerous products on learning how to write characters, such as *NJ Star, Wenlin, Clavis Sinica, eStroke,* and *Chinese Writing Master*, to name just a few.

The rise of internet technology has consequently led to a profound proliferation of Chinese CALL resources. For example, Xie and Yao (2009) listed a great number of programs and websites both for teachers preparing instructional materials and for students learning Chinese. These resources cover various tools for typing Chinese characters, converting characters in between simplified and traditional conventions, and typing and converting tone marks. Furthermore, they feature concordance programs for retrieving a particular word or phrase, online dictionaries, and glossing engines. Their list also includes web resources geared for pronunciation, listening (also recording, videoing, podcasting), speaking, reading, writing, and text-to-speech software. *Learn to Write Characters*, (https://home.csulb.edu/~txie/azi/page1.htm), for example, is the most complete and popular site for learning Chinese characters, created by Tianwei Xie to feature animated Chinese characters one stroke after another. From the 1990s on, most of publications on the topic of Chinese CALL would recommend novel programs, applications, tools, and websites (e.g., Yao, 1996; Zhang, 1998; Bourgerie, 2003; Xie & Yao, 2009; Zhang, 2019). Worth noting is that while learning programs were created in the early days, Chinese testing via computer was not overlooked. Yao's (1995) Computer-Adaptive Test for Reading Chinese and Ke and Zhang's (2002) Chinese Computerized Adaptive Listening Comprehension Test are two exemplary products. There is also research on how technology was integrated in advancing students' skills in listening and speaking (e.g., Chang, 2007), speaking skills (e.g., Shi & Stickler, 2019), and writing skills (e.g., Gao, 2019).

One important work in Chinese CALL that should be highlighted is Shei and Hsieh (2012). In this research, which aims to resolve the problems encountered by English-speaking college learners of Chinese, the authors designed an integrated CALL system. The English-speaking students' learning challenges center around the understanding of the concepts of syllables, characters, and words in the Chinese language. Specifically, how Chinese syllables correspond to characters and how characters are mapped to words is not straightforward on a one-to-one relation, as is the case in the English language. Called *Linkit*, this system comprises core engine, knowledge base, interface, and external resource. The core engine is used to process user requests by drawing data from internal and external resources. The knowledge base stores the data of frequency of linguistic elements such as syllables, characters, words, and phrases. The interface is where students interact with the tutor. The external resources refer to dictionaries or other machine translation apps. Armed with these four crucial components, *Linkit* powerfully allows phonological, morphological, and orthographic parts to present together so that learners can see how the individual linguistic items across different levels are interconnected with each other. Exposed with characteristics of a particular level of language (either sounds or characters, or words or phrases) in paradigmatic formats, students are empowered not only to learn details of a given character but also to appreciate how this character is related to other characters if they are homophonic and how it develops into a word or a phrase. The essence of Linkit is its emphasis of "continuity," that is, "close relationships and interactions between the levels of phonology, morphology, orthography, vocabulary, and phraseology in Chinese." This "gives the learner unlimited access to language data online and offers consolidated multi-level analysis to help speed up learners' empirically based learning processes" (p. 331). According to the authors, *Linkit* can be used with a textbook or a corpus for students to practice what they have learned.

For the current state of Chinese CALL in the USA, Zhang (2019) included two milestones as the primary accomplishments. One is the International Conference and Workshops on Technology and Chinese Language Teaching (TCLT) in the 21st Century, which, initiated at Hamilton College in 2009, is held every other year in the US or in Asia to discuss issues related to technology, teaching methodology, and curriculum, as well as to enhance the exchange on technology-based Chinese language teaching. The other is the launch of the online *Journal of Technology and Chinese Language Teaching (JTCLT)* in 2010 to address the research and application of educational technology in Chinese language learning and teaching. Apart from the biannual TCLT conference and the peer-reviewed semiannual online publication of the *JTCLT*, Zhang listed studies on over three dozen advanced technologies applied in Chinese classrooms. Furthermore, Zhang discussed as many as nine future trends in the development of CALL with the teaching and learning of Chinese into consideration (p. 495–497).

A summary of Chinese CALL would not be complete without highlighting some notable publications in the field. Four volumes appeared over the recent five years: Amber Navarre's (2019) *Technology-Enhanced Teaching and Learning of Chinese as a Foreign Language*, Miao-fen Tseng and Yan Gao's (2021) *Teach Chinese Online: An Essential Guide*, and Shijuan Liu's (2022a, 2022b) two edited collections: *Teaching the Chinese Language Remotely: Global Cases and Perspectives*, and *Online Chinese Teaching and Learning in 2020–2020* 中文线上教学. For a review of Chinese CALL development chronologically, refer to Dew (1989), Albert (1989, 1996), Zhang (1998), Xie (2001), Bourgerie (2003), Liu (2007), Xie and Yao (2009), Yao (1995, 1996, 2003, 2009), Xu (2004, 2005, 2013, 2015), Wu (2016), Da and Zheng (2018), Bai et al. (2019), Shi and Stickler (2019), Zhang (2019), Liu and Da (2022).

2.5 Different Stages of CALL

Warschauer and Healey (1998) is the first attempt to examine the history of CALL from the perspectives of second language acquisition (SLA). In this account, CALL has three stages. Behavioristic (1960s–1970s) is the first stage, which takes advantage of the features of computer technology to engage learners with repeated tasks in hopes to make them react to stimuli. The second stage is Communicative CALL (1970s–1980s), which contains three models regarding the role of technology: *computer as tutor* (i.e., the CALL activities providing learners with right answers); *computer as stimuli* (i.e., the CALL programs providing language material to stimulate learners' discussion, writing, and critical thinking); and *computer as tool* (i.e., the CALL programs such as word processors and spelling and grammar checkers empowering learners to use the language). As more advanced technological means burgeoned with multimedia technology and internet towards the late 1990s, the third stage of Integrative CALL occurred, which promotes the learner-centered approach to language learning through media and interactions via CMC. For Warschauer and Healey (1998), what drives the development of each stage is computing technology, that is, the mainframe computer for the Behavioristic CALL, the personal computer for the Communicative CALL, and the multimedia networked computer for the Integrative CALL.

In his subsequent work, Warschauer (2000) repeated the same tripartite classification of the CALL development but postponed the time period to around 10 years later for each phrase: 1970s-1980s for Structural CALL, 1980s-1990s for Communicative CALL, and 2000s onwards to the present for Integrative CALL. Also, to describe the first stage, Warschauer used the term Structure CALL instead of Behaviorist CALL. Thomas et al. (2012) supported the analysis of Warschauer and Healey (1998) and Warschauer (2000) by advocating a fourth stage, Social CALL, to reflect the CALL development in response to the arrival of Web 2.0 technology and portable digital devices including smartphones, tablets, and e-readers. This stage is also underpinned by the constructivist principles that promote collaborative learning and participation experience. Social CALL is, therefore, far more significant than the drill-and-practice tutorials, or transmission of teaching and passive experience. Through activities of web-based synchronous and asynchronous communication to enhance learner engagement, collaboration, and learning motivation, Social CALL aims to encourage students to develop higher-order critical thinking skills and creative communication skills rather than discrete skills like grammar, spelling, and text decoding. According to Thomas et al. (2012), while the four CALL phrases appear like a chronological development, there is no strict linear order among them because each successive stage did not emerge as a result of winning over the preceding one. Some of them, for example, Communicative CALL and Integrative CALL, may overlap or co-exist with each other for a period of time.

Bax (2003) criticized this classification. First, the terminologies are confusing and incorrect. For example, while Communicative CALL seemed to match the CLT in terms of time frame, Warschauer and Healey (1998) did not mention the purpose of language communication, the most important aspect of CLT. With a chronological order of Integrative CALL following Communicative CALL, it mistakenly gives the impression that CLT no longer exists for language education. Second, this classification fails to consider factors such as the teacher's role, students' roles, and the roles of CALL, which are significant in the learning process. Third, no clear criteria are used for differentiating the three stages, hence causing inconsistencies in terms of time periods. To correctly capture the characteristics of CALL development, Bax (2003) considered it crucial to look at its history from the angle of learning theory, teachers' roles, activity types, hardware, and software. To that end, Bax proposed three phrases of CALL. The first is Restricted CALL (1960s–1980s), by which the use of CALL or computer is limited because instructors, students, or hardware/software programs were all not ready to apply CALL in classroom. The second is Open CALL (1980s–2003), which covers Warschauer and Healey's (1998) time periods for Communicative CALL and Integrative CALL. In contrast to the Restricted CALL, the attitudes of teachers and administrators were now much more open towards using computers. For example, instructors were able to use computers to engage students for more interactions among one another via the internet, the web, and email systems along the lines of CLT. Likewise, students embraced the novel computer technology with higher enthusiasm and motivation. The third is Integrated CALL, which is the stage when the use of technology would become invisible, embedded in everyday classroom environments. In other words, as technology is applied in every teacher's instructional practice for the needs of learners, nobody is consciously aware of its presence as a technology. In addition, the application of technology plays an effective role in the language learning process.

Bax's classification of the CALL history into three aspects may coincidently match with the three phrases defined by Warschauer and Healey (1998) and Warschauer (2000) in terms of time frame. However, according to Bax (2003), his three approaches should not be regarded as three historical times. Instead, they represent three different attitudes to dealing with CALL, from being hesitant and uncomfortable with the use of CALL, to being ready and willing to try it, to finally using it happily. At the time when the article was written, Bax claimed that the third approach, Integrated CALL, was not fully available yet though it "exists in a few places and a few dimensions only" (p. 22). Based on Bax, only when the technology is gradually seen as something normalized does the technology become invisible.

What is the "normalization" of CALL now? Bax (2011) pointed out that CALL has evolved to become more integrated and perhaps more normalized in some formal classrooms. According to Davies et al. (2012),

> We are now entering a fully integrated and naturalized phase of CALL. Digital tools for learning have become integrated elements both in the real world and also in foreign language syllabuses. CALL has reached the stage of normalization insofar as so-called Web 2.0 applications have become a common social phenomenon.
>
> (p. 34)

If CALL was considered as entering an integrated phrase in 2012 in view of the development of even more flexible tools for social networking and knowledge sharing, then after in-person teaching was shifted pivotally into online mode due to the breakout of a global pandemic in 2020 and since some part of online teaching has remained active, it might be safe to say that CALL is being normalized. Indeed, the COVID-19 pandemic has rendered technology commonplace to people's ways of working, shopping, and educating. As a result, instructors as well as learners can hardly continue their language teaching and learning respectively without CALL. Reinhardt and Oskoz (2021) claimed that CALL "has [also] become not less but more ubiquitous in everyday life and informal contexts, leading to a blurring of boundaries among the times when and spaces where we engage in what we might call CALL" (p. 4). Bax (2011) noted that his concept of normalization was cited and addressed differently. It is possible that more questions will arise about the notion of normalization, some of which may include the following: Can all technologies be normalized to the same degree and in the same fashion? Does each technology need to be normalized before it can be effectively utilized? What is the relationship between normalization of technology and effectiveness of technology application? Regardless of answers to these questions, "It is indisputable that technology has in fact become more integrated into language learning and is well on the way to becoming a normal part of everyday practice" (Otto, 2017, p. 21).

With respect to TCFL, Xu (2015) also proposed four stages of Chinese CALL: (i) the Pioneering Stage (1970–1985), corresponding to Warschauer and Healey's (1998) Behaviorist or Structural CALL (1970s-80s); (ii) Starting (1986–1993) and Developing (1994–1999) Stage, corresponding to Warschauer and Healey's (1998) Communicative CALL (1980s-90s); (iii) Omni-Directional Development Stage (2000–2004), corresponding to Warschauer and Healey's (1998) Integrative CALL (after 2000); and (iv) New Trend Stage (2005–2015), corresponding to Social CALL by Thomas et al. (2012). Regarding Bax's (2003) normalization of CALL, Xie (2008) noted that some technologies such as *Blackboard, Moodle*, and other online learning platforms have already become part of the education in the digital age because they are no longer regarded as novel. Shi and Stickler (2019) also held a similar view, as evidenced in their statement, "In the late 2010s, we can safely say that this development has taken place and Integrated CALL can be observed in language education" (p. 512).

2.6 Benefits of CALL

Computers were initially incorporated into instruction because of their capabilities of repeating a job at a good speed. Therefore, repetition is deemed as an advantage for language instruction. As reported in the news article mentioned at the beginning of this chapter, according to the head of the Chinese program at Seton Hall University, "the need for Chinese teachers was rapidly increasing and that computers would reduce the time for training them" (Browne, p. 67). This suggests another benefit of using computer technology—efficiency, that is, the time that was taken to train teachers could be shortened. In the case of PLATO for language education, it enabled many students to have interactive, self-paced, and self-selected drills on vocabulary and grammar outside class simultaneously. In this way, the teacher would have time to devote to more significant instructional activities in class, while students could concentrate on expressing themselves in the target language. Thus, both instructor and students benefit from CALL as to how to make use of class time. In fact, a wide variety of advantages of integrating technology in language instruction has been reported in the literature, see the two lists, as given next.

Warschauer and Healey's (1998) benefits of CALL (p. 59):

- Multimodal practice with feedback
- Individualization in a large class
- Pair and small group work on projects, either collaboratively or competitively
- The fun factor
- Variety in the resources available and learning styles used
- Exploratory learning with large amounts of language data
- Real-life skill-building in computer use

Ozturk's (2013) strengths of CALL (p. 38):

- Affective factors; interest and motivation
- Learners' differences leading to individualization and independence
- Flexible learning; free from time and place
- An opportunity for native language input

Other than the overall advantages, research has been conducted exploring the effectiveness of computer programs in view of language aspects like vocabulary or skills such as listening, speaking, reading, and writing. As reported in Shrum and Glisan (2010), technology has been used to (i) facilitate the acquisition of vocabulary; (ii) support reading via reading assistant software with integrated video and the internet; (iii) increase writing through writing assistant software, email, and chat rooms; (iv) enhance listening comprehension and retention; and (v) promote exploration of authentic language use through email or the internet (p. 454). Blake (2016) observed that in the context of the TBLT approach supported by CALL, students engaged in a speaking task to make video postings cannot overlook listening or writing. While working on a listening task, they will inevitably pay attention to details like reading captions; likewise, writing will be carried out as a result of collaborative chatting, videoconferencing, and negotiations of their linguistic and cultural competence. In other words, under the TBLT approach with contemporary technology, second language development became more integrated with multimodal communication rather than concentrating on a set of discrete categories such as speaking, listening, reading, and writing.

Godwin-Jones (2021) noted two more advantages owing to the emergence of smartphone phone technology and online learning technology. For example, being an almost indispensable necessity in our daily life, smartphones have added additional benefits because of their "easy text entry in multiple script systems, ability to combine different languages in a single text, the anytime-anywhere access to authentic L2 materials, the availability of L2 support services (dictionaries, translators, flashcards, etc.) and more" (p. 7). A major benefit of engaging learners to have online exchanges for learning is its "potential for gaining insight into the importance of language pragmatics, the use of language in culturally and contextually appropriate ways" (p. 11).

Among the educators who have observed the contributions of CALL for the teaching and learning of Chinese, Zhang (1998, pp. 54–56) lists the following six advantages:

- Interactivity—implementing learner-centered teaching methods
- Multimedia—e.g., character stroke order showing the animated demonstration
- Random and rapid access—allowing instant retrieval of learning materials
- Store and manipulate the data—allowing to track learner performance
- Consistency and patience—creating association and repeated exposure
- Graphic display of acoustic properties—helping perception and production of sounds

In his recent study, Zhang (2019) addressed the potential of technological advances for the teaching of Chinese tones, characters, vocabulary, reading, and grammar. According to Zhang, to integrate technology in instruction, Chinese teachers should first achieve a sound understanding of the structure of the language. Targeting each challenging characteristics in the language, Zhang recommended differentiated technological tools. For example, of the four different basic tones in Chinese, the third tone—a dipping pattern with a falling pitch going down first followed by a rising pitch (Chao, 1968)—is often pronounced as half third tone, that is, only the first part of the pitch pattern. In addition, the third tone involves tone changes when used in different contexts. However, in the real-world classroom, the third tone is usually mistaught as a full third tone due to the misleading pinyin tone mark (e.g., Simmons, 2014; Zhang, 2019), resulting in various problems for students of Chinese at the beginning stage. To help learners with the subtleties related to the third tone, Zhang (2019) advocated for turning to useful programs like *WaveSurfer* for assistance because it aids production of tones by tracking pitch features. For the learning issues related to the Chinese writing due to its logographic nature, Zhang suggested the animation feature of the *Pleco* program. The Chinese language distinguishes characters from words and sometimes a character is a word, but, in many cases, two or more characters are combined to form a compound word, creating confusion for learners. Moreover, sharing no cognates with other languages adds more difficulty for students to learn Chinese vocabulary. Thus, Zhang recommended *ClozeMaster* to help learners to beef up vocabulary in context. Due to the challenges with characters, coupled with the convention to present each character without a space in Chinese, Zhang recommended *Decipher Chinese*, *The Chairman's Bao*, and *Du Chinese* to improve students' reading skills in segmenting words and providing meaning glosses. He recommended *Duolingo* and the *JMix* module of *Hot Potatoes* to rearrange different lexical elements in an appropriate order.

With respect to the learning of characters for beginners, Zhang (2019) highlighted the use of the typing technique, which he proposed in Zhang (2002). Typing technique is a general basic feature available for any computer, laptop, or mobile device with a simple configuration of keyboard settings. Chen (2005) developed a web-based Chinese learning program, which, through "inputting" or "typing," enables the learning of pinyin, pronunciation, characters, words, and sentences simultaneously. Zhang (2019) spelled out 10 advantages that the simple action of typing can assist students with the learning of a particular character because it is capable of (p. 501):

1 Strengthening pinyin/pronunciation skills (with phonetic input)
2 Strengthening association between sound and shape of characters
3 Strengthening character recognition through necessary homonym selection
4 Increasing awareness of homophony through homophone selection
5 Increasing awareness of phonetic components in characters (characters with same phonetic components tend to appear together on homophone lists)
6 Increasing awareness of the concept of wordhood (using multisyllabic words yields higher accuracy/efficiency)
7 Lessening the difference between traditional and simplified characters
8 Lowering psychological pressure (especially in test situations)
9 Developing a necessary skill for messaging and online communication
10 Ease of editing, searching, and archiving

All these empower learners to achieve not only a full grasp of characters but also a good command of pronunciation and communication. In this regard, typing is considered a substantive asset of Chinese CALL, which is one of the three examples that Zhang used to illustrate the significance "to tap the full potential of basic general resources" of a technology (p. 501).

Some points are in order about CALL benefits for language education. First, as observed by Hubbard (2009), when discussing advantages of CALL, not only should the learning performance brought by CALL be included but also the improvement of learning be considered. The latter may include six perspectives: (i) learning efficiency, or whether it helps to learn quickly, easily, and effectively; (ii) learning effectiveness, or whether it helps lead to solid learning and long-term retention; (iii) access, or whether materials are easier to access and use; (iv) convenience, or whether it provides equal effective learning and practice across different times and places; (v) motivation, or whether it helps promote learning interest and enjoyment; and (vi) institutional efficiency, or whether it helps save teaching time and resources (p. 2). Improved conditions are part of supportive learning environments, which are necessary and useful for successful learning (Chun, 2016).

Second, it should be clear that no matter how beneficial CALL proves for language learning, technology is not a "panacea" for success (Martinez-Lage & Herren, 1998; Bax, 2011). It is never too much to emphasize the fact that technology cannot replace an instructor. Generally speaking, a language instructor needs to develop curricular objectives based on language standards. In accordance with the backwards design postulated by Wiggins and McTighe (2005), after identifying learning priorities, the instructor should design and determine assessments to measure whether the students achieve the objectives. With goals and assessments decided, the instructor starts to design lesson plans, which s/he next implements in class. During the teaching process, the instructor engages students to learn and practice by scaffolding and evaluating student learning. To make each of these dynamic steps work well in the process, the teacher should be knowledgeable, flexible, reasonable, resourceful, and strategic, among others. While a computer program or an app may help in some areas, it cannot handle the complexity of a classroom, let alone produce a competent language learner (Cuban, 1986, 2001; Thomas et al., 2012).

Third, benefits obtained from applying computer programs in a language classroom should not be presumed to come from the tools and software themselves but mostly from how they are used in language instruction. Hence, it is the pedagogy or the instructional strategies that influence the quality of teaching and the effects of learning. While both technology and pedagogy assist language teaching and learning, pedagogy is more crucial than technology. On this notion, Zhang (1998, 2019) suggested that technology and pedagogy should go together to achieve better outcomes. Abdallah (2021) pointed out that it is pedagogy that guides and informs the choice and use of technology (p. 26).

Fourth, as noted by Thomas et al. (2012), the emergence of Web 2.0 technologies and a great variety of social media apps brought a new dimension to the original environments for language learning. Through web-based synchronous and asynchronous CMC means of various technologies, L2 learners are able to interact seamlessly with other learners of the same target language and/or native speakers. Thomas et al. (2012) pointed out that such a networked global learning environment is, citing the words of Reinders and Darasawang (2011), much more "decentralized, democratic and learner-centric" as compared with the traditional classroom (p. 7). Therefore, it engages and empowers learners to explore the use of language with a high motivation and collaboration. Unlike previous CALL technologies, Social CALL contains pedagogies to foster students' higher-order critical thinking rather than a narrow subset of discrete skills like grammar, spelling, and text decoding (Thomas et al., 2012). In other words, CALL is not just a simple tool. Instead, it is an "any-time, any-place provision through networked digital means" (Otto, 2017, p. 21). It is important to note that as CALL evolved from "its ancillary role in the curriculum to become a core source of content and a conduit for authentic language learning experiences" (Otto, 2017, p. 17), students became "creator[s] of digital texts and media" and "co-constructor[s] of knowledge both in and out of the classroom" (p. 19).

Finally, as technologies constantly evolve, the apps or websites that are built on them must be upgraded accordingly. In consequence, it is normal that a program or a resource that is effective today may no longer work well tomorrow if the technology that supports it is phased out. This "ephemeral" nature of a technology suggests that CALL professionals must always stay abreast of emerging technologies. Let me end the discussion of CALL benefits with a remark from Godwin-Jones (2021):

> Technology in and of itself, no matter how powerful the advances, cannot solve the world's problems, but if we find ways to harness its help in language learning, cultural understanding, and interconnections, that can be a boon to both individuals and society as a whole.
>
> (p.18)

2.7 Issues Associated With CALL

Despite an extensive range of advantages, there are issues in the field of CALL, such as misunderstanding of the function of technology and a lack of research methods or its own theoretical framework. In early years, CALL development was mostly a passive response to emerging technologies, leading to an inaccurate understanding. For example, some teachers thought that new technologies should be used simply because they were novel, as noted by Salaberry (2001). Bax (2003) listed two divided viewpoints among teachers and school administrators regarding the role of technology in the past. The "awe" view is that technology is so powerful that it can solve any problems, while the "fear" view is that technology is so complicated that it can hardly be implemented in the classroom without problems (p. 25). As can be seen, the issue is placing too much emphasis on what technology can or cannot add to the learning process. To fix the issue, knowledge and training of technology and understanding of curricular goals should be considered (Alsuhaibani, 2019).

The misunderstanding of technology is also related to how technology is viewed in relation to pedagogy. Zhang (1998) observed some asymmetries between technology and pedagogy as reflected by more work done on listening and reading skills, with less on speaking and writing skills in TCFL. For example, regarding the accessibility of technology, there was more focus on the use of technology provided for beginners, less so for those having an advanced level of proficiency. As for the elements of language, technology was geared more for pronunciation, vocabulary, and characters, with less attention to grammar. According to Zhang (1998), such imbalance could be due to restrictions in technology itself or the inability to utilize its function by CALL program developers or practitioners. Zhang (1998) thus suggested identifying strengths and limitations of technology in order to understand the potential of a certain technology. Furthermore, whether a given technology could well serve pedagogy also depends on how it is implemented and whether its exploitation is informed by the theory of language and pedagogy (p. 57). Twenty years later, Zhang (2019) suggested that teachers should capitalize on the use of existing technology to its full maximum or repurpose general resources instead of following the latest technology, which may come and go due to the rapid development. As mentioned previously, Zhang called for achieving a good understanding of the Chinese language before applying a technology to enhance the teaching and learning of a linguistic phenomenon. In his words, "however rapidly technology may change, pedagogical soundness is a constant that will not change" (p. 504).

What should be the methods to evaluate CALL in order to design effective CALL programs? Earlier research adopted a comparative approach, under which the learning outcomes from a CALL-involved teaching curriculum were compared with those without CALL. Studies of this kind are archived on the website (https://detaresearch.org/research-support/no-significant-difference/), which contains articles that document no significant differences between students' performance via technology and students' performance without technology as well as the articles that report significant differences. Pederson (1987) criticized these comparative studies because they (i) did not address the cause of the outcomes, (ii) did not connect with any language-learning theories, and (iii) could not be replicated (p. 106). Chapelle (1997) argued that "needs exist for perspectives and research methods that can guide in the development and evaluation of CALL activities " (p. 23). In Chapelle (2016), she pointed out that for CALL research, questions relevant to CALL should be specified, and how they can be examined through empirical research should be identified. Failure to do so would result in product-oriented comparison studies about learning outcomes, which had no theoretical explanatory basis. She suggested adopting second language acquisition (SLA) research methods (p. 160).

What serves as theoretical framework for CALL? Some CALL researchers exploited diverse perspectives from cross-disciplinary sources to understand instructional activities. For example, in the early studies on intelligent tutoring systems for foreign language learning, Oxford (1995) drew insights from learning theories including the theory of novice vs. expert learning, constructivism, and individual differences theory. According to Oxford, the theories on how people learn or how they learn best were more important than those of computational linguistics, whose focus is on natural language processes. MacWhinney (1995) used psycholinguistics, human-computer interaction, and psychology. Others like Salaberry (1996) looked to research in the disciplines like anthropology, cognitive psychology, communication theory, linguistics, and SLA to build a theoretical foundation for the pedagogical tasks in CMC. Unlike these researchers, Chapelle (1997) proposed utilizing research approaches used in instructed second language classroom research, such as Gass' (1997) interactionist model of SLA, under which a learner acquires the target language through interaction with other learners or native speakers by using the target language. Chapelle argued that in applying the interactionist approach, CALL practitioners will focus on the face-to-face interactions between the teacher and students in the classroom, for example, the language forms that the teacher used when speaking to students, the reaction that students showed to the teacher, the target language that students used, etc. An examination of these interactions, which constitute a learning environment for students to attend to language form, comprehend message meaning, and produce output, will allow the researcher to observe learners' language performance so as to evaluate the classroom CALL-enabled activities.

Chapelle's proposal of using instructed SLA approaches to assess the CALL effect in language-learning processes has impacted the field, into which other theoretical accounts of SLA such as language socialization, sociocultural theory, and activity theory have been adopted to explore language learning via CALL. For example, sociocultural learning, which promotes the idea that language users socially interact in the learning process (Lantolf & Pavlenko, 1995; Lantolf, 2000), is investigated in research on CMC and telecollaboration. Through interacting with peers and native speakers by emails or chat tools, students learn how to express themselves appropriately in the target language (e.g., Thorne, 2008; Kern, 2014; Dooly, 2017; Culpeper et al., 2018). In the process, pragmatics is highlighted in the context, which is usually ignored in classroom (González-Lloret, 2019, 2021). On the other hand, Nick Ellis' (e.g., 2002, 2017) usage-based learning model of SLA not only emphasizes the frequency with which learners encounter specific linguistic patterns in the input and the frequency with which language units occur but also highlights the word groupings and chunks of language conventionally used together. This kind of learning has been supported by Boulton and Vyatkina's (2021) analysis of 30-year data-driven learning and Reinders and Lan's (2021) examination of big data in language education and research. As observed by Godwin-Jones (2021), related to the usage-based learning is incidental or informal language learning. The latter engages students to watch TV programs or movies made available by streaming video services or do online activities outside the classroom. Research in this regard shows that students of English advanced their learning as a result of accessing English media online for leisure purposes (Sockett, 2014) and that primary and secondary students developed their language skills through extramural English activities (Sundqvist & Sylvén, 2016). Also, Kusyk (2017) reported how university French and German students' participation in online informal learning of English helped improve their English writing complexity, accuracy, and fluency.

On the other hand, Hubbard and Levy (2016) pointed out that CALL does not have its own theoretical framework, based on Hubbard's (2008) review of theories used in articles published in the *CALICO Journal* over a period of time from 1983 to 2007. However, Hubbard and Levy (2016), agreeing with Chapelle (2009), claimed that the SLA theories, such as the interaction account, sociocultural theory, and constructivism, serve as a basis for CALL research and evaluation. In the latest work that synthesizes CALL research over a period of 42 years (from 1980 to 2021) through a comprehensive scientometric analysis of 4,631 original articles, Mohsen et al. (2023) found that CALL research is supported by robust theoretical frameworks and grounded in sociocultural and second language acquisition theories.

2.8 Conclusion

CALL has evolved from the early passive response to emerging technology, to the subsequent quest for methods of designing and evaluating CALL in late 1990s (e.g., Chapelle, 1997), and to the current proactive search for guidance from SLA theories and research (e.g., Chapelle, 2016; Godwin-Jones, 2021; Reinhardt & Oskoz, 2021). Scholars like Chapelle (1997, 2016) and Godwin-Jones (2021) are happy about applying SLA theories and related research methods to the studies of

CALL. Researchers like Thomas et al. (2012) consider CALL as an independent discipline, shaped by trends in language pedagogy and second language acquisition (SLA) theories as well as the state of computer technology.

Is CALL an independent discipline? What is the relationship between CALL and SLA, on the one hand, and CALL and DH, on the other? Chanier (2013) briefly questioned the connection among SLA, CALL, and DH. In this book, I will argue that CALL overlaps with SLA, but both are part of DH. In Chapter 4, I will argue why CALL belongs to the domain of DH, why language educators need CALL and DH, and how both can be reconciled through the innovative approach of Project-Based Language Learning (PBLL). Should a theory emerge from a CALL perspective for CALL? What should serve as the theoretical framework for CALL? Regardless of answers in terms of these questions, it is crucial to face the reality that CALL is part of language education, and it is the responsibility of the instructor to utilize technology to make language learning efficient and effective. This has become especially important in the post-COVID learning environment: "Now more than ever, language teachers need to understand technology and how to use it effectively" (Hubbard, 2021, p. 5).

References

Abdallah, M. (2021). *Computer-assisted language learning (CALL) for 4th year EFL student teachers*. https://files.eric.ed.gov/fulltext/ED615246.pdf

Albert, C. J. (1989). Technology in language teaching. *Journal of the Chinese Language Teachers Association, 24*(2), 85–108.

Albert, C. J. (1996). Citizens of a global village: Information technology and Chinese language instruction-A search for standards. In S. McGinnis (Ed.), *Chinese pedagogy: An emerging field (Chinese Language Teachers Association Monograph No. 2)* (pp. 229–253). National Foreign Language Resource Center at Ohio State University.

Alderman, D. L., Appel, L. R., & Murphy, R. T. (1978). PLATO and TICCIT: An evaluation of CAI in the community college. *Educational Technology, 18*(4), 40–45.

Alpert, D., & Bitzer, D. L. (1970). Advances in computer-based education: The PLATO program will provide a major test of the educational and economic feasibility of this medium. *Science, 167*(3925), 1582–1590. https://doi.org/10.1126/science.167.3925.1582

Alsuhaibani, Z. (2019). Using computer-assisted language learning in classrooms: What does research say about teachers' beliefs and practices? *Theory and Practice in Language Studies, 9*(6), 723–728. http://doi.org/10.17507/tpls.0906.17

Arneil, S., Holmes, M., & Street, H. (1998–2009). *Hot Potatoes*. University of Victoria and Hal-Baked Software, Inc.

Arnold, N., & Ducate, L. (2019). *Engaging language learners through CALL: From theory and research to new directions in foreign language teaching* (3rd ed.). Equinox.

Bai, J., Li, C., & Yeh, W. C. (2019). Integrating technology in the teaching of advanced Chinese. *Journal of Technology and Chinese Language Teaching, 10*(1), 73–90.

Bassein, R., & Underwood, J. (1985). *Juegos comunicativos: Games for communicative practice in Spanish, based on Puntos de Partida*. Random House, Inc.

Bax, S. (2003). Call-past, present, and future. *System: An International Journal of Educational Technology and Applied Linguistics, 31*(1), 13–28. https://doi.org/10.1016/s0346-251x(02)00071-4

Bax, S. (2011). Normalisation revisited: The effective use of technology in language education. *International Journal of Computer Assisted Language Learning and Teaching, 1*(2), 1–15. https://doi.org/10.4018/ijcallt.2011040101

Blake, R. (2016). *Technology and the four skills.* https://scholarspace.manoa.hawaii.edu/server/api/core/bitstreams/7febd85f-e4d6-4a25-98a7-ad5f6fa4b74d/content

Boulton, A., & Vyatkina, N. (2021). Thirty years of data-driven learning: Taking stock and charting new directions over time. *Language Learning & Technology, 25*(3), 66–89. http://hdl.handle.net/10125/73450

Bourgerie, D. (2003). Computer assisted language learning for Chinese: A survey and annotated bibliography. *Journal of Chinese Language Teachers Association, 38*(2), 14–32.

Browne, M. (1967, July 30). Computers ready to teach Chinese. *The New York Times*, p. 67. www.nytimes.com/1967/07/30/archives/computers-ready-to-teach-chinese-seton-hall-will-use-machine-to.html

Bunderson, C. V. (1974). *A status report on the TICCIT project.* Proceedings of the May 6–10, 1974, National Computer Conference and Exposition, 167. https://doi.org/10.1145/1500175.1500209

Chao, Y. R. (1968). *A grammar of spoken Chinese.* U of California P.

Chang, L. (2007). The effects of using CALL on advanced Chinese foreign language learners. *CALICO Journal, 24*(2), 331–353. https://journal.equinoxpub.com/Calico/article/view/17462

Chanier, T. (2013, September). *A viewpoint on the place of CALL within the Digital Humanities: Considering CALL journals, research data and the sharing of research results* [Paper presentation]. EUROCALL 2013, Learning from the Past, Looking to the Future. https://edutice.archives-ouvertes.fr/edutice-00862024

Chapelle, C. A. (1997). CALL in the year 2000: Still in search of research paradigms? *Language Learning & Technology, 1*(1), 19–43.

Chapelle, C. A. (2009). The relationship between second language acquisition theory and computer-assisted language learning. *The Modern Language Journal, 93*, 741–753.

Chapelle, C. A. (2016). CALL in the year 2000: A look back from 2016. *Language Learning & Technology, 20*(2), 159–161. http://llt.msu.edu/issues/june2016/chapelle.pdf.

Chapelle, C. A., & Sauro, S. (Eds.). (2017). *The handbook of technology and second language teaching and learning.* Wiley-Blackwell. https://doi.org/10.1002/9781118914069

Chen, D. (2005). Empowering Chinese language instruction via technology. *Global Chinese Journal on Computers in Education, 4*(1&2), 159–182.

Cheng, C. (1973). Computer-based Chinese teaching program at Illinois. *Journal of the Chinese Language Teachers Association, 8*(2). 75–79.

Chun, D. M. (2016). The role of technology in SLA research. *Language Learning & Technology, 20*(2), 98–115.

Cuban, L. (1986). *Teachers and machines: The classroom use of technology since 1920.* Teachers College Press.

Cuban, L. (2001). *Oversold and underused: Computers in classrooms, 1980–2000.* Harvard University Press.

Culpeper, J., Mackey, A., & Taguchi, N. (2018). *Second language pragmatics: From theory to research.* Routledge.

Da, J., & Zheng, Y. (2018). Technology and the teaching and learning of Chinese as a foreign language. In C. Ke (Ed.). *The Routledge handbook of Chinese second language acquisition* (pp. 432–447). Routledge.

Davies, G., & Steel, D. (1981, April). *First steps in computer-assisted language learning at Ealing College of Higher Education* [Paper presentation]. CAL 81 Symposium.

Davies, G., Otto, S. E., & Rüschoff, B. (2012). Historical perspectives on CALL. In T. Michael, R. Hayo, & W. Mark (Eds.), *Contemporary computer-assisted language learning* (pp. 19–38). Bloomsbury.

Dew, J. E. (1989). Typeable national phonetic letters—Computerize Juhin Fwuhaw for teaching materials. *Journal of the Chinese Language Teachers Association, 24*(3), 91–100.

Dooly, M. (2017). Telecollaboration. In C. A. Chapelle & S. Sauro (Eds.), *The handbook of technology and second language teaching and learning* (pp. 169–183). Wiley-Blackwell.

Ellis, N. C. (2002). Frequency effects in language processing: A review with implications for theories of implicit and explicit language acquisition. *Studies in Second Language Acquisition, 24*(2), 143–188. https://doi.org/10.1017/s0272263102002024

Ellis, N. C. (2017). Cognition, corpora, and computing: Triangulating research in usage-based language learning. *Language Learning, 67*(S1), 40–65. https://doi.org/10.1111/lang.12215

Farr, F., & Murray, L. (Eds.). (2016). *The Routledge handbook of language learning and technology*. Routledge.

Gale, L. E. (1983). Montevidisco: An anecdotal history of an interactive videodisc. *CALICO Journal, 1*(1), 42–46. https://doi.org/10.1558/cj.v1i1.42-46

Gao, Z. (2019). Towards automatic identification of Chinese collocation errors. In C. Shei, M. Zikpi, & D. Chao (Eds.), *The Routledge handbook of Chinese language teaching* (pp. 526–543). Routledge.

Gass, S. (1997). *Input, interaction, and the second language learner*. Lawrence Erlbaum.

Godwin-Jones, R. (2021). Evolving technologies for language learning. *Language Learning & Technology, 25*(3), 6–26. http://hdl.handle.net/10125/73443

González-Lloret, M. (2019). Task-based language teaching and L2 pragmatics. In N. Taguchi (Ed.), *Routledge handbook of SLA and pragmatics* (pp. 338–352). Routledge.

González-Lloret, M. (2021). L2 pragmatics and CALL. *Language Learning & Technology, 25*(3), 90–105. http://hdl.handle.net/10125/73451

Gray, E. F. (1992). Interactive language learning: A la rencontre de Philippe. *The French Review, 65*(3), 499–507. www.jstor.org/stable/pdf/395140.pdf?casa_token=uG7VkzK6-0sgAAAAA:irVHUKAehGnRpz3mbrrIbye4Pit3_4zwEUQVrvOdcBLGOgcLHUwccTSrCqcZA64gDVVrXqaCKOoMVujFWsqcPPoOdeV1sE_kQBF1xD2ryFmmv8wKwGU

Hubbard, P. (2008). Twenty-five years of theory in the CALICO Journal. *CALICO Journal, 25*(3), 387–399.

Hubbard, P. (Ed.). (2009). *Computer assisted language learning: Critical concepts in linguistics* (Vol. I-IV). Routledge. https://web.stanford.edu/~efs/callcc/

Hubbard, P. (2021). *An invitation to CALL: Foundations of computer-assisted language learning*. APACALL. www.apacall.org/research/books/6/

Hubbard, P., & Levy, M. (2016). Theory in computer assisted language learning research and practice. In F. Farr & L. Murray (Eds.), *The Routledge handbook of language learning and technology* (pp. 50–64). Routledge.

Jones, R. L. (1995). TICCIT and CLIPS: The early years. Thirty years of computer-assisted language instruction: Festschrift for John R. Russell (R. Sanders, Ed.). *CALICO Journal, 12*(4), 84–96. https://doi.org/10.1558/cj.v12i4.84-96

Ke, C., & Zhang, Z. (2002). *Chinese computerized adaptive listening comprehension test*. The Ohio State University Foreign Language Publication, http://ccalt.osu.edu/

Kern, R. (2014). Technology as pharmakon: The promise and perils of the internet for foreign language education. *The Modern Language Journal, 98*(1), 340–357. https://doi.org/10.1111/j.1540-4781.2014.12065.x

Kusyk, M. (2017). The development of complexity, accuracy, and fluency in L2 written production through informal participation in online activities. *CALICO Journal, 34*(1), 75–96. https://doi.org/10.1558/cj.29513

Lantolf, J. P. (2000). *Sociocultural theory and second language acquisition*. Oxford University Press.

Lantolf, J. P., & Pavlenko, A. (1995). Sociocultural theory and second language acquisition. *Annual Review of Applied Linguistics, 15*, 108–124. https://doi.org/10.1017/s0267190500002646

Last, R. (1984). *Language teaching and the microcomputer*. Wiley-Blackwell.

Levy, M. (1997). *Computer-assisted language learning: Context and conceptualization*. Oxford University Press.

Levy, M., & Hubbard, P. (2005). Why call CALL CALL? (editorial). *Computer Assisted Language Learning, 18*(3), 143–149.

Liu, P. (2007). Computer technology and Chinese language teaching: Looking into the past and the future. *Journal of the Chinese Language Teachers Association, 42*(3), 81–100.

Liu, S. (Ed.). (2022a). *Teaching the Chinese language remotely: Global cases and perspectives*. Springer Nature. https://doi.org/10.1007/978-3-030-87055-3

Liu, S. (Ed.). (2022b). *Online Chinese teaching and learning in 2020–2020中文线上教学*. National Foreign Language Resource Center.

Liu, S., & Da, J. (2022). Technology in Chinese language teaching. In Z. Ye (Ed.), *The Palgrave handbook of Chinese language studies* (pp. 1–41). Palgrave Macmillan. https://doi.org/10.1007/978-981-13-6844-8_3-2

MacWhinney, B. (1995). Evaluating foreign language tutoring systems. In V. M. Holland, J. D. Kaplan, & M. R. Sams (Eds.), *Intelligent language tutors: Theory shaping technology* (pp. 317–326). Lawrence Erlbaum Associates.

Martinez-Lage, A., & Herren, D. (1998). Challenges and opportunities: Curriculum pressures in the technological present. In J. Harper, M. Lively, & M. Williams (Eds.), *The coming of age of the profession: Issues and emerging ideas for teaching of foreign languages* (pp. 141–167). Heinle & Heinle.

Mohsen, M. A., Althebi, S., Alsagour, R., Alsalem, A., Almudawi, A., & Alshahrani, A. (2023). Forty-two years of computer-assisted language learning research: A scientometric study of hotspot research and trending issues. *ReCALL*, 1–20. www.cambridge.org/core/services/aop-cambridge-core/content/view/6A18E83D2D3DCFA3E42AA420BB1FF018/S0958344023000253a.pdf/div-class-title-forty-two-years-of-computer-assisted-language-learning-research-a-scientometric-study-of-hotspot-research-and-trending-issues-div.pdf

Navarre, A. (2019). *Technology-enhanced teaching and learning of Chinese as a foreign language*. Routledge.

Otto, S. E. (2017). From past to present: A hundred years of technology for L2 learning. In C. A. Chapelle & S. Sauro (Eds.), *The handbook of technology and second language teaching and learning* (pp. 10–25). Wiley-Blackwell.

Oxford, R. L. (1995). Linking theories of learning with intelligent computer-assisted language learning (ICALL). In V. M. Holland, J. D. Kaplan, & M. R. Sams (Eds.), *Intelligent language tutors: Theory shaping technology* (pp. 359–369). Lawrence Erlbaum Associates, Inc.

Ozturk, N. (2013). Using CALL in language teaching and learning, in consideration of its strengths and limitations. *Journal of European Education, 3*(1), 35–41. www.eu-journal.org/index.php/JEE/article/view/189

Pederson, K. M. (1987). Research on CALL. In W. F. Smith (Ed.), *Modern media in foreign language education: Theory and implementation* (pp. 99–132). National Textbook Company.

Reinders, H., & Darasawang, P. (2011). Diversity in learner support. In G. Stockwell (Ed.), *Computer-assisted language learning: Diversity in research and practice* (pp. 49–70). Cambridge University Press.

Reinders, H., & Lan, Y. J. (2021). Big data in language education and research. *Language Learning & Technology, 25*(1), 1–3. http://hdl.handle.net/10125/44746

Reinhardt, J., & Oskoz, A. (2021). Twenty-five years of emerging technologies. *Language Learning & Technology, 25*(3), 1–5. http://hdl.handle.net/10125/73442

Richards, J., & Rodgers, T. (2014). *Approaches and methods in language teaching* (3rd ed.). Cambridge University Press.

Salaberry, M. R. (1996). The theoretical foundation for the development of pedagogical tasks in computer mediated communication. *CALICO Journal, 14*(1), 5–34. https://doi.org/10.1558/cj.v14i1.5-34

Salaberry, M. R. (2001). The use of technology for second language learning and teaching: A retrospective. *Modern Language Journal, 85*(1), 39–56. https://doi.org/10.1111/0026-7902.00096

Sanders, R. (1995). Thirty years of computer-assisted language instruction: Introduction. *CALICO Journal, 12*(4), 6–14. https://journal.equinoxpub.com/Calico/issue/view/1661

Sanders, R., & Sanders, A. (1995). History of an AI spy game: Spion. *CALICO Journal, 12*(4), 114–127. https://doi.org/10.1558/cj.v12i4.114-127

Shei, C., & Hsieh, H. (2012). Linkit: A CALL system for learning Chinese characters, words, and phrases. *Computer Assisted Language Learning*, *25*(4), 319–338. https://doi.org/10.1080/09588221.2011.589390

Shi, L., & Stickler, U. (2019). Using technology to learn to speak Chinese. In C. Shei, E. Monica, M. Zikpi, & D. Chao (Eds.), *The Routledge handbook of Chinese language teaching* (pp. 509–525). Routledge. https://doi.org/10.4324/9781315104652-32

Shrum, J. L., & Glisan, E. W. (2010). *Teacher's handbook* (4th ed.). Heinle & Heinle.

Simmons, R. V. (2014, February). *Teaching pronunciation and grammar, tricks and keys*. [Keynote speech]. K–12 Chinese-Language Teachers Roundtable.

Sockett, G. (2014). *The online informal learning of English*. Springer.

Sundqvist, P., & Sylvén, L. K. (2016). *Extramural English in teaching and learning*. Palgrave Macmillan.

Thomas, M., Reinders, H., & Warschauer, M. (2012). The role of digital media and incremental change. In M. Thomas, H. Reinders, & M. Warschauer (Eds.), *Contemporary computer assisted language learning* (pp. 1–12). Bloomberg Academic.

Thorne, S. L. (2008). Transcultural communication in open internet environments and massively multiplayer online games. In S. Magnan (Ed.), *Mediating discourse online* (pp. 305–327). John Benjamins.

Tseng, M., & Gao, Y. (2021). *Teach Chinese online: An essential guide*. Phoenix Tree Publishing.

Warschauer, M. (1996). Computer-assisted language learning: An introduction. In S. Fotos (Ed.), *Multimedia language teaching* (pp. 3–20). Logos International.

Warschauer, M. (2000). The death of cyberspace and the rebirth of CALL. *English Teachers' Journal*, *53*(1), 61–67. https://education.uci.edu/uploads/7/2/7/6/72769947/cyberspace.pdf

Warschauer, M., & Healey, D. (1998). Computers and language learning: An overview. *Language Teaching*, *31*, 57–71.

Wiggins, G., & McTighe, J. (2005). *Understanding by design, expanded 2nd Edition*. Association for Supervision and Curriculum Development.

Winke, P., & MacGregor, D. (2001). Review of hot Potatoes. *Language Learning & Technology*, *5*(2), 28–33. http://llt.msu.edu/vol5num2/review3/default.html

Wu, Y. (2016). Technology in CFL education. In J. Ruan, C. Leung, & J. Zhang (Eds.), *Perspectives on Chinese as a foreign language education* (pp. 97–122). Springer.

Xie, T. (2001). E-Generation's Chinese language teachers: Meet the new challenges. *Journal of Chinese Language Teachers Association*, *36*(3), 75–80.

Xie, T. 谢天蔚 (2008, August). 电脑教学日常化是必由之路 (*Normalization of CALL is the only way forward*). [Paper presentation]. 第六届中文电化教学国际研讨会发言稿. 韩国又松大学 (Speech at the Sixth International Symposium of Call for Chinese. Woosong Univerisity, Korea).

Xie, T., & Yao, T. C. (2009). Technology in Chinese language teaching and learning. In M. Everson & Y. Xiao (Eds.), *Teaching Chinese as a foreign language: Theories and applications* (pp. 151–172). Cheng & Tsui Company.

Xu, D. B. (2004, May). *Adapting the past, facing the future, an overview of the development of multimedia Chinese language teaching* [Plenary speech]. The 3rd International Conference on Technology and Chinese Language Teaching (TCLT3).

Xu, D. B. (2005, June). *An overview of the development of multimedia Chinese language teaching during the past 35 years* [Plenary speech]. International Conference on Internet Chinese Education.

Xu, D. B. (2013, July). *Current trend in technology and Chinese language teaching* [Paper presentation]. TCLT Forum at The 7th International Conference on Internet Chinese Education, Pasadena, CA.

Xu, D. B. (2015). Issues in CALL studies. *Journal of Technology and Chinese Language Teaching*, *6*(2), 1–16.

Yao, T. C. (1995). A computer-adaptive test for reading Chinese: A preliminary report. *Journal of Chinese Language Teachers Association*, *30*(1), 75–85.

Yao, T. C. (1996). A review of some computer assisted language learning (CALL) software for Chinese. In S. McGinnis (Ed.), *Chinese pedagogy: An emerging field* (pp. 255–284). Foreign Language Publications

Yao, T. C. (2003, October). *The current situation and future of Internet Chinese teaching in the United States* [Paper presentation]. The 3rd International Conference on Internet Chinese Education. Taipei.

Yao, T. C. (2009). The current status of Chinese CALL in the United States. *Journal of Chinese Language Teachers Association, 44*(1), 1–23.

Yao, T. C., & Peterson, M. (1986). Chinese character tutor: An example of Chinese language instruction using personal computers. *Journal of the Chinese Language Teachers Association, 21*(2), 1–18.

Zhang, Z. (1998). CALL for Chinese: Issues and practice. *Journal of Chinese Language Teachers Association, 33*(1), 51–82.

Zhang, Z. (2002). "Writing" characters using the computer. In *Proceedings of the third international conference on Chinese pedagogy*. Nanjing University Press.

Zhang, Z. (2019). The current status of CALL for Chinese in the United States. In C. Shei, M. Zikpi, & D. Chao (Eds.), *The Routledge handbook of Chinese language teaching* (pp. 493–508). Routledge. https://doi.org/10.4324/9781315104652-31

Ziegler, N., & González-Lloret, M. (Eds.). (2022). *The Routledge handbook of second language acquisition and technology*. Routledge.

3 Digital Humanities

3.1 Introduction

In the third volume of *Modernism/Modernity,* as published on April 11, 2018, Buurma and Heffernan wrote an article, which starts as follows:

> From this day forward, every time you see the name Roberto Busa invoked as a—or *the*—founding scholar of either quantitative or computational method in the humanities, we want you to mentally search and replace with another name: Josephine Miles.
>
> Miles was a poet and an English professor at Berkeley. In the 1930s, as a graduate student at Berkeley, she completed her first distant reading project: an analysis of the adjectives favored by Romantic poets. In the 1940s, with the aid of a Guggenheim, she expanded this work into a large-scale study of the phrasal forms of the poetry of the 1640s, 1740s, and 1840s. In all of this distant reading work, Miles created her tabulations by hand, with pen and graph paper. She also directed possibly the first literary concordance to use machine methods. In the early 1950s, Miles became project director of an abandoned index-card-based Concordance to the Poetical Works of John Dryden. Partnering with the Electrical Engineering department at Berkeley, and contracting with their computer lab and its IBM tabulation machine, Miles used machine methods to complete the concordance. It was published in 1957, six years after she and several woman graduate students and woman punch-card operators began the work. It was thus begun around the time that Busa circulated early proof-of-concept drafts of his concordance to the complete works of St. Thomas Aquinas, and published 17 years before the first volumes of the 56-volume *Index Thomasticus* began to appear.
>
> (p. 1)

Here, Buurma and Heffernan claim that it is Miles, not Busa, who should be considered the founding pioneer in "computational method in the humanities." This is because Miles is the first scholar to launch a distant reading project to analyze Romantic poets' use of adjectives with quantitative methods and later to direct a concordance project to examine John Dryden's poetical works. Furthermore, Miles

DOI: 10.4324/9781003292081-3

not only involved female collaborators to prepare the punch cards but also recognized their contribution to her research. Specialized in poetics, Josephine Miles, in completing these unprecedent projects at the time, transformed her own writing of poetry as well as teaching of poetry composition and initiated the era of computing humanities, now known as Digital Humanities (DH), which started up new ways of teaching and researching about humanities.

Many scholars (e.g., Hockey (1980, 2004), Terras (2006), Sevensson (2009), Burdick et al. (2012), and Nyhan and Flinn (2016)) identified Robert Busa as the forebearer of Humanities Computing because of his completion of large-scale projects on works of St. Thomas Aquinas, whereas some like Oakman (1980) named John W. Ellison, due to his project *Computerized Concordance to the Revised Standard Version of the Bible* completed in 1957 (Vanhoutte, 2013). I am not attempting to enter the debate by arguing with Buurma and Heffernan about instating Miles as the first forerunner for the field of computing humanities. I merely want to draw attention to the three keywords: distant reading, concordance, and computing humanities. So-called *distant reading* is a fairly new term coined by Moretti (2000, 2005) in contrast with close reading, referring to the use of computational methods to quantify the examination of literary works, typically by "aggregating and analyzing massive amounts of data" (Schulz, 2011). Such method differs from the traditional approach of close reading, which focuses on appraising particular words and phrases, identifying general patterns of description, and exploring underlying themes of the work. Undoubtedly, both distant reading and close reading are valuable methodologies for literary studies, with one supplementing the other. However, the former, through embracing new technologies such as text mining and data mining tools for probing literature and culture, has sparked a broader interest among humanists. As for *concordance*, it can mean either a compilation of all the occurrences of a word in a text or corpus showing the words that appear before or after it or a software program that can automatically generate such a list of each occurrence of the item along with some contexts. Concordancing, a valuable tool for understanding the meaning and patterns within a text, is useful for linguistic and literary analysis because it reveals a rich array of information, including literal meanings and implied connotations, collocation within a context, and frequency with respect to individual words. It is important to note that the earliest concordances were dated to the 13th century, when preachers of the Bible used concordancing methodologies for scriptural interpretation (Wisbey, 1962; McCarty, 1993; Sinclair & Rockwell, 2015; Rockwell & Sinclair, 2016).

Empowered by computing technologies, the methodologies like distant readings, concordance, and other quantitative techniques motivated scholars to embark on novel approaches to textual analysis in a multitude of captivating projects. In consequence, the discipline of computing humanities was established (e.g., Rockwell, 1999; Terras, 2006). Over the past several decades, different terms were used to refer to the activities and practices of these kinds of text analyses, such as computing humanities, humanities computing, humanist informatics, literary and linguistic computing, digital resources in the humanities, and eHumanities occasionally to be found in literature from continental Europe (Nyhan et al, 2013, p. 2). In 2004,

Digital Humanities was chosen to replace the previous terms and has since been used in the field. Why did the field change its name from computing humanities to DH? What is computing humanities? What is DH? What do digital humanists do? What is the history of the DH evolution? What contributions has DH brought to the study of humanities? What are the issues in the field of DH? What are the future directions for DH? I will address some of these questions in this chapter.

3.2 What Is DH?

I will follow Vanhoutte (2013) in distinguishing the capitalized *Digital Humanities* to refer to the field and digital humanities without capitalization to refer to the activity in and for the humanities. What is DH? This is not a straightforward question. On the one hand, many working in the field endeavored to develop a definite and definitive definition of what Digital Humanities is, while, on the other hand, the field is emerging and changing so rapidly due to the advancing of information technologies that it is hard to describe who belongs to DH and what they do. To understand the field, let us begin with the task of defining "Humanities Computing," because that is what Digital Humanities has inherited from. In addition, Humanities Computing is "relatively established and well-defined," and "many of the issues, considerations and parameters relevant to Humanities Computing are also relevant to digital humanities more generally" (Sevensson, 2009, para. 8).

In his work, "The Gates of Hell: History and Definition of Digital | Humanities | Computing," Vanhoutte (2013) stated the following: "By 'Humanities Computing' I mean the practice of using computing *for* and *in* the humanities from the early 1950s to 2004 when 'Digital Humanities' became the prominent name for the field" (p. 120). This definition is specific about the period of time when Humanities Computing lasted as a field but vague about its "practice." Earlier, Unsworth (2002) defined "Humanities Computing" as something one can do,

> in which the computer is used as tool for modeling humanities data and our understanding of it, and that activity is entirely distinct from using the computer when it models the typewriter, or the telephone, or the phonograph, or any of the many other things it can be.
>
> (p. 71)

Then what is that "something"? Unsworth elaborated on the "something" by stating the following:

> So, given that humanities computing isn't general-purpose academic computing—isn't word-processing, email, web-browsing [. . .] [h]umanities computing is a practice of representation, a form of modeling or [. . .] mimicry. It is [. . .] a way of reasoning and a set of ontological commitments, and its representational practice is shaped by the need for efficient computation on the one hand, and for human communication on the other.
>
> (p. 73)

With that lengthy definition, Unsworth used examples to illustrate each of his assertions, which are the statements that he drew from Davis et al. (1993). Concordance, for example, is a case that he adopted to explain the assertion that Humanities Computing is a way of reasoning. As discussed before, a concordance software is able to sort keywords based on their frequency, word lengths, or other morphological features in a context. To accomplish that functionality, the software needs to use intelligent inference to detect patterns in a text and allow for certain kinds of stylistic analysis.

Unsworth's view of Humanities Computing is reiterated by other scholars. For example, Burdick et al. (2012) claimed that

> the mere use of digital tools for the purpose of humanistic research and communication does not qualify as Digital Humanities. Nor is Digital Humanities to be understood as the study of digital artifacts, new media, or contemporary culture in place of physical artifacts, old media, or historical culture.
>
> (p. SG2)

This perspective further ignited debates as to who should belong to the field. On this topic, roughly speaking, two schools of thought can be categorized. Headed by Melissa Terras is the school of "Big Tent Digital Humanities," as first expressed in her blog (Terras, 2011). Under this "big tent" gathered the scholars and practitioners whose research includes a wide variety of disciplines, including African American literature, American studies, arts and arts classics, computing and computer sciences, education, engineering, history, languages and literatures, linguistics, mathematics and statistics, media studies, medieval literature and culture, music, philosophy, religious studies, social sciences and cultural studies, women's studies, gender and sexuality studies, and postcolonial studies (e.g., Terras, 2006, 2011; Sula & Hill, 2019). For this group of scholars, DH is open and accessible to all so as to reflect diverse human experiences and perspectives. Unlike the inclusive scholars who advocate diversity and inclusivity in DH are the exclusive people, who endeavor to embrace digital technologies and methodologies to explore new avenues for research and education in the digital age, as postulated in *The Digital Humanities Manifesto 2.0* (Presner et al., 2009). Stephen Ramsay, one extreme representative of exclusive scholars, claimed that if scholars do not possess technical skills like coding, they should be excluded from the DH (Ramsay, 2013a). He highly promoted the idea of "building" for DH by arguing that if "you aren't building, you are not engaged in the 'methodologization' of the humanities, which, to me, is the hallmark of the discipline" (Ramsay, p. 241). According to Ramsay (2013b), "building" is a new kind of hermeneutic. Things like "data mining, xml encoding, text analysis, GIS, Web design, visualization, programming, tool design, database design" involve building (p. 245). Patrik Svensson suggested a "no tent" approach" (2012), which considered DH as "a fractioned (not homogenous) collaborative (not coerced) trading zone and a meeting place that supports deeply collaborative work, individual expression, unexpected connections, and synergetic power" (p. 46).

McCarty (2003) called for "self-reflection" about different approaches towards defining the field by arguing that the question of what constitutes and defines Humanities Computing should be continually explored and refined rather than answered definitively (McCarty, 2003, p. 1233). Similarly, Terras (2006) claimed that with an absence of definition about the field, practitioners in the field of DH would be "free to develop their own research and career paths, which may not fit into the normal mode of operation for academic subjects, but could allow the subject to remain fluid and undefined" (p. 242). Along these lines of arguments, Nyhan et al. (2013), in their introduction to the book, *Defining Digital Humanities: A Reader*, stated the following:

> We do not try to define digital humanities ourselves: our editorial perspective is to highlight the range of discussions that attempt to scope out the limits and purview of the discipline. We hope that this volume is of interest both to those new to the discipline and established scholars in the field, to frame the debate on how best to define digital humanities.
>
> (p. 7)

Clearly, as can be seen, instead of defining DH, they urged continued reflection on what and how humanists can contribute by using new methodologies and tools in their research. During the first 15 years of this century, as DH was still an emerging field with scholars coming from various disciplines to explore and examine, it was impractical or unproductive to expect a comprehensive definition that a majority, if not everyone, would agree upon. That view is further manifested in Vanhoutte's (2013) statement, "A definition therefore formally freezes the meaning of a term and since Humanities Computing as a field of activity was in constant flux, a formal description was therefore impossible" (p. 137).

Despite the difficulty in reaching a consensus with respect to viewing the field, numerous scholars have endeavored to define DH, as evidenced in Gibbs's (2013) 170 responses to the question "How do you define Humanities Computing/Digital Humanities" collected in 2011, and Terras et al.'s (2013) selection of a range of thoughts regarding what DH should or can be for the project Day of Digital Humanities Definitions, spanning from 2009 to 2012. I highlight Burdick et al.'s (2012) definition, which goes as follows:

> Digital Humanities refers to new modes of scholarship and institutional units for collaborative, transdisciplinary, and computationally engaged research, teaching, and publication [including] . . . the opportunities and challenges that arise from the conjunction of the term digital with the term humanities to form a new collective singular.
>
> (p. 122)

This definition takes into consideration both "opportunities" and "challenges" as a result of combining "digital" with "humanities." By "opportunities," Burdick et al. acknowledged new prospects whereby more traditional classroom learning is animated with digital tools and innovative methods like "hands-on project-based learning." When specialists collaborate across disciplines, "new inquiry and knowledge production" cultivates a technologically enhanced generation of "humanists." While traditional concerns associated with "the Humanities" remain essential in DH, the "challenges" are how to address these fundamental questions in the information age through digital instruments. Classroom teaching conducted under such an approach can nurture students with innovative minds and creative hands. This definition aligns with the observation made in Hockey (2004) that the field "has had to embrace 'the two cultures,' to bring the rigor and systematic unambiguous procedural methodologies characteristic of the sciences to address problems within the humanities that had hitherto been most often treated in a serendipitous fashion" (p. 3). It also accords with what is proclaimed in *The Digital Humanities Manifesto 2.0*. That is, DH "can serve as an umbrella under which to group both people and projects seeking to reshape and reinvigorate contemporary arts and humanities practices and expand their boundaries." It does not imply "a digital turn that might somehow leave the Humanities intact," neither does it mean that "the humanities are being modified by the digital, as it were, 'from the outside' with the digital leading and the Humanities following" (Presner et al., 2009, p. 13). This definition serves as the basis for the current work.

Let me end the discussion with a recent definition provided by Davis et al. (2020):

> Digital humanities is an area of research, teaching, and creation concerned with the intersection of computing and humanities research questions. Developed from an earlier field called humanities computing, today, digital humanities embraces a variety of topics ranging from curating online collections to data mining large cultural data sets. Digital humanities currently incorporates both digitized and born-digital materials and combines methodologies from the traditional humanities disciplines (such as history, philosophy, linguistics, literature, art history, archaeology, music, and cultural studies) with tools provided by computing (such as data visualization, information retrieval, text encoding, data mining, statistics, and computational analysis) and digital publishing.
>
> (p. 24)

This definition is extensive, encompassing a broad spectrum of disciplines and involving research, teaching, and services pertaining to the intersection of humanities and computing.

3.3 What Do Digital Humanists Do?

With a general picture of the issues related to defining DH accompanied with some definitions, let us take a look at who digital humanists are and what they do. For the purposes of this book, I will only examine the areas that involve literary text analysis, such as distant reading and concordance. In particular, I will show how literary scholars conduct their teaching and research.

Based on Terras (2006), part of which analyzes the presentations of the 2005 Humanities Computing Conference held at the University of Victoria, Canada, the participants were mostly faculty members from a broad range of academic disciplines such as library studies, English, linguistics, computer science, arts and social sciences, archaeology, communication, economics and business, philosophy, and sociology (p. 86). A decade later, Sula and Hill (2019) completed a study on the corpus that consisted of 1,334 research articles published in the journals *Computers and the Humanities (CHum)* (1966–2004) and *Literary and Linguistic Computing (LLC)* (1986–2004). One of their major findings is that text is the most frequently studied medium, totaling 59% of all *CHum* articles and 72% of *LLC* articles. In terms of disciplines, English language and literature is studied the most (i.e., taking up 13.9% for *CHum* and 15.3% for *LLC*). The findings supported Kirschenbaum's observation that DH's "professional apparatus . . . is probably more rooted in English than any other departmental home" (Kirschenbaum, 2010, p. 55). In addition to the faculty of English who published their DH research on the two journals are those who were from the area of languages and literatures other than English (12.5% and 15.2%), followed by linguists (8.2% and 12.4% for *CHum* and *LLC* respectively) and the humanists in a variety of fields including library sciences, music, history, classics, philosophy, religious studies, arts and art history, education, social sciences, and sciences (p. 198). These two studies offer a glimpse of the individuals engaged in researching DH activities between 1966 and 2004.

Sula and Hills (2019) called for further examination as to why, in the early days, literature studies scholars involved in DH were mostly from the areas of English as compared to other disciplines. It might not be too difficult to speculate given that English language and literature studies faculty deal with texts as part of their research and teaching. As shown by the case of Miles who was mentioned at the beginning of this chapter, she was an English professor, specializing in poetry analysis and writing. Some examination of how English professors teach in literature classrooms sheds light on the question. In the collection *Teaching With Digital Humanities: Tools and Methods for Nineteenth-Century American Literature*, editors Travis and DeSpain (2018) presented innovative ways instructors of 19th-century American literature involved their students to improve skills and interests while advancing the study of the academic content. For example, a study by Cynthia L. Hallen required her students to participate in developing the database *Emily Dickinson Lexicon* with the help of *WordCruncher*, a free app. Years of collaboration between the instructor and her students of different classes eventually resulted in a website hosting the digital dictionary of all the words that appear in Dickinson's poems. In addition, Hallen provided her seminar students with a digital copy of the complete poems of Eliza R. Snow and asked them to compare and contrast the two poets' word choices. In this way, students were able to better appreciate the poems of the two authors. In the 15 case studies comprising Travis and DeSpain's collection, instructors engaged students in active learning through technology-supported assignments or projects in the format of either making, archiving, acting and playing, or curating, etc. Consequently, the students developed archives or worked as authors, editors, lexicographers, project managers, and/or collaborators while learning the subject matter. In the process of doing this, students dealt with critical analysis of literature in novel ways and comprehended multiple uses of literary studies. One notable aspect is that students in these American literature classrooms not only engaged in the traditional practice of reading masterpieces to comprehend the meanings of important works but also utilized available digital tools to create products, thereby developing higher-level thinking and collaboration skills. Teaching literature in this way, as noted by Travis and DeSpain, demonstrated "an important shift in emphasis to DH pedagogy, moving from a focus on digital humanities writ large to how particular DH methods and practices operate at a field-specific level" (p. ix). The editors invited scholars of literary study and beyond to discuss how to "deepen their own objectives for student learning and scholarship" (p. ix).

Another example involves distant reading, which has been proved effective when used to analyze a *corpus* of oral texts to generate trends and patterns. As reported in Burdick et al. (2012), the University of Southern California Shoah Foundation's Visual History Archive employs the methodology of distant reading to provide online access to videos wherein cultural data had been extracted from the 2-hour-long taped testimonies of over 52,000 Holocaust and other genocide survivors. With help from the computing analyses, machine reading, advanced filming techniques, and specialized display technologies, users can quickly access any one video out of the thousands for watching. Additionally, in a few cases, users are able to not only interpose their own reactions to what they are viewing but also to actually converse with the survivor whose interview was prerecorded (To engage in virtual conversation with Holocaust survivor Pinchas Gutter, visit [https://iwitness.usc.edu/dit/pinchas]). Such a fascinating interactive "conversation" between the user and a survivor achieved by the use of "new and impactful technology" shows that research with the distant reading methodology enables expansive studies of humanities and achieves scholarly insights previously unattainable without impossibly difficult and/or costly methodology.

Related to distant reading is concordance, which is at the core of text analysis. As mentioned before, concordance predated the age of computer technology, which emerged when a table or an index to the Bible was made by hand for effective preaching of scriptures (Wisbey, 1962; Howard-Hill, 1979; McCarty, 1993; Rockwell & Sinclair, 2016). With no assistance from any machine, staff working for the handmade concordance projects had to spend an extremely large amount of time or even their whole life repeating the same mechanical work such as cutting a slip of a particular item and then pasting it (Rockwell & Sinclair, 2016). With the advent of the computer, which was ready and willing to repeat tedious work without any complaint, creating a concordance became more efficient. However, it still cost much time and energy in the era of mainframe computers because data had to be keyed using the technique of punching cards due to the lack of effective inputting methods. McCarty (1993) considered Busa's *Index Thomisticus* as the first computer-assisted lemmatized concordance, though it was produced by "machine but designed to be printed" in accordance with Howard-Hill's (1979) classification of concordance. The Busa project took a staff of 60 people 33 years to, among other works, produce millions of punch cards, before a concordance of 118 of Thomas

Aquinas' texts and further texts by another 61 related authors was created, which led to a 56-volume set, later put on CD-ROM, and now a web service (Vanhoutte, 2013). The invention of the World Wide Web rendered the concordancing methodology web-based and interactive. Unlike the early concordances, which were organized by theme or logic of the text, the contemporary electronic concordances are organized alphabetically. Such user-friendly and interactive concordances have become "ubiquitous analytics" (Rockwell & Sinclair, 2016). For example, the publication of President George W. Bush's seventh State of the Union address in the *New York Times* of January 23, 2007, contained a built-in visual analytics tool, which enabled readers to see the frequency of each word used in the address. Through a couple of simple clicks, readers could immediately find out that "Afghanistan," a most-frequently-used word in the 2002 State of the Union address, is replaced by the word "Iraq" in 2007 (Rockwell & Sinclair, 2016). In another case, Amazon's *Click to Look Inside!* feature offers users a quick overview of the table of contents and introduction regarding a given e-book. The *Google Ngram Viewer*, an online search engine, provides the information found in printed sources published in between 1500 and 2019 by charting the frequencies of any set of search strings that users put in. All these are made possible by using the methodology of concordance (Rockwell & Sinclair, 2016).

In sum, the work described here was conducted by humanists mostly specialized in literary analysis or culture studies. Some scholars engaged their students in hands-on projects, resulting in a product or a tool as a result. Through the projects, students as well as faculty achieved "procedural literacy" (Ramsay, 2013b, p. 245), which should be a valuable asset for both groups. The process of making or building while researching or teaching through data mining, text analysis, web design, visualization, database design, etc. is unique to the characteristics of DH inquiries, different from those of traditional humanities research focusing more on analysis and criticism. DH and non-DH activities and practices have their own approaches, yet the two can be materialized in the works of the same scholar. This is reflected in Franco Moretti, a well-known Italian literary historian and theorist; he conducted both kinds of research and managed to publish his *Distant Reading* (DH book) and *The Bourgeois* (non-DH book) on the same day. When interviewed by Melissa Dinsman, Moretti shared his reflections on the process of writing the two books by saying that "I do things in the mode of *Distant Reading* that I could never do in the mode of *The Bourgeois*. But it also works the other way around" (Dinsman, 2016). The examples as discussed that integrate the methodologies of text analysis, distant readings, and concordance have benefited the general public.

3.4 The Historical Developments of DH

Hockey (2004) outlined four historical periods regarding DH development. They are as follows: (i) Beginnings: 1949 to early 1970s; (ii) Consolidation: 1970s to mid-1980s; (iii) New Developments: mid-1980s to early 1990s; and (iv) The Era of the Internet: early 1990s to the present. This categorization of DH development corresponds to the chronological progression of information technology related to

CALL, as discussed in Chapter 2. Vanhoutte (2013) reviewed the earlier development of the field by telling the interesting stories of how the warfare technologies such as cryptanalysis resulted in machine translation for the social function of textual computing, which not only further led to many well-known accomplishments including the Text Encoding Initiative (TEI) but finally grew into a discipline of DH. Nyhan and Flinn (2016), which presented a collection of oral histories told by those who worked in the field in the earlier days, outlined two stages for DH history, with Humanities Computing (c.1949–2006) as the first and Digital Humanities (c.2006–present) as the second. This division is marked by the change of terminology that replaced Humanities Computing with Digital Humanities around 2004. Unlike the previous scholars' approaches and accounts, Sula and Hill (2019) recorded the history by analyzing the articles published in the two founding journals in the field of DH, covering the time from 1966 to 2004. By tracing publications of two major journals for around 40 years, Sula and Hill obtained the empirical evidence that the early DH work heavily involved text experiments. However, the study also indicated a broader trend in which DH scholarship was expanded to include sound, multimedia, and other disciplinary investigations, with researchers from under-represented locations. Hopkins (2022) offered a personal account of DH history from 1981 to 2021, listing technical milestones in accordance with his anecdotal experience. All theses investigations provide a holistic view showing how Humanities Computing emerged and was branded into Digital Humanities chronologically.

I will, in the following pages, describe the DH evolution from an alternative perspective, focusing on two central questions: (i) how was the professional infrastructure of DH built up? and (ii) how did academia respond to the rise of DH? By tracking the milestones in the establishment of associations, organization of conferences, launching of journals, institutionalization of DH education, and development of curriculum over the past six decades, I aim to show how the field of DH has developed its disciplinary identity, thereby providing a glimpse into its overall growth.

Establishing Associations How is the professional infrastructure of DH formed? To answer this question, I will start with Roy Wisbey, a British specialist on medieval German literature. In the early 1960s, inspired by Busa's seminal work, Wisbey concorded "Wiener Genesis," an Old Testament in early Middle High German, which consisted of over 6,000 lines in rhyming couplets and was of great linguistic as well as literary importance (Wisbey, 1962). Seeing the potential of this kind of work, Wisbey established the Literary and Linguistic Computing Centre (LLCC) at the University of Cambridge in 1963 to carry out lexicographical and linguistic research (Hockey, 2004; Vanhoutte, 2013). As the founding director, Wisbey succeeded in archiving machine-readable texts of medieval German literature, for which he was considered as "the first in his discipline to publish a series of computer-generated indices and concordances" (Short, 2020). Wisbey moved to King's College London in 1971, where he founded the Centre for Computing in the Humanities in 1996, which became an academic department in 2002, and finally changed its name to the Department of Digital Humanities in 2011. Wisbey was instrumental in pioneering and laying out foundational work for the field.

Following early initiatives on hosting conferences and publishing conference proceedings which will be described shortly, the Association for Literary and Linguistic Computing (ALLC) was founded in 1973 in Europe and the Association for Computers and the Humanities (ACH) in 1978 in America, which, as remarked by Vanhoutte (2013), led the research on Humanities Computing from both sides of the Atlantic Ocean. As the field continued to grow, accompanied by increasing demands for institutional support, the Alliance of Digital Humanities Organization (ADHO) was established in 2005 to coordinate the endeavors of different regional organizations. At present, ADHO comprises 11 constituent organizations, including ACH and ALLC. In 2011, ALLC was renamed as the European Association for Digital Humanities (EADH) to encompass the expanded scope of DH and cater to the special requirements of European DH initiatives as well.

Organizing Conferences Around the period of time between 1964 and 1965, several important conferences were organized in the USA. One such early conference, titled *Computers for the Humanities?*, was held at Yale University in January 1965, resulting in the publication of the proceedings under the same title (Pierson, 1965). Later, 6 similar conferences were organized, all sponsored by IBM, attended by some 1,200 academics from the USA (Vanhoutte, 2013). Selected papers were published in *Computers in Humanistic Research: Readings and Perspectives* (Bowles, 1967), addressing the topics on computational applications in anthropology, archaeology, history, political sciences, language, literature, and musicology. Five years later, in Europe, under Wisbey's leadership, two international conferences on the use of the computer in literary and linguistic research were organized by LLCC in 1970 and 1972 respectively, with the first proceedings, *The Computer in Literary and Linguistic Research,* published by Cambridge University Press (Wisbey, 1971). Starting in 1970, ALLC organized its biannual conference on literary and linguistic computing in Europe, which later alternated with the biannual series of the International Conference on Computers in the Humanities in North America (Hockey, 2004; Vanhoutte, 2015b). While the focus then was mostly on literary studies and linguistic computing, it spurred huge interests in the role of technology among humanists. One year after ADHO was established in 2005, it began organizing an annual Digital Humanities conference. According to *The Index of Digital Humanities Conferences*, a recent creation out of a collaborative project (Eichmann-Kalwara et al., 2020), up to now, there have been a total of 8,777 presentations from 506 digital humanities conferences spanning 63 years, contributed by 10,393 different authors from 2,663 institutions and 86 countries. From founding a computer center to establishing an alliance with a number of associations, encompassing the transition from the ALLC to EADH, and progressing from publishing conference proceedings to archiving an online index of DH conferences, each marked a milestone, exemplifying a remarkable evolution of DH in quantity, quality, scope, and scale.

Launching Journals Related to the growing number of conferences is the launching of academic journals, which directly attests to its rich history. According to Sula and Hill (2019), ACH launched its journal *Computers and the Humanities* (*CHum*) in 1966, while ALLC published *Literary and Linguistic Computing* (*LLC*) in 1986. From 2005 onward, after *CHum* was terminated in 2004, *LLC* became the official journal for both ALLC and ACH, whose focus was on textual and text-based literary analysis. While the journal has played a profound role in establishing the field of Humanities Computing (Sevensson, 2009), *LLC* was renamed in 2015 as *Digital Scholarship in the Humanities* (*DSH*) to reflect the broader scope of the field. According to the chief editor of *DSH*, the first issue of *LLC* featured papers on authorship, style, meaning, text processing, linguistics, and lexicometrics, whereas the inaugural issue of its successor included the studies on oral history, film, ontologies, digital collections, and data modeling, in addition to research articles focusing on literary and linguistic themes. In order to reach out to a wide audience, *DSH* publishes not only digital scholarship but also "(interdisciplinary) contributions from fields akin to or related to the Digital Humanities" (Vanhoutte, 2015a).

In between the termination of *CHum* and the rebranding of *LLC* into *DSH*, a number of journals emerged, of which two should be highlighted: Digital Humanities Quarterly (*DHQ*) and *The Journal of Interactive Technology and Pedagogy* (*JITP*). *DHQ* is a digital journal covering all aspects of digital media in the humanities. Launched by ACH and ADHO in 2007, the open-access and peer-reviewed *DHQ* presents novel ways to operate. For example, it explores new publishing formats and the rhetoric of digital authoring; it delivers content by using open standards; and it provides multilingual reviewing services (www.digitalhumanities.org/dhq/). *JITP* is another open access and peer-reviewed online journal. Inaugurated in 2012 by the Interactive Technology and Pedagogy Certificate Program at the Graduate Center of the City University of New York and published in multimedia forms as well as traditional written formats, *JITP* invites voices from across academic disciplines. It is open in terms of topic, format, review process, and operation modes (https://jitp.commons.gc.cuny.edu/). For example, the editorial board includes graduate students who participate in the daily operation of the journal, such as to determine the type of content for the journal and to co-edit each issue with a faculty member. Furthermore, the journal incorporates a blog-style platform for general readers to post comments about each paper, facilitating direct communication between readers and authors for further discussions. It is evident that the innovative features of the two digital journals as described here differentiate them from a traditional paper journal in several significant ways.

Institutionalizing DH Education The establishment of professional associations and the organization of conferences, alongside the launching of journals, have built the necessary infrastructure that laid a solid foundation for DH to strive and thrive. In response to this development, academia started to open a new major/minor on DH, which is the second aspect that I will examine now. In the earlier days when computing humanities was considered as nonserious academic research on humanities, work in this regard was often overlooked. A typical example was when McMaster University developed a degree program in Humanities Computing in 1985, the faculty had to choose the word *multimedia* for the program Combined Honors in Multimedia and Another Subject instead of "Humanities Computing." This decision was made out of the concern that the latter might not appeal to either prospective students or university administrators (Rockwell,

1999). Since early researchers in Humanities Computing were usually located in "liminal and academically precarious institutional spaces" such as "instructional technology support units" and "grant-funded research groups," they had to be engaged in discussion on "how and whether this domain could become a discipline" and whether their faculty positions were academically legitimate (Flanders, 2012, p. 292). To solve this and other problems, research centers on DH were built on campus (Hirsch, 2012) (e.g., the Center for Digital Humanities at UCLA, Stanford Literary Lab, The Center for New Media and History at George Mason University, and the Maryland Institute for Technology in the Humanities, to name just a few in the USA). Observed by Fraistat (2012), centers like these are "key sites for bridging the daunting gap between new technology and humanities scholars, serving as the crosswalks between cyberinfrastructure and users," which not only promote genuine "collaborative and interdisciplinary work" but also bring together graduate students and faculty to work on "projects of common intellectual interest" (p. 281).

Amid the success of the opening of research centers with ongoing debates surrounding the question whether Humanities Computing is an academic discipline, programs developed on campuses slowly. For example, McCarty and Kirschenbaum (2003) published a list of departments, centers, institutes, and other institutional forms that conduct research or offer courses in the field, of which nine teaching programs provided an option or concentration on Humanities Computing. Terras (2006) compared the teaching focus of four university graduate programs, two from the UK and one from Belgium and the USA respectively. Just 5 years later, Spiro (2011) analyzed as many as 134 English language syllabi from DH courses, offered in between 2006 and 2011 and housed either in DH departments or in the departments of a wide varieties of disciplines (p. 9). By examining the assignments, readings, media types, key concepts, and technologies covered in these courses, Spiro found that the DH courses were characterized by (i) combining theory to practice; (ii) involving collaboration-based projects; (iii) utilizing social media such as blogging or *Twitter*; (iv) focusing on a wide range of media such as video, audio, images, games, maps, simulation, and 3D modeling as well as text; and (v) reflecting contemporary issues such as data and databases, openness and copyright, networks and networking, and interaction.

Sula et al. (2017) reported as many as 37 DH programs in the Anglophone world (Australia, Canada, Ireland, the United Kingdom, and the United States), and 93 DH programs in Europe. It was found that the majority of Anglophone programs were certificates, minors, specializations, and concentrations, except the Department of Digital Humanities at King's College, London, which offered DH degrees ranging from BA in digital culture and MA in digital humanities to Mphil/PhD in digital humanities research. In contrast, most European programs are degree-granting, often at the master's level. About one-third of Anglophone DH programs were offered by centers, initiatives, or jointly with the library, issued mostly from colleges/schools of arts and humanities, while most DH concentrations and specializations programs are located within English departments. This study showed two significant discoveries: (i) the sharp rise of DH programs in the English-speaking countries beginning in 1991 and (ii) a steady increase of several programs each year since 2008 (p. 7).

Developing Curriculum A well-designed curriculum is a crucial element contributing to the success of an academic program. It took decades before DH curricula were shaped up. Initial discussions regarding the development of Digital Humanities curriculum took place during teaching workshops and conferences, where the question of whether programing should be taught sparked debates (e.g., Hockey, 1986, 2001; Clement, 2012). Thirty years later, the same question remained relevant in Dinsman's (2016) DH interview series, again, prompting diverse opinions. Clement (2012) claimed that what should be included as part of the undergraduate education in DH is determined by the big questions *what*, *how*, and *why* DH should be taught to college students. Taking into consideration Mark Bauerlein's (2008) labeling of teens and twenty-somethings as "the dumbest generation" because of the web, Clement argued that "digital humanities can enhance students' skills in writing and reading the Web, in interpreting, discerning, and critiquing the Web, and ultimately, in becoming more engaged citizens in the world" (Clement, 2012, p. 366). She proposed cultivating students' "multiliteracies" by incorporating the following four major components. That is, (i) James Paul Gee's 36 key learning principles (Gee, 2003); (ii) Henry Jenkin's 11 skills that the Participatory Culture engages (Jenkins, 2009); (iii) Cathy Davidson's 20 "interrelated literacies" (Davidson, 2010); and (iv) Costa and Kallick's 16 habits of mind (a composite of many skills, attitudes, cues, past experiences, and proclivities) (Costa & Kallick, 2007). According to Clement (2012), the multiliteracies skills are considered as "essential to undergraduate student learning outcomes in the twenty-first century" (p. 374).

With respect to the curriculum content, here are three cases presented chronologically when they were proposed. The master's degree program in DH at the University of Virginia comprises two-year core courses, concentration electives, projects, teaching, and practicum/internships. Two points are worth noting. First, they used the term "Digital Humanities" after debating over "Humanities Informatics" vs "Humanities Computing." Second, they required students to achieve competency in major computer operating systems, visual programming software, and multimedia authoring tools as well as markup languages and programming languages (Unsworth, 2001). The world's first PhD program in Digital Humanities was established in 2005 at King's College, London (McCarty, 2012). The program was initially hosted by the Centre for Computing in the Humanities, which became the Department of Digital Humanities in 2011. In order to show the interdisciplinary collaboration of faculty working across disciplines (e.g., classics; culture, media and creative industries; English and American studies; Hellenic studies; history; music; philosophy; Portuguese; theology and religious studies; translation studies; communication and media studies) at the Royal Institute of Technology, they created multiple names for the same program, for example, PhD program in digital classics or PhD program in digital culture. While the program offers a wide range of concentrations, the objective of the PhD in DH is "to produce culturally literate and critically as well as digitally adept scholars" (p. 37). Students begin with MPhil status and then submit an application to upgrade to the PhD upon successful completion of the first year of full-time work or its equivalent. Throughout the program of up to a maximum of four years full-time, students are required to report on progress each year. For this "research-only" program, students are encouraged to "do research of any kind that involves critical work with digital tools and methods" (p. 45).

The recently established DH minor program at Singapore University of Technology and Design told another interesting story (Gornall, 2022). Unlike the aforementioned programs that cater to students pursuing diverse humanities disciplines, this DH program was designed specifically for aspiring computer scientists, who major in either computer science and design or engineering systems and design. The program aims to (i) teach students to use digital tools and computing techniques for cultural analysis and interpretation and (ii) enhance their critical thinking skills regarding computation and digital culture through a humanities lens. The curriculum mandates an introductory DH course for computational skills in understanding human culture as well as four humanities electives, divided into two categories. Some electives explore digital methods and culture from a humanistic viewpoint, while others involve digital research projects to investigate, using computational methods, aspects of human culture related to traditional subjects such as history, literature, and philosophy. Due to the local cultural settings, some elective course material may be presented in non-English with an English translation. In some scenarios, the datasets to analyze are even represented in Singaporean English (Singlish), which the popular tools do not support because they are usually trained only on American or British English. When encountering these difficulties, students must develop solutions to deal with the challenges. As is seen, this DH minor program explores the links between humanities and computer science epistemologies, with a focus on humanities research methods and projects rooted in humanities research inquiries, reflecting the Singaporean accent in nature.

The case reported by Gornall (2022) has English used as the mandatory medium of instruction in the university (though the national language of Singapore is Malay, with English, Chinese, Malay, and Tamil as four commonly used languages). The other two DH programs are both from the English-speaking countries. Similarly, the data reported in Sula et al. (2017) is collected only from the institutions of higher education located in English-speaking countries and the European world. Therefore, what has been discussed does not present a comprehensive global picture. However, the growth in the number of academic programs and the expanding scope of curriculum in DH education offer valuable insights into development of the field, indicating its steady advances.

To conclude this session on the evolution of DH, I will use the quotes from three editorial introductions for the well-known series *Debates in the Digital Humanities*, as they provide a compelling view of the recent historical developments of DH. When the first volume came out in 2012, the editor Matthew K. Gold, in his introduction "The Digital Humanities Moment," wrote with pride that "the digital humanities experienced a banner year that saw cluster hires at multiple universities, the establishment of new digital humanities centers and initiatives across the globe, and multimillion-dollar grants distributed by federal agencies and charitable foundations" (Gold, 2012, p. ix). As the second collection appeared in 2016, editors Klein and Gold's (2016) introduction "Digital Humanities: The Expanded Field" contains the following statements,

> The digital humanities, as a field, has arrived … DH now encompasses a wide range of methods and practices: visualizations of large image sets, 3D modeling of historical artifacts, "born digital" dissertations, hashtag activism and the analysis thereof, alternate reality games, mobile makerspaces, and more.
> (p. ix)

In the third volume published in 2019, editors Gold and Klein (2019), in the introduction "A DH That Matters," claimed that "we are convinced that digital humanists can contribute significantly to a larger technically and historically informed resistance" (p. ix). As can be seen, each piece records a stride: going from an activity marginal to a prosperous field and flushing from a new field of inquiry to a focus on social justice and community engagements. While each records a momentum, they all suggest the potential of DH in transforming humanistic inquiry and engaging with broader social and political issues.

3.5 The Accomplishments of DH

In 2016, Melissa Dinsman conducted a special interview series holding conversations with 12 "leading practitioners" in the field of DH and "vocal critics" on a number of questions (Dinsman, 2016). The last question she asked of the interviewees, "What do you think the digital in the humanities has accomplished so far?", solicited diverse answers from different perspectives. In my evaluation of DH's contributions, the fact that DH has grown into a discipline following the emergence and evolution of information technology is a miracle per se. DH accomplishments spanning over six decades are too countless to enumerate. However, I want to concentrate on one project initiated, one set of tools crafted, and one teaching method developed over the years. Therefore, I will first describe the emergence of the Text Encoding Initiative (TEI) and then introduce Voyant Tools followed by an example and a review of some studies on the tools. I will finally examine how digital pedagogy is formed and how it has affected language education in the digital age.

Text Encoding Initiative To conduct text analysis through computers, a fundamental issue to consider is how to encode texts. To that end, a standard should be established. In November 1987, 32 humanities scholars engaging in text archives and analysis met at Vassar College, Poughkeepsie, NY, USA, to discuss how to represent texts in order for computers to understand them (Vanhoutte, 2013). As a result, the "Poughkeepsie Principles," that is, text encoding guidelines for literary, linguistic, and historical research, were formulated. These principles adopted the Standard Generalized Markup Language (SGML), known as "the ancestor of XML" (Romary, 2008, p. 8), and International Organization for Standardization (ISO) standards as the recommended formats to encode electronic texts (Ide & Sperberg-McQueen, 1995; Vanhoutte, 2013). After joint efforts of scholars from various disciplines through numerous revisions with multiple phases, the first proposal of the TEI Guidelines appeared in 1990, with *Guidelines for Electronic Text Encoding and Interchange* published in 1994 (Sperberg-McQueen & Burnard, 1994) and many more updated versions in the following years. The TEI Guidelines, which provide "more than 500 XML elements together with a thick documentation coming in 23 chapters, ranging from manuscript description to dictionary encoding" (Romary, 2008, p. 9), offer a comprehensive and adaptable framework for describing various elements and features of a text, such as titles, paragraphs, headings, footnotes, citations, annotations, tables, and images, thereby empowering practitioners to capture and convey rich information about the content. In 1999, Extensible Markup Language (XML) was chosen to replace SGML as an industry standard, and the TEI Consortium was formed in 2000 to sustain and develop the project (Vanhoutte, 2013). As TEI-encoded texts are stored in XML format, which is compatible with different software tools and systems that support XML, TEI has become a widely adopted standard for structuring, representing, and transmitting data. Hence, Hockey (2004) considered TEI as "one humanities computing activity to be highlighted above all others. It represents the most significant intellectual advances that have been made in our area, and has influenced the markup community as a whole" (p. 16). Rockwell and Sinclair (2016) recognized TEI as "one of the great innovations of the Digital Humanities community" (p. 51) because, among others, it establishes a standardized organization and presentation of texts and offers seamless data sharing and transmission.

Voyant Tools Of the numerous tools created by digital humanists, Fraistat (2012) mentioned *Zotero* and *Omeka*, free and open-source reference and content management software respectively, developed by the University of George Mason's Rosenzweig Center for History and New Media. I want to give a special recognition to Voyant Tools, a free web-based application for text analysis and distant reading. Designed and developed by DH scholars, Stéfan Sinclair, Geoffrey Rockwell, and their team, Voyant Tools offers a valuable platform to explore, analyze, and visualize textual data in an accessible and user-friendly manner (http://voyant-tools.org). Among its multiple powerful functions, Voyant Tools can perform an on-site analysis of a text/corpus, generating an interactive visualization of the words by displaying the information such as the total count of a given word in the corpus, the number of unique words out of the total, the frequency of keywords, the distribution of the words in the context, vocabulary density, readability index, and average words per sentence, to name just a few. In addition, Voyant Tools empowers users to add its functionality to one's writings so other readers can see through the texts with analytical results. Furthermore, Voyant Tools enables users to develop their own tools using the functionality and code offered by the application ([https://voyant-tools.org/docs/#!/guide/about]; Sinclair & Rockwell, 2015; Rockwell & Sinclair, 2016). These functionalities support both scholarly reading and interpretation of texts/corpus and analysis of words, hence proving invaluable and efficient for academic research as well as for the interests of the general public.

To illustrate the application of Voyant Tools, I used the drafts of my Chapter 2 and Chapter 3 of this manuscript for analysis. By copying and pasting the texts of the chapters in the "Add Texts" box of the application and then clicking the

"Reveal" button separately, a visualization of the words used in the chapters is generated instantly. Table 3.1 shows the information about the two chapters, including each of their cirri and summaries of vocabulary density, readability index, and average words per sentence. The most frequent words used in each chapter are also listed. The two chapters are on different topics, therefore, *language, learning,* and *computer* are the most frequent words used in the chapter on CALL, and *digital, humanities,* and *technology* are the most frequent words used in the chapter on DH. There are two interesting points: (i) both utilize *computer* or *computing* at a similar frequency (55 vs 57) and (ii) *pedagogy* is related to DH but not CALL.

As can be seen, not only do Voyant Tools empower text analysis at a fast speed with fascinating visualization and information but also offer new interpretation of the written words (Welsh, 2014). For example, Lynch (2015) integrated Voyant Tools in his English class to produce a line graph depicting the relative frequency of Virginia Woolf's use of the character names in her novel *Mrs. Dalloway*. The visual presentation of how often the author mentioned three main characters' names throughout the novel helped students gain a better understanding of the work. In Maramba et al. (2015), medical practitioners explored the feasibility of web-based text processing tools with the aim to discover new methods to extract valuable information from the extensive free-text commentary on patient experience. They concluded that Voyant Tools, such as the text clouds tool, distinctive word extraction tool, and key words in context tool, helped them extract useful information, which paved the way for further research. In a study that documented the use of Voyant Tools with respect to the digital scholarship project on Tennessee's history at Middle Tennessee State University, Miller (2018) found that the data generated through Voyant Tools offered insights for the exploration of the texts. It was also found that Voyant Tools worked well with the school's Drupal Content Management System, allowing others to interact with live data. Hendrigan (2019) showed that Voyant Tools could serve as a viable heuristic for librarians to understand complex and multidisciplinary research publications of applied science faculty, suggesting that librarians add text mining in Voyant Tools to their traditional methods when learning about their faculty's activities. Hetenyi et al. (2019) demonstrated that the four subtools of Voyant they explored yielded valuable visualized information, suggesting that Voyant Tools can be conveniently applied to explore qualitative business data on the sales-marketing interface. While there are some negative and limited aspects, the authors recommended Voyant Tools for its being a free and open source of analyzing qualitative data with impressive sophisticated statistical functionality. In a recent study written in Lithuania that used Voyant Tools to examine a corpus comprising 404 articles on the topic of DH, Kairaitytė-Užupė et al. (2023) revealed that the predominant focus of research employing quantitative methods revolved around distant reading and interactive reading capabilities. The authors evaluated the benefit of data visualization in facilitating research and interpretation. Evidently, the Voyant Tools created by humanists for the DH field have gone beyond the initiating territory, benefiting a larger community.

Digital Pedagogy Pedagogy, one of the crucial issues explored in the current book, is the most significant contribution that DH has offered for education in the

Digital Humanities 61

Table 3.1 Information about Chapter 2 and Chapter 3 Generated by Voyant Tools

Information About Chapter 2 	Information About Chapter 3 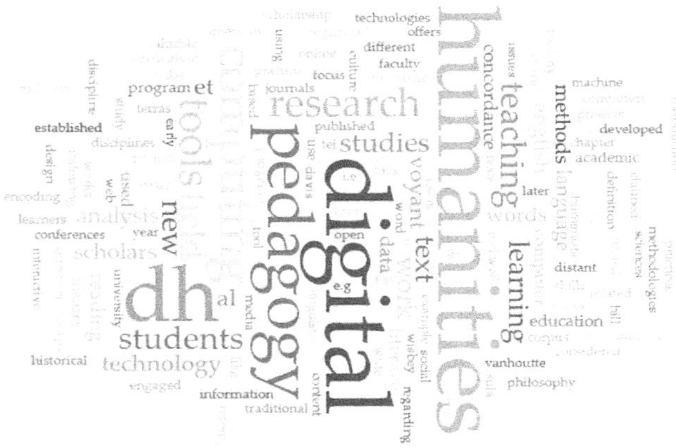

Figure 3.1 Cirrus of the Frequent Words Used in Chapter 2

Summary:
This corpus has 1 document with 7,994 total words and 2,018 unique word forms.
Vocabulary Density: 0.252
Readability Index: 15.078
Average Words Per Sentence: 26.7
Most frequent words in the corpus:
language (107); learning (92); technology (62); Chinese (60); computer (55)

Figure 3.2 Cirrus of the Frequent Words Used in Chapter 3

Summary:
This corpus has 1 document with 11,237 total words and 2,591 unique word forms.
Vocabulary Density: 0.231
Readability Index: 15.016
Average Words Per Sentence: 29.2
Most frequent words in the corpus:
digital (181); humanities (144); DH (106); pedagogy (79); computing (57)

digital age. Generally speaking, pedagogy is overshadowed by research. But it is not the case for DH. In fact, pedagogy held a pride of place in the field from the late 1980s through the mid-1990s due to internal factors such as administrative and curricular developments within institutions and external support from professional organizations and granting agencies (Hirsch, 2012). However, its favored status seemed to have waned until 2006 when Melissa Terras called for a recognition of pedagogy by arguing that "research and teaching methods peculiar to Humanities Computing have to be promoted and developed as useful adjuncts to usual training for Humanities students" (Terras, 2006, p. 243). In 2011, Paul Fyfe published the article "Digital Pedagogy Unplugged," claiming that "it is irresponsible to teach with technology without a digital pedagogy" (Fyfe, 2011, para. 20). Such a statement, which demystified the confusion that many had held about teaching with technology and teaching with pedagogy, urged DH scholars to pay attention to pedagogy. Subsequently, a series of great endeavors were made, resulting in the development of digital pedagogy.

First, *Hybrid Pedagogy: The Journal of Critical Digital Pedagogy* and *The Journal of Interactive Technology and Pedagogy* were launched in 2011 and 2012 respectively to openly publish studies that explore, among others, the interconnectedness of teaching, learning, research, and technology. The word *pedagogy*, in the names of both journals, highlights a focus on the use of methodology for teaching and learning with respect to technology. Second, various annual events were organized concentrating on the topic of pedagogy, with each leading to incremental progress. For example, the 2011 Modern Language Association (MLA) convention panel on "The Future and History of Digital Humanities" organized by Kathleen Fitzpatrick proposed placing pedagogy as part of DH work. When a Digital Pedagogy National Institute for Technology & Liberal Education (NITLE) seminar was held a year later, Katherine D. Harris claimed that "collaboration, playfulness/tinkering, focus on process, and building" should be the key components of Digital Pedagogy (2012). During the first weeklong workshop Digital Pedagogy in the Humanities in 2012, participants reached an understanding that "pedagogy must be recognized as part of digital humanities work" (Davis et al., 2020). In the introduction to the 2013 MLA Digital Pedagogy Unconference, Brian Croxall and Adeline Koh stated that digital pedagogy "is the use of electronic elements to enhance or to change the experience of education" (2013). In the same year, the publication of two-part articles on decoding digital pedagogy (i.e., Morris (2013) and Stommel (2013)) further defined the field of digital pedagogy and elaborated on its significance. In the opening plenary session at the Digital Pedagogy Institute 2014, Rebecca Frost Davis gave a presentation titled "Big Ideas in Digital Pedagogy." She called participants to situate

> the development of digital pedagogy in the current discourse about higher education; offer a vision for transformative digital pedagogy; suggest both barriers to and strategies for achieving that vision; and engage participants in a thought experiment to design an integrated curriculum articulated by digital pedagogy.
>
> (Davis, 2014)

In 2012, Sean Michael Morris and Jesse Stommel founded the Digital Pedagogy Lab at the University of Wisconsin-Madison, which, starting in 2015, offered annual international events to address issues related to digital and online teaching regarding technology and pedagogy. Third, after ten years of hard work from four editors along with several hundred language and literature instructors, the special online collection *Digital Pedagogy in the Humanities* was published (Davis et al., 2020). This peer-reviewed publication, in the format of curation, organized by 59 keywords, comprises 573 unique artifacts, which "are both direct samples of digital pedagogy in action and models of teaching ideas that can be reused and remixed" (Davis et al., 2020). I will shortly provide an example that uses "language learning" as a keyword to demonstrate its curation.

So, what is digital pedagogy? There are different definitions. According to *Hybrid Pedagogy: The Journal of Critical Digital Pedagogy*,

> Digital Pedagogy is precisely not about using digital technologies for teaching and, rather, about approaching those tools from a critical pedagogical perspective. So, it is as much about using digital tools thoughtfully as it is about deciding when not to use digital tools, and about paying attention to the impact of digital tools on learning.
> (https://hybridpedagogy.org/tag/what-is-digital-pedagogy/)

The co-founder of the Digital Pedagogy Lab, Jesse Stommel, stated that digital pedagogy

> is inextricably bound up in the work of teaching and learning . . . is not a path through the woods. It's a compass (one that often takes several people working in concert to use) . . . Digital pedagogy demands that we rethink power relations between students and teachers—demands we create more collaborative and less hierarchical institutions for learning.
> (2013)

In the preface to the timeline that he developed, "Digital Pedagogy: A Genealogy," written for the 2015 MLA Digital Humanities panel, Stommel (2015) further claimed that digital pedagogy is "an orientation toward pedagogy that does not fetishize digital tools." Along that line, Davis et al. (2020) defined digital pedagogy as "a rich area of pedagogical practice that makes use of digital tools, platforms, and methods and that both shapes and is shaped by emerging digital ecosystems."

Davis et al. (2020) considers digital pedagogy as an *approach*, which contains six key concepts: openness, collaboration, play, practice, student agency, and identity. Briefly, as a vital feature of digital pedagogy, openness refers to transparency of practice; removal of boundaries; and sharing of content, tools, and ideas. Openness of individual practice enables collaboration, which is another key element characterizing digital pedagogy. The next common characteristic shared by digital pedagogues is play, that is, the willingness to experiment, to try something new just to see what will happen. Practice, the applied learning, in the form of assignments, creation, making, and doing, is attached with importance in digital pedagogy. Through doing or making, students are encouraged to develop agency, a sense of ownership, control, and efficacy, which assists students as they apply learning in new contexts. Finally, identity is the last valuable element in digital pedagogy. Digital environments provide many opportunities for students to explore and express themselves, which enables them to further develop their selfhood and preserve identity.

To demonstrate the concept of digital pedagogy, here is how Oskoz (2020) curated the key term of *language learning*. As is known, language learning is usually regarded as primarily a matter of acquiring vocabulary and grammar. However, with digital pedagogy, language learning has "increasingly transformed communicative practices both outside and within the language classroom" into "a multimodal endeavor" (Oskoz, 2020). For example, language instructors involved students with various technology-enabled projects to facilitate their learning, such as (i) the collaborative writing via *wikis* (a tool that allows learners to write and edit collaboratively in a document) by learners of German; (ii) the telecollaboration among learners of Spanish in the USA and learners of English in Spain through *Google+* (a social network, but not used any more) and *Skype*; and (iii) the use of an educational social platform like *NING* (an online educational social network website, [www.ning.com/]) for English learners to achieve grammatical competence, meaningful participation, and digital competency. Through talking about these case studies, which reflect some of the concepts in digital pedagogy, Oskoz claimed that new digital pedagogy coupled with digital tools should empower teaching methods, enrich receptive and productive capacity, encourage multiple modes to convey meanings, and enhance learner agency, thereby creating a better learning experience.

It is crucial to point out that there are scholars outside of the field of DH who are also aware of the value of "digital pedagogy." For example, Craig Blewett, a computer scientist, observed a paradox with digital learning, in which instructors simply copied the practices of teaching in an offline classroom and moved them to the online instructional settings directly. Blewett (2016) claimed that taking such a "copy/paste" approach that may have functioned well in the in-person classroom would not work effectively in the online environment powered by smartboard, e-books, and *YouTube*. This is because the potential benefits of these digital tools are not optimized to align with curricular goals of teaching and learning. In the face of these challenges, Blewett (2016) proposed his digital pedagogy, which can be summarized into four shifts away from the traditional teaching methods: (i) a move from a pedagogy of consumption towards a pedagogy of creation; (ii) a move from content to conversation; (iii) a move from correct to correcting; and (iv) a move from control to chaos. By the shift to a pedagogy of creation, the methodology engages a true learner-centered approach, which focuses on enhancing learners' ability to creatively apply what is being learned or produce new things rather than just consuming the knowledge and skills. For a shift to focusing on conversation, learners are encouraged to co-construct with other learners or the teacher so as to connect with what they already know. This method would reinforce learning as compared to the case where learners merely work on the content for the purposes of rote memorization. As for the shift to correcting, it fosters learners to actively participate in the process of correcting errors. The final shift to pursuing chaos promotes the idea of being willing to make noise, and even make mistakes, and then resolve them. Known as active approaches for the digital learning world, Blewett tackled teaching and learning by leveraging the opportunities offered by technology, thus distinguishing his digital pedagogy from that of Davis et al. (2020), though there are some commonalities. Bećirović (2023) is another scholar who addresses digital pedagogy by discussing what digital pedagogy involves and what characteristics it constitutes for the future of digital education. When discussing the learning issues regarding education in the digital age, Bećirović incorporates the views on digital pedagogy from both inside and outside the field of DH.

3.6 Conclusion

DH has evolved from the time when there was only "a singular focus on text analysis" during the last century, to the time when the field becomes "DH in its current varieties" (Sula & Hill, 2019, p. 192). For a long period of time, digital humanists had to "define or defend digital humanities to skeptical outsiders," but now we are to "translate the subtleties of our research to others within the expanded field" (Gold & Klein, 2019, p. xiii). As much as DH is championed, it is criticized as well (e.g., Liu, 2012; Grusin, 2014). Media studies scholars like Richard Grusin considered DH as part of "neoliberalism," causing "the economic crisis in the humanities in higher education" (Grusin, 2014, p. 79). In the contrast, scholars like Chun and Rhody (2014) argued that

> the dark side of the digital humanities is its bright side, its alleged promise—its alleged promise to save the humanities by making them and their graduates relevant, by giving their graduates technical skills that will allow them to thrive in a difficult and precarious job market.
>
> (p. 2)

On this topic, Kirschenbaum (2014) made a good point,

> Everything produced by digital humanities . . . may be subject to criticism and critique on the basis of its methods, assumptions, expressions, and outcomes. All of that is completely normative and part of the routine conduct of academic disciplines.
>
> (p. 47)

Gold and Klein (2019) strongly advocate for digital humanists to actively embrace the world by undertaking the following crucial tasks: (i) to set an "orientation toward the public in its scholarship, pedagogy, and service"; (ii) to call "attention to issues of academic labor and credit for the same"; (iii) to "question ossified institutional structures and outmoded scholarly systems"; and (iv) to draw "its attention to how digital methods can help prepare students for both academic and nonacademic careers" (p. x). Inspired by Gold and Klein's enthusiasm about DH's responsibilities, I will set my orientation towards "pedagogy" and pay a particular attention to how digital pedagogy can help Chinese language professionals to prepare students for both academic and nonacademic careers. By digital pedagogy, I have three points to make. First, integrating digital pedagogy is not the same thing as teaching DH. To teach with digital pedagogy, one should adopt a "DH style"—with the six "key concepts" in the sense of Davis et al. (2020) and with digital pedagogy as a "compass" (Stommel, 2013). Guided under digital pedagogy, students are taught by focusing on "how instructors' interaction through machines could affect teaching and learning" (Davis et al., 2020) and evaluated by having them complete hands-on project-based work. Reflecting the "DH style" ideas, Travis and DeSpain's (2018) case studies in teaching American literature and Oskoz's (2020) work on foreign language education have exemplified how digital pedagogy can deepen teaching objectives and scholarship. Second, I assume the philosophy and concepts of digital pedagogy originated from DH. While digital pedagogy emerges in the middle of DH and "flourishes within DH," it "lives beyond DH." (Davis et al., 2020). Just as it offers influence over the studies of DH, it will impact language education. Third, I will adopt the perspectives of Stommel (2013, 2015) and Davis et al. (2020) in that digital pedagogy extends beyond mere technology or digital tools. Although digital pedagogy inevitably involves the application of technology and digital tools, its primary goal is to facilitate transformative teaching and learning experiences. As an approach, digital pedagogy informs and guides humanists in their teaching and research endeavors. In the next chapter, I will argue how DH combined with CALL will augment PBLL in enforcing the teaching and learning of Chinese as a foreign language.

References

Bauerlein, M. (2008). *The dumbest generation: How the digital age stupefies young Americans and jeopardizes our future (or, don't trust anyone under 30)*. Penguin.
Bećirović, S. (2023). *Digital pedagogy: The use of digital technologies in contemporary education*. Springer Nature.
Blewett, C. (2016). From traditional pedagogy to digital pedagogy: Paradoxes, affordances, and approaches. In M. A. Samuel, R. Dhunpath, & N. Amin (Eds.), *Disrupting higher education curriculum: Undoing cognitive damage* (pp. 265–287). Springer. https://link.springer.com/chapter/10.1007/978-94-6300-896-9_16
Bowles, E. A. (Ed.). (1967). *Computers in humanistic research: Readings and perspectives*. Prentice Hall.
Burdick, A., Drucker, J., Lunenfeld, P., Presner, T., & Schnapp, J. (2012). *Digital humanities*. The MIT Press. https://doi.org/10.7551/mitpress/9248.001.0001
Buurma, R. S., & Heffernan, L. (2018). Search and replace: Josephine Miles and the origins of distant reading. *Modernism/Modernity, 3*(1). https://works.swarthmore.edu/cgi/viewcontent.cgi?article=1376&context=fac-english-lit
Clement, T. (2012). Multiliteracies in the undergraduate digital humanities curriculum: Skills, principles, and habits of mind. In B. D. Hirsch (Ed.), *Digital humanities pedagogy: Practices, principles and politics* (pp. 365–388). Open Book Publishers. https://doi.org/10.2307/j.ctt5vjtt3.20
Chun, W. H. K., & Rhody, L. M. (2014). Working the digital humanities: Uncovering shadows between the dark and the light. *Differences, 25*(1), 1–25. https://summit.sfu.ca/_flysystem/fedora/sfu_migrate/18199/WorkingDH_WHKChun_LMRhody-2014.pdf

Costa, A. L., & Kallick, B. (2007). Describing 16 habits of mind. In *Habits of mind: A developmental series* (pp. 93–110). Intel Corp. https://peertje.daanberg.net/drivers/intel/download.intel.com/education/Common/my/Resources/EO/Resources/Thinking/Habits_of_Mind.pdf

Croxall, B., & Koh, A. (2013). Digital pedagogy. *A digital pedagogy unconference*. http://web.archive.org/web/20130410071518/www.briancroxall.net/digitalpedagogy/

Davidson, C. (2010, December 31). *21st century literacies: Syllabus, assignments, calendar* [Paper presentation]. HASTAC 2010: Grand Challenges and Global Innovations. Virtual Conference.

Davis, R. F. (2014). *Big ideas in digital pedagogy*. https://rebeccafrostdavis.wordpress.com/2014/08/11/big-ideas-in-digital-pedagogy/

Davis, R., Shrobe, H., & Szolovits, P. (1993). What is a knowledge representation? *AI Magazine*, *14*(1), 17–33. https://mit-medg.github.io/publications.html

Davis, R. F., Gold, M. K., & Harris, K. D. (2020). Curating digital pedagogy in the humanities. In R. F. Davis, M. K. Gold, K. D. Harris, & J. Sayers (Eds.), *Digital pedagogy in the humanities: Concepts, models, and experiments*. Modern Language Association. https://digitalpedagogy.hcommons.org/introduction/

Dinsman, M. (2016). The digital in the humanities: A special interview series. *The los angeles review of books* (p. 2). https://lareviewofbooks.org/feature/the-digital-in-the-humanities/

Eichmann-Kalwara, N., Weingart, S. B., Lincoln, M., et al. (2020). *The index of digital humanities conferences*. Carnegie Mellon University. https://doi.org/10.34666/k1de-j489

Flanders, J. (2012). Time, labor, and 'alternate careers' in digital humanities knowledge work. In M. K. Gold (Ed.), *Debates in the digital humanities* (pp. 292–308). University of Minnesota Press. https://doi.org/10.5749/minnesota/9780816677948.003.0029

Fraistat, N. (2012). The function of digital humanities centers at the present time. In M. K. Gold, (Ed.), *Debates in the digital humanities* (pp. 281–291). University of Minnesota Press. https://doi.org/10.5749/minnesota/9780816677948.003.0028

Fyfe, P. (2011). Digital pedagogy unplugged. *Digital Humanities Quarterly*, *5*(3). www.digitalhumanities.org/dhq/vol/5/3/000106/000106.html

Gee, J. P. (2003). What video games have to teach us about learning and literacy. *Computers in Entertainment (CIE)*, *1*(1), 20. https://doi.org/10.1145/950566.950595

Gibbs, F. (2013). Digital humanities definitions by type. In M. Terras, J. Nyhan, & E. Vanhoutte (Eds.), *Defining digital humanities: A reader* (pp. 289–297). Routledge.

Gold, M. K. (2012). Introduction: The digital humanities moment. In M. K. Gold (Ed.), *Debates in the digital humanities* (pp. ix–xvi). University of Minnesota Press. https://doi.org/10.5749/minnesota/9780816677948.001.0001

Gold, M. K., & Klein, L. F. (2019). Introduction: A DH that matters. In M. K. Gold & L. F. Klein (Eds.), *Debates in the digital humanities* (pp. ix—xiv). University of Minnesota Press. https://doi.org/10.5749/j.ctvg251hk.3

Gornall, A. (2022). Digital humanities inside out: Developing a digital humanities curriculum for computer scientists in Singapore. *DHQ: Digital Humanities Quarterly*, *16*(4). https://dhq-static.digitalhumanities.org/pdf/000647.pdf

Grusin, R. (2014). The dark side of digital humanities: Dispatches from two recent MLA conventions. *Differences: A Journal of Feminist Cultural Studies*, *25*(1), 79–92. https://doi.org/10.1215/10407391-2420009

Harris, K. D. (2012). *NITLE (National Institute for Technology & Liberal Education) digital pedagogy seminar*. https://triproftri.wordpress.com/2012/03/27/nitle-digital-pedagogy/

Hendrigan, H. (2019). Mixing digital humanities and applied science librarianship: Using voyan tools to reveal word patterns in faculty research. *Issues in Science and Technology Librarianship*, (91). https://journals.library.ualberta.ca/istl/index.php/istl/article/view/3

Hetenyi, G., Lengyel, A. Dr., & Szilasi, M. Dr. (2019). Quantitative analysis of qualitative data: Using Voyant Tools to investigate the sales-marketing interface. *Journal of Industrial Engineering and Management*, *12*(3), 393–404. https://doi.org/10.3926/jiem.2929

Hirsch, B. D. (2012). Digital humanities and the place of pedagogy. In B. D. Hirsch (Ed.), *Digital humanities pedagogy: Practices, principles and politics* (pp. 3–30). Open Book. www.openbookpublishers.com/books/10.11647/obp.0024

Hockey, S. (1986). Workshop on teaching computers and the humanities courses. *Literary and Linguistic Computing, 1*(4), 228–229. https://doi.org/10.1093/llc/1.4.228

Hockey, S. (2001, November). *Towards a curriculum for humanities computing: Theoretical goals and practical outcomes* [paper]. The Humanities Computing Curriculum/The Computing Curriculum in the Arts and Humanities, Nanaimo, British Columbia.

Hockey, S. (2004). The history of humanities computing. In S. Schreibman, R. Siemens, & J. Unsworth (Eds.), *A companion to digital humanities* (pp. 1–19). John Wiley & Sons https://doi.org/10.1002/9780470999875.ch1

Hockey, S. M. (1980). *A guide to computer applications in the humanities.* Johns Hopkins University Press.

Hopkins, A. (2022). Digital humanities 1981–2021: A personal timeline. *Journal of Art Historiography*, 1–6. https://arthistoriography.wordpress.com/27s-dec22/

Howard-Hill, T. H. (1979). *Literary concordances: A guide to the preparation of manual and computer concordances.* Pergamon Press.

Hybrid Pedagogy. What is digital pedagogy? https://hybridpedagogy.org/tag/what-is-digital-pedagogy/

Ide, N. M., & Sperberg-McQueen, C. M. (1995). The TEI: History, goals, and future. *Computers and the Humanities, 29*, 5–15. https://link.springer.com/article/10.1007/BF01830313

Jenkins, H. (2009). Confronting the challenges of participatory culture: Media education for the 21st century. In D. John & T. C. MacArthur (Eds.), *Foundation reports on digital media and learning.* MIT Press. https://doi.org/10.7551/mitpress/8435.001.0001

Kairaitytė-Užupė, A., Ramanauskaitė, E., & Rudžionis, V. E. (2023). Teksto analizės įrankio "Voyant Tools" panaudojimas mokslinės informacijos analizei. *Information & Media, 97*, 25–48. www.zurnalai.vu.lt/IM/article/view/29024

Kirschenbaum, M. (2010). What is digital humanities and what's it doing in English departments? *ADE Bulletin, 150*, 55–61.

Kirschenbaum, M. (2014). What is "Digital Humanities," and why are they saying such terrible things about it? *Differences: A Journal of Feminist Cultural Studies, 25*(1), 46–63. https://doi.org/10.1215/10407391-2419997

Klein, L. F., & Gold, M. K. (2016). Introduction: Digital humanities: The expanded field. In M. K. Gold & L. F. Klein (Eds.), *Debates in the digital humanities 2016* (pp. ix– xvi). University of Minnesota Press. https://doi.org/10.5749/j.ctt1cn6thb.3

Liu, A. (2012). The state of the digital humanities: A report and a critique. *Arts and Humanities in Higher Education, 11*(1–2), 8–41. https://doi.org/10.1177/1474022211427364

Lynch, T. L. (2015). Soft(a)ware in the English classroom counting characters: Quantitative approaches to literary study. *English Journal, 104*(6), 71–74. www.jstor.org/stable/24484439

Maramba, I. D., Davey, A., Elliott, M. N., Roberts, M., Roland, M., Brown, F., Burt, J., Boiko, O., & Campbell, J. (2015). Web-based textual analysis of free-text patient experience comments from a survey in primary care. *JMIR Medical Informatics, 3*, e20. https://medinform.jmir.org/2015/2/e20/

McCarty, W. (1993). Handmade, computer-assisted, and electronic concordances of Chaucer. *CCH Working Papers, 3*, 49–65.

McCarty, W. (2003). Humanities computing. *Encyclopedia of library and information science* (pp. 1224–35). Marcel Dekker.

McCarty, W. (2012). The PhD in digital humanities. In B. D. Hirsch (Ed.), *Digital humanities pedagogy: Practices, principles and politics* (pp. 33–46). Open Book Publishers. www.openbookpublishers.com/books/10.11647/obp.0024

McCarty, W., & Kirschenbaum, M. (2003). Institutional models for humanities computing. Literary and Linguistic *Computing, 18*(4), 465–489. www.kcl.ac.uk/humanities/cch/allc/imhc/

Miller, A. (2018). Text mining digital humanities projects: Assessing content analysis capabilities of Voyant Tools. *Journal of Web Librarianship, 12*(3), 169–197. https://doi.org/10.1080/19322909.2018.1479673

Moretti, F. (2000). Conjectures on world literature. *New Left Review, 1,* 54–66. https://newleftreview.org/II/1/franco-moretti-conjectures-on-world-literature

Moretti, F. (2005). *Graphs, maps, trees: Abstract models for literary history.* Verso.

Morris, S. M. (2013). Decoding digital pedagogy, pt. 1: Beyond the LMS. *Hybrid pedagogy.* https://hybridpedagogy.org/decoding-digital-pedagogy-pt-1-beyond-the-lms/

Nyhan, J., & Flinn, A. (2016). *Computation and the humanities: Towards an oral history of digital humanities.* Springer.

Nyhan, J., Terras, M., & Vanhoutte, E. (2013). Introduction. In M. Terras, J. Nyhan, & E. Vanhoutte (Eds.), *Defining digital humanities: A reader* (pp. 1–11). Routledge.

Oakman, R. L. (1980). *Computer methods for literary research.* University of South Carolina Press.

Oskoz, A. (2020). Language learning. In R. F. Davis, M. K. Gold, K. D. Harris, & J. Sayers (Eds.), *Digital pedagogy in the humanities: Concepts, models, and experiments.* Modern Language Association. https://digitalpedagogy.hcommons.org/keyword/Language-Learning

Pierson, G. W. (Ed.). (1965). *Computers for the humanities?* A record of the conference sponsored by Yale University on a grant from IBM, January 22–23.

Presner, T., Schnapp, J., & Lunenfeld, P. (2009). *Digital humanities manifesto 2.0. UCLA Mellon seminars in the digital humanities.* University of California. https://www.humanitiesblast.com/manifesto/Manifesto_V2.pdf

Ramsay, S. (2013a). Who's in and who's out. In M. Terras, J. Nyhan, & E. Vanhoutte (Eds.), *Defining digital humanities: A reader* (pp. 239–241). Routledge.

Ramsay, S. (2013b). On building. In M. Terras, J. Nyhan, J., & E. Vanhoutte (Eds.), *Defining digital humanities: A reader* (pp. 243–245). Routledge.

Rockwell, G. (1999, November). *Is humanities computing an academic discipline?* An Interdisciplinary Seminar Series, University of Virginia. www.iath.virginia.edu/hcs/rockwell.html

Rockwell, G., & Sinclair, S. (2016). From the concordance to ubiquitous analytics. In G. Rockwell & S. Sinclair (Eds.), *Hermeneutica: Computer-assisted interpretation in the humanities* (pp. 45–68). MIT Press. https://doi.org/10.7551/mitpress/9522.003.0004

Romary, L. (2008). *Questions & answers for TEI newcomers.* Jahrbuch für Computerphilologie: Hinweise zum Einrichten des Manuskripts (Yearbook of Computational Philology: Notes on Setting Up the Manuscript), 1–22. https://arxiv.org/ftp/arxiv/papers/0812/0812.3563.pdf

Schulz, K. (2011, June 24). What is distant reading? *New York Times.* www.nytimes.com/2011/06/26/books/review/the-mechanic-muse-what-is-distant-reading.html

Sevensson, P. (2009). Humanities computing as digital humanities. *DHQ: Digital Humanities Quarterly, 3*(3). www.digitalhumanities.org/dhq/vol/3/3/000065/000065.html

Svensson, P. (2012). Beyond the big tent. Debates in the digital humanities. In M. K. Gold, (Ed.), *Debates in the digital humanities* (pp. 36–49). University of Minnesota Press. https://doi.org/10.5749/minnesota/9780816677948.003.0004

Short, H. (2020, November 30). *Roy Wisbey 1929–2020.* Alliance of Digital Humanities Organizations. https://adho.org/2020/11/30/roy-wisbey-1929-2020/

Sinclair, S., & Rockwell, G. (2015). Text analysis and visualization: Making meaning count. In S. Schreibman, S. Siemens, & J. Unsworth (Eds.), *A new companion to digital humanities* (pp. 274–290). John Wiley & Sons. https://doi.org/10.1002/9781118680605.ch19

Sinclair, S., & Rockwell, G. (2016). *Voyant tools.* http://voyant-tools.org/

Sperberg-McQueen, C. M., & Burnard, L. (Eds.). (1994). *Guidelines for electronic text encoding and interchange.* TEI P3 Text Encoding Initiative Chicago. Oxford. https://tei-c.org/Vault/GL/p4beta.pdf

Spiro, L. (2011, June). *Knowing and doing: Understanding the digital humanities curriculum*. [Digital Humanities Conference]. https://pdfs.semanticscholar.org/8f15/5abedf0ad4cb9ecf8bbe0219b3a59670e70d.pdf

Stommel, J. (2013, March 5). Decoding digital pedagogy, pt. 2: (Un) Mapping the terrain. *Hybrid Pedagogy*. https://hybridpedagogy.org/decoding-digital-pedagogy-pt-2-unmapping-the-terrain/

Stommel, J. (2015). Digital pedagogy: A genealogy. *Tiki-Toki*. www.tiki-toki.com/timeline/entry/392826/Digital-Pedagogy-a-Genealogy/

Sula, C. A., Hackney, S. E., & Cunningham, P. (2017). A survey of digital humanities programs. *The Journal of Interactive Technology and Pedagogy*, *11*. https://jitp.commons.gc.cuny.edu/a-survey-of-digital-humanities-programs/

Sula, C. A., & Hill, H. V. (2019). The early history of digital humanities: An analysis of computers and the humanities (1966–2004) and literary and linguistic computing (1986–2004). *Digital Scholarship in the Humanities*, *34*(1), 190–206. https://doi.org/10.1093/llc/fqz072

Terras, M. (2006). Disciplined: Using educational studies to analyse 'Humanities Computing'. *Literary and Linguistic Computing*, *21*(2), 229–246. https://doi.org/10.1093/llc/fql022

Terras, M. (2011). *Peering inside the big tent: Digital Humanities and the crisis of inclusion*. https://melissaterras.org/2011/07/26/peering-inside-the-big-tent-digital-humanities-and-the-crisis-of-inclusion/

Terras, M., Nyhan, J., & Vanhoutte, E. (2013). Introduction. In M. Terras, J. Nyhan, & E. Vanhoutte (Eds.), *Defining digital humanities: A reader* (pp. 1–10). Routledge.

Travis, J., & DeSpain, J. (2018). *Teaching with digital humanities: Tools and methods for nineteenth-century American literature*. University of Illinois Press.

Unsworth, J. (2001, May). *A master's degree in digital humanities: Part of the media studies program at the University of Virginia* [paper]. Congress of the Social Sciences and Humanities, Québec. https://johnunsworth.name/laval.html

Unsworth, J. (2002). What is humanities computing, and what is it not? In G. Braungart, K. Eibl, & F. Jannidis (Eds.), *Jahrbuch für Computerphilologie* (Vol. 4, pp. 71–84). Mentis Verlag. www.digital-humanities.de/jahrbuch/jb4-content.html

Vanhoutte, E. (2013). The gates of hell: History and definition of digital humanities computing. In M. Terras, J. Nyhan, & E. Vanhoutte (Eds.), *Defining digital humanities: A reader* (pp. 119–156). Routledge.

Vanhoutte, E. (2015a). *The journal is dead, long live the journal!* Oxford University Press. https://academic.oup.com/dsh/pages/DSH_name_change

Vanhoutte, E. (2015b). Special and thematic issues then and now. *Digital Scholarship in the Humanities*, *30*(3), 315–321. https://doi.org/10.1093/llc/fqv029

Welsh, M. E. (2014). Review of Voyant Tools. *Collaborative Librarianship*, *6*(2), 96–97. https://digitalcommons.du.edu/collaborativelibrarianship/vol6/iss2/8

Wisbey, R. A. (1962). Concordance making by electronic computer: Some experiences with the "Wiener Genesis." *The Modern Language Review*, *57*(2), 161–172. www.jstor.org/stable/3720960?origin=crossref

Wisbey, R. A. (Ed.). (1971). *The computer in literary and linguistic research. Papers from a Cambridge symposium*. Cambridge University Press.

4 Project-Based Learning

4.1 Introduction

In this chapter, I will first introduce the Project-Based Learning (PBL) approach, its essence, and its corresponding teaching practices as defined by Buck Institute for Education (BIE, [www.bie.org]). Subsequently, I will explore the evolution of PBL for language learning, starting from its application in teaching English as a foreign or second language to its expansion to encompass foreign and second language education, resulting in Project-Based Language Learning (PBLL). I will next review the literature research on PBLL, examining its theoretical underpinnings and enumerating its benefits for language learning. Additionally, I will provide an overview of the standards for foreign language learning in the USA and Europe, along with the essential 21st century skills. I will argue that PBLL represents an optimal instrument for language educators to address standards and cultivate skill sets needed for contemporary society. Finally, I will propose combining CALL and DH and adding it to PBLL to form a DH-Augmented Technology-Enhanced PBLL (DATEPBLL) model. This integrated approach will leverage the strengths of PBLL as well as both DH and CALL, presenting a powerful means to transform foreign and second language learning.

4.2 What Is PBL?

Buck Institute for Education (BIE) considers Project-Based Learning (PBL) as a teaching method to foster active learning by engaging students with a project, which focuses on a challenging real-world problem in hopes for a solution (www.pblworks.org). Unlike the traditional approach that emphasizes acquisition of knowledge typically presented by a teacher-centered lecture, PBL promotes the student-centered "learning through doing" practice as proposed by John Dewey (Dewey, 1916). To complete a project, individual preparation as well as collaborative learning requires each participant to work together towards a goal, thereby enabling students to gain knowledge of subject matter while developing skills in communication and collaboration. The concept was first initiated by the educator David Snedden (1868–1951) to teach science in the early 20th century (Beckett, 1999, 2002). But it was William Heard Kilpatrick (1871–1965), a student of John Dewey, who later conceptualized it into a practical method though his influential essay titled "The Project Method" (Kilpatrick, 1918). Over the past several decades, PBL has gradually become popularized among educators of different subjects for teaching English as a second language (Fried-Booth, 1982, 1986; Brumfit, 1984; Legutke & Thomas, 1991/1999; Hedge, 1993; Laverick, 2018); learning in secondary English language arts (Boardman et al., 2021); foreign and second language study (Beckett & Miller, 2006; Beckett & Slater, 2019; Thomas, 2017; Gras-Velázquez, 2019; Thomas & Yamazaki, 2021); STEM education (Capraro et al, 2013); and general education in the K–12 setting (Bender, 2012; Krauss & Boss, 2013; Lenz et al., 2015; Larmer et al., 2015; Boss & Larmer, 2018).

We live in a world that is filled with projects. Unlike the projects that employees are assigned to undertake at work or those we do at home for improvement purposes, a project in PBL for education must possess seven essential design elements: (i) a challenging problem or question, (ii) sustained inquiry, (iii) authenticity, (iv) students' voice and choice; (v) reflection, (vi) critique and revision, and (vii) public product (Boss & Larmer, 2018, p. 3). First and foremost, there must exist a real-world problem or issue, without which there is no need for students to participate in the activities related to a project. Such an issue should be challenging and significant enough to hold learners' curiosity and desire to invest in time and energy. In addition to its appeal, a project should constitute authenticity and have relevance to learners. As to how to do the project, learners should be allowed to air their opinions on problem-solving and decision-making. Throughout the process, all the parties involved not only reflect upon their own work but also critique each others' to advance student learning. In the end, the completion of the project results in a public product, benefiting a community, big or small. While each of these design elements contributes to the project's success, it is the last four attributes that assure quality learning, through which learners are engaged to strive for excellence, thereby making the PBL project different from other projects.

With respect to these seven fundamentals as postulated by Boss and Larmer (2018), seven teaching practices were recommended to effectively deliver a PBL curriculum. Namely, an instructor should (i) integrate a real-world problem in designing a project, (ii) follow standards, (iii) build a PBL culture for learning, (iv) manage all activities, (v) provide scaffolding support, (vi) assess student learning throughout the process, and (vii) act as coach (p. 5). At the outset, when identifying a problem, the instructor must prioritize the most crucial knowledge and essential skills that students are expected to take away for a given subject matter. To that end, the instructor should follow the standards and curricular objectives and always bear in mind the learning goals. Once the project is assigned to students, the instructor should create a supportive learning environment so that students would feel encouraged to explore in the friendly atmosphere. Throughout the entire process, the instructor manages all the activities, providing scaffolding to support learners and assessing student learning. Last but not least, an instructor should guide, support, and empower individuals or the group to achieve their goals. In the PBL model, the instructor acts like a designer, planner, mentor, guide, facilitator, assessor, and coach, in addition to the role of a teacher, engaging students to dedicate themselves to each step for success.

In sum, PBL is an instructional method that centers teaching activities around projects with a goal to make student learning deep and meaningful. Educators have explored the approach in order to produce knowledgeable, skillful, and collaborative world citizens.

4.3 Development From PBL to PBLL

The concept of projects was applied to teaching English as a foreign language (EFL) in the 1980s to engage student learning with authentic material, emphasizing learner-centered teamwork experience, encouraging students to be responsible for learning by concentrating on the activities outside the class and involving different language skills (Fried-Booth, 1982, 1986; Brumfit, 1984). In Fried-Booth's real-world project, advanced learners of English were assigned to conduct research on the challenges faced by disabled tourists in the city of Bath with objectives to gather information about facilities available for the visitors with disabilities. The author highlighted the usefulness of incorporating such projects in EFL, along with valuable details for their implementation. As for Brumfit (1984), teaching English as a foreign language is to cultivate learners' English fluency and accuracy. To achieve that goal, one of the projects that Brumfit assigned to adult students was to produce a radio program about their own country on topics like ethnic groups, religion, and education. In this case, students were engaged to work together in a group, researching their topic, writing a script, and rehearsing it. As is seen, these two projects provided students with a unique opportunity to study, during the process of which they learned to communicate in English by speaking, listening, reading, and writing as they were planning, organizing, and discussing in order to complete the project.

The PBL method was formally introduced into EFL as a key concept by Hedge (1993), who claimed that

> a project is an extended task which usually integrates language skills work through a number of activities. These activities combine in working towards an agreed goal and may include planning, the gathering of information through reading, listening, interviewing, etc., discussion of the information, problem solving, oral or written reporting, and display.
>
> (p. 276)

Hedge listed some features that projects in the EFL curriculum present. For example, the English materials that students are exposed to are authentic; student-centered experience is emphasized; students are responsible for planning, carrying out and presenting the task; a period of time is given to do fieldwork, prepare information, and present the work; a range of language skills are used; and all activities take place outside of the classroom. As Krashen's (1982) comprehensible input hypothesis proved insufficient for successful L2 acquisition (Beckett, 1999, 2002; Beckett et al., 2019), motivating Swain to propose her comprehensible output hypothesis (1985), PBL naturally appealed to language educators due to its authenticity, meaningfulness, relevance, and practicality.

Moss and Van Duzer (1998) summarized PBL characteristics in nine principles for adult English language learning:

- building on prior knowledge;
- including four aspects of language such as speaking, listening, reading, and writing;
- cultivating skills in collaboration, problem-solving, negotiating, and other interpersonal social capabilities;
- engaging learners with independent work;
- challenging learners to use English in real-world contexts;
- encouraging learners to make their own decision about the focus of the project and the planning process;
- guiding learners to acquire new information;
- resulting in clear outcomes; and
- incorporating assessment by oneself, peers, and the instructor.

(p. 3)

Some of these principles reflect concepts of innovative models or approaches for L2 teaching and learning, which became popular in the 1980s and afterwards, such as experiential learning, learner autonomy, collaborative learning, critical thinking, task-based language teaching (TBLT), and Content-Based Instruction (CBI) (e.g., Larsen-Freeman & Anderson, 2013; Richards & Rodgers, 2014). Under the PBL instructional approach, the language classroom serves as an authentic language-using environment, while teamwork among students challenges them for communication and collaboration. For language beginners, although they are not linguistically proficient enough to carry a conversation in the target language, they learn to negotiate for meaning (Long, 1983). In the process of conducting the project, students learn to communicate and also develop other social skills, such as critical thinking and collaboration. In this regard, PBL functions as a bridge between learning English in class and using it in real life outside of class (Moss & Van Duzer, 1998).

Mohan (1986) recognized PBL as an ideal approach for teaching English language, subject matter content, and cognitive and social skills in an integrated manner. Following Mohan's language and content approach, Beckett (1999) defined projects as

> a series of individual or group activities designed to engage students in language and content learning through planning, researching (empirical and/or document), analyzing and synthesizing data, and reflecting on the process and product orally and/or in writing by comparing, contrasting, and justifying alternatives.

(p. 4)

As more language professionals, including both researchers and practitioners of second and foreign language, explored and experimented with PBL, Project-Based Language Learning (PBLL) emerged, which is, according to Beckett et al. (2019), "content-based activities composed of a series of tasks for solving problems, thinking critically, making decisions, producing products, and articulating the process and products" (p. 6).

Along with Alan and Stoller's (2005) ten steps to maximize the benefits of project work in foreign language classrooms, Stoller (2006) specified ten conditions in order for effective PBLL to take place. An analysis shows that five of the conditions are the same as or similar to those outlined in Boss and Larmer's (2018) seven essential project design elements, such as, authenticity of the material, sustained inquiry, voice and choice for students, critique reflection, and public product. However, Stoller added five more conditions for PBLL to target at language learning, including an emphasis on both process and product, a learning of both language and content, an obligation of students working both in groups and on their own, a requirement of holding students responsible for their learning, and an assignment of new roles to both students and teacher. While the element of a challenging problem or question appears to be absent from Stoller's list as compared to Boss and Larmer's (2018), her third condition explicitly states that the project should span over an extended period of time rather than a single class session. This requirement implies complexity of the project and its multifaceted nature.

Beckett et al. (2019) identified four primary pillars that sustain PBLL. First is Dewey's education philosophy (Dewey, 1916; Dewey & Dewey, 1915) that advocates experiential learning, student-centered learning, and learning by doing, among others. Incorporating these ideas in the study of a foreign or second language is to cultivate a lifelong learner, which aligns with the learning goal of L2 acquisition. Second are Vygotskian social-constructivist learning theories (Vygotsky, 1978). They include concepts like hands-on learning, learning by creating, personal meaning and relevance, collaborative learning, problem-solving and critical thinking, social interaction and cultural tools, and ownership of learning. As these concepts are implemented during the process of language learning, learners are cultivated to use the language for communication. Third is Halliday's systemic functional language view that proposes various functions of language, such as instrumental (to achieve objectives), regulatory (to control behavior), interactional (to engage with others), personal (to express feelings and meanings), heuristic (to learn and discover), imaginative (to create an imaginative world), and representational (to communicate information) functions (Halliday, 1975, pp. 11–17). This theory suggests that the ultimate aim of learning a foreign language is to utilize it for diverse purposes. Under the functionalist paradigm, language learning involves both learning language and learning about the world, calling for an integration of language with content (Mohan, 1986; Beckett, 1999; Stoller, 2006; Beckett et al., 2019). The fourth is Schieffelin and Ochs' (1986) theory of language socialization, or "socialization through the use of language and socialization to use language" (Schieffelin & Ochs, 1986, p. 163). According to Schieffelin and Ochs,

> socialization is an interactive process, in which the child or the novice (in the case of older individuals) is not a passive recipient of sociocultural knowledge but rather an active contributor to the meaning and outcome of interactions with other members of a social group.
>
> (p. 165)

This idea suggests that to acquire a language one needs to be involved in socialization.

The previous four theories have distinct historical backgrounds and perspectives. However, the first two are closely tied to the concept of active learning, and the last two are related to the concept of interaction. They all share a common ground in focusing on interaction, relevance, communication, meaning, and the learner's role in the language learning process. These commonalities, which underscore the importance of understanding language as a dynamic and social phenomenon that occurs within specific sociocultural contexts, enrich the PBLL in advocating and emphasizing the necessity for learners' collaboration and interaction. In this regard, I argue that the established second language acquisition theories such as Long's (1983, 1996) interaction hypothesis and Schmidt's (1990, 2001) noticing hypothesis should also be included to the theoretical underpinnings for PBLL because of their psycholinguistic insights. Doing a group project offers L2 learners plenty of opportunities first to notice and then pay attention to a new language's form and function. When encountering unfamiliar forms and functions, learners inevitably negotiate for meaning so they can comprehend and keep communication flowing. Noticing of and attention to language along with negotiation for meaning are essential aspects of the language learning process, as they help learners internalize the language more effectively and foster genuine communication. With these second language acquisition theories added, a cohesive and comprehensive foundation would be formed for the PBLL teaching model, which should guide language educators as they seek effective practices to promote intellectual growth and language development in students.

4.4 Literature Review of PBLL and Its Benefits

In the upcoming literature review, Project-Based Instruction (PBI) and PBL may be used interchangeably with PBLL. This is because various researchers at different time periods adopted different terms for their research purposes. However, all refer to the application of project work to teach a language. In the early days, empirical research on PBL was limited. Eyring (1989) and Beckett (1999) are two exceptions. As doctoral dissertations, both empirically studied the ESL teacher's experience implementing project work and students' responses to the approach through comparison with the traditional teaching methods. Unlike positive views about PBL that the students of general education held, ESL participants' perceptions of projects were mixed, as reported in Beckett (2002). The 11 students in Eyring's (1989) research preferred studying vocabulary and grammar separately rather than learning the language in an integrated manner as in the PBL method, and they enjoyed listening to the instructor rather than taking an initiative to plan their own curriculum for learning, suggesting that students preferred the traditional teacher-centered approach. In Beckett's (1999) study, 73 grade 8–12 Chinese-speaking ESL students in Canada from the project class completed their projects by going through each step (i.e., planning the project, conducting the research, talking with native speakers, synthesizing the data, and presenting their findings).

However, over half of them (57%) disliked this kind of learning, with 25% showing mixed feelings. Only 18% of the students liked the PBL instruction. As far as instructors were concerned, again, different from those teachers of general education who rated project-based instruction positively, L2 teachers' evaluations of this unconventional way of teaching were inconsistent, with Eyring's (1989) teachers disliking it and Beckett's (1999) teachers enjoying it.

Since the work by Eyring (1989) and Beckett (1999), an increasing number of researchers delved into exploring the application of PBLL from both qualitative and quantitative perspectives. As a result, numerous publications emerged. Beckett and Miller's (2006) *Project-Based Second and Foreign Language Education: Past, Present, and Future* is a groundbreaking collection contributed to by pioneers in the field from Canada, Israel, Japan, Singapore, and the US. The volume contains 16 works, covering theoretical examination of PBLL, practical research on challenges of implementing PBLL, exploration of project models, and assessments. For example, one chapter discusses the theories that have influenced PBLL, providing implications of the research findings for second and foreign language teaching and learning. One chapter outlines the goals of the teachers for PBLL instruction of ESL in a secondary school, which are to offer students an opportunity to socialize through the learning of English as well as help them learn the language. One case study addresses the assessment issues related to PBLL instruction by proposing an evaluation model derived from science projects to assesses the learning of the English language, content understanding, and other skills. As the first book-length publication with a comprehensive account of issues related to the topic of PBLL, the volume provides insights and implications for those exploring the field. A decade later, Beckett and Slater (2019) published a new collection that contains 14 works contributed to by 33 authors from 10 countries, involving PBLL teaching and research in the Catalan, Chinese, English, German, Japanese, Spanish, Swedish, and Turkish contexts. Subjects engaged in the research include TCFL teachers in America, bilingual teachers in Spain, as well as L2 learners of Chinese, German, and linguistics in addition to the teachers and students of ESL from the K–12 setting to the institutions of higher education. This volume offers an updated account of key theoretical thoughts for PBLL, wide-ranging empirical research, and insightful research-based frameworks to help further PBLL implementation and research.

In addition to the previously mentioned two collections are a few more books on PBLL published recently. One is Michael Thomas' (2017) *Project-Based Language Learning With Technology: Learner Collaboration in an EFL Classroom in Japan*. Concentrating on Japanese learners of English collaboration in a real-world setting, this book highlights how technology-mediated Project-Based Language Learning research can contribute to our understanding of both learner interaction in specific cultural contexts and the role of technology in language learning more generally. Laverick's (2018) *Project-Based Learning* offers an overview of the topic, covering implementation examples, strategies for overcoming challenges, and rubric design for assessments and reflection as well as showcasing how PBL can improve students' language and critical thinking skills. In *Project-Based Learning in Second Language Acquisition: Building Communities of Practice in Higher*

Education, Gras-Velázquez (2019) explores how PBLL can be utilized to facilitate student second language development while providing service to the community simultaneously. It demonstrates diverse PBLL activities including environmental projects, social activism, study abroad, and in-service learning, which form an interdisciplinary, multilingual, and multicultural higher education learning environment to enhance student learning and growth. Thomas and Yamazaki's (2021) *Project-Based Language Learning and CALL: From Virtual Exchange to Social Justice* is the first substantive book on project-based and cross-curricular language learning using digital technologies with collaborative literacies, problem-solving, civic engagement, social justice, and telecollaboration. The book offers insights into foreign language education in the context where a multidisciplinary approach is applied.

In addition, some journal articles addressing various issues of PBLL are worth mentioning. Again, the target language engaged is mostly English as a foreign language. However, learners have different language backgrounds. For example, Grant (2017) reported on a university English for Academic Purposes (EAP) writing course case study of 16 Chinese-speaking students at an English medium university in Macau. During this four-week project, intermediate-level students worked in pairs first to identify a particular problem in their academic writing they wanted to tackle and then to seek guidance from an experienced writer on campus. They next set up an interview with the chosen writer, for which they needed to prepare questions, and conducted the interview. Finally, students submitted all the materials, including the email correspondences with the interviewee, questions, and the recorded interview. Grant found that the students presented stronger motivation and willingness to take charge of their academic writing development autonomously.

Pitura and Berlińska-Kopeć (2018) required upper-secondary school students of English in Poland to work in a team of three or five members to complete a project of their own choice of two tasks. Task 1 involved writing an online article about the learners' own reflections on one Warsaw mural, which may show a current topic, reality, achievements, problems, or weaknesses. Task 2 involved producing an online book in English that presented a tale from the well-known Polish philosopher Leszek Kołakowski's *Tales From the Kingdom of Lailonia & The Key to Heaven*. To finish the tasks, students were required to analyze and write about their own reflections. In addition, they needed to learn some digital tools, such as blogging and *Padlet*, to publish their finished work on the students' blog page. This project showed how Polish students learned English while simultaneously appreciating their own language and culture.

Wang (2019) reported on an email exchange project involving 28 Chinese and 28 Korean EFL college students of English in China and South Korea. The two-month e-pal project enabled the Chinese-speaking English majors who enrolled in the practical writing course to communicate in the target language with someone from another cultural setting. The author found that many participants held positive attitudes towards the activity for its authentic way to practice English though their communication with the Korean counterparts was limited.

Greenier (2020) presented a longitudinal investigation of Korean middle school students' attitudes towards a PBL Teachers of English to Speakers of Other Languages (TESOL) curriculum, in which ten students at a low-intermediate to intermediate level of English proficiency in a private academy were assigned to create a brochure for an imaginary high school. To guide the students throughout the project, Greenier designed ten stages: Coaching, Concept Generation, Confrontation, Comprehension, Creation, Critique, Change, Culmination, Collaborative Reflection, and Composition. For an element of closure, students presented their finished brochure to the class and wrote an essay on their experience of making this product. The Composition stage helped students think about what they learned and how they might use the acquired knowledge of the language. Greenier concluded that PBL provided ways and strategies to develop students' social and affective capabilities, linguistic knowledge, and communication skills.

As far as teaching Chinese as a foreign language is concerned, research on the use of the PBL approach is scant. In the book *Exploring Task-Based PBL in Chinese Teaching and Learning*, edited by Du and Kirkebæk (2012), a theoretical model of the task-based PBL for the teaching and learning of Chinese in the Danish context was proposed. Under this framework, the principles driven by a task are combined with the ideas of pedagogy motivated by a project. Tasks were designed and implemented in teaching oral Chinese and Chinese culture at lower secondary schools and Chinese characters in an upper secondary school. The findings of the project suggest the effectiveness of new teaching methods. It should be noted that the studies in this collection were conducted under the framework of task-based language teaching (TBLT) (e.g., Ellis, 2003), which differs from PBL in terms of design, goal, engagement, and scale, among other aspects, though there are some similarities between the two (Thomas, 2017; Thomas & Yamazaki, 2021).

Zhao and Beckett (2014) implemented an action research project carried out in an American high school. The teaching of beginning Chinese via PBI—Project-Based Instruction—was studied to investigate students' views about project activities and the teacher's experiences with and perceptions of PBI. Seven mini projects were involved, each of which took students two weeks to complete. Feedback and experience of both students and the instructor were collected through students' project diaries, teacher reflective journals, classroom observation, students' project products, interviews, and surveys. It was found that PBI was effective in teaching the language, culture, and other skills simultaneously. However, some students expressed difficulty using the target language during the process of doing the projects, specifically with sentence structure and character memorization and recognition. Zhao (2015) focused on students' encounters with PBI using the same methodologies employed in (Zhao & Beckett, 2014). It was found that PBI motivated students in learning, enriched cultural knowledge, and enhanced their language skills. While students regarded PBI as more beneficial and supportive of their learning, they wanted to keep both traditional learning activity and PBI. In a subsequent study, Zhao (2019) examined four Chinese-speaking teachers' practices with technology-enriched PBLL in American secondary classrooms. The author, through a seven-month observation of their classroom teaching, studied the roles of PBLL in these teachers' adaptation to the American educational system and their perceptions towards and use of PBLL in teaching. The results shows that PBLL served as an instructional bridge for the teachers to transit from the Chinese ways of teaching to an American pedagogy. However, two teachers expressed concerns and doubts about PBLL, suggesting that they were not fully embracing or trusting the PBLL concepts due to their linguistic, cultural, and philosophical traditions.

Chen and Du (2022) examined a project-based learning activity for non-native beginners learning Chinese as a foreign language in Denmark. Two parallel classes were involved, using the same content taught by the same instructor through PBL instruction, with the experimental class having additional online collaborative learning sessions with Chinese college students in China. The learners of Chinese in the two classes were assigned with two sequential projects: the first was to design a tourist guidance booklet for people traveling to China from Denmark, and the second was to make a concept map, comparing the similarities and differences in education and family between China and Denmark. Quantitative data from knowledge tests and project assessments, along with qualitative data from communicative records and interviews, showed no significant difference between the two classes in terms of the knowledge test. However, the students in the experimental class, who had an additional collaborative online learning option with Chinese native speakers studying at Beijing Normal University in China, performed better than those in the control class in terms of project outcomes such as "intercultural awareness" and "originality" during the communication with their partners. The author concluded that the PBL approach positively impacted the beginners of Chinese, but intercultural collaboration deepened their understanding of the target culture.

In summary, since the inception of the project method a century ago, PBL has remained a popular means of instruction. While it continues to shape contemporary education, its application has expanded from instructing English as a foreign language to include second language teaching, giving rise to PBLL. Most published research concerns teaching English as a second language, with limited studies that looked at the integration of PBLL in TCFL. It is imperative to outline the benefits that are attributed to project work in second and foreign language settings. Following is a compilation of advantages reported in various resources, summarized by Stoller (2006, p. 24), and arranged in the order from the most commonly cited to the least cited in the literature:

1. Authenticity of experience and language
2. Intensity of motivation, involvement, engagement, participation, enjoyment, creativity
3. Enhanced language skills: repeated opportunities for output, modified input, and negotiated meaning; purposeful opportunities for an integrated focus on form and other aspects of language
4. Improved abilities to function in a group (including social, cooperative, and collaborative skills)
5. Increased current knowledge

6 Improved confidence, sense of self, self-esteem, attitude towards learning, comfort for using language, satisfaction with achievement
7 Increased autonomy, independence, self-initiation, and willingness to take responsibility for own learning
8 Improved abilities to make decisions, be analytical, think critically, and solve problems

4.5 Standards for Foreign Language Learning and 21st Century Skills

In the US, K–12 schools are required to adhere to, among others, Common Core State Standards (CCSS, 2012) for general education and specific standards for world languages. With respect to the latter, the American Council on the Teaching of Foreign Languages (ACTFL) proposed principles for foreign language learning in the 21st century, known as five Cs: Communication, Cultures, Connections, Comparisons, and Communities (ACTFL, 1996, 1999, 2006). First and foremost is Communication, the core of foreign language education—the objective of which is to develop proficiency in terms of: (i) the interpersonal (i.e., the ability to engage in conversation, provide or obtain information, express oneself, and exchange ideas); (ii) the interpretative (i.e., the ability to understand or interpret spoken and written language on different topics); and (iii) the presentational (i.e., the ability to convey information to listeners or readers). The next core component is Cultures, or gaining knowledge and understanding of the target culture. Language learning without culture is incomplete, as the two should go hand in hand. Third is Connection by which students are trained to associate the learning of a foreign language with other disciplines so that they can further reinforce their knowledge or understanding of those disciplines through the language. Fourth is Comparisons, which encourages new insights into the nature of language and culture through comparing the target language with the mother tongue as well as developing a new appreciation of the concept of culture through comparing the target culture with the native culture. Finally is Communities, where learners participate in multilingual communities, thereby utilizing the language beyond the context of school and becoming lifelong learners.

The ACTFL foreign language education standards reflect the most effective aspects of theoretical perspectives from second language learning theories. As a consensus on the objectives of foreign language learning, the standards guide state and local policymakers, curriculum developers, and instructors in making decisions about the content of high-quality world language programs (ACTFL, 1996, 1999, 2006).

In 2015, ACTFL updated the standards to a new version, known as world-readiness standards. Among the key changes in the edition is the call for attention to foster literacy and the 21st century skills of communication, collaboration, critical thinking, and creativity. The newly added content is part of the 21st century skills, deemed as prerequisites for entering society as a responsible citizen or moving into college for academic success.

Why should the foreign language learning standards include the component of world-readiness skills? What are the 21st century skills? Who proposed them? How can a language instructor help students acquire these skills while teaching a world language? Let me shed light on the origin and definition of the 21st century skills first before discussing the *how* question. In 2009, Partnership for 21st Century Learning, a nonprofit organization, started to work with educators in institutions of higher education and research, business leaders of 500 strong corporations, and government agencies addressing two important questions: What kind of students should high schools develop? What should high schools do in order to produce competent graduates who are capable of dealing with the challenges at colleges/ universities or at work in various sectors? The discussion led to the establishment of a set of special qualities, abilities, and dispositions identified as essential for success in the current society (Partnership for 21st Century Learning, 2009).

Briefly, the 21st century skills have four modules: (i) key subjects and 21st century themes; (ii) learning and innovative skills; (iii) information, media, and technology literacy skills, and (iv) life and career skills. The first module includes what is known as 3Rs, which contains the basic skills of reading, writing, and arithmetic, and common core subjects such as English as language arts, foreign language, history, economics, science, etc. The second module involves the abilities to learn and be innovative, or the 4Cs: communication, collaboration, critical thinking, and creativity. The third module covers information literacy, media literacy, and technology literacy, with which one knows where to retrieve required information, whether the information provided by a given media is true and reliable, and whether one knows how to avail technology to get work done. Finally, the fourth module comprises a series of life skills such as being flexible, acting like a leader, taking initiative, having adaptability and productivity, and other social skills so as to survive and thrive in a society. In a word, the 21st century skills encompass knowledge of key subjects and 12 different skills, including 3 digital literacy skills (i.e., information literacy, media literacy, technology literacy), the 4Cs (i.e., critical thinking, collaboration, communication, and creativity), and 5 life skills (i.e., flexibility, leadership, initiative, adaptability, social skills). Collectively, the knowledge and these skills empower students with capabilities and dispositions to address challenges in today's complex world (Partnership for 21st Century Learning, 2009).

ACTFL is not the only organization that imposes the cultivation of world-readiness skills as part of foreign language education standards. Outside the USA, the Common European Framework of Reference for Languages was proposed as the content and performance standards for foreign language education (Council of Europe, 2001). Furthermore, European educational policy mandates the cultivation of students' 21st century skills, including independent learning, critical thinking and problem-solving, communication and collaboration, creativity, and information and communication technology (ICT) skills (Lewin & McNicol, 2015). In Poland, for example, English is learnt by most students during primary and secondary education as the first foreign language (Pitura & Berlińska-Kopeć, 2018). As such, *Core Curriculum for Modern Languages* is in place to require school graduates to effectively communicate in L2 in speech and writing (MEN, 2009). The curricular provisions prescribe not only balanced development of all language activities covering speaking, writing, reading, listening, and each component of the language systems but also digital and civic competences, viewed as essential for effective functioning in the modern world.

Miller (2006) called for an integration of PBI and standards because he believes that PBI lends itself to meeting the standards set forth by ACTFL. Through a thematic, project-based unit about French gastronomy, Miller demonstrated how PBI is able to serve as an effective instrument to prepare students concerning each of the 5Cs. Similarly, Bellanca and Brandt (2010) also claim that PBL has the potential to serve as an effective teaching method for developing students' 21st century skills because when students are involved in a project with a team, they are inevitably engaged in building up some of the skills while learning new knowledge. The process challenges the learners to think critically, plan their own learning, collaborate with team members, and assess partners' work. In demonstrating how Polish students of English improved the target language while brushing up the understanding of their own native culture, Pitura and Berlińska-Kopeć (2018) concluded that PBL is a way to help students develop their skills while learning the language.

The rational of using PBL/PBLL to address standards is further supported by other works (e.g., Lenz et al., 2015; Allison, 2018; Gleason & Link, 2019). Lenz et al. (2015) is a compelling case study of a high school that provides a project-based, cooperative, and *graduate profile*–oriented educational experience to address Common Core standards and help students develop skills to be successful in college and professional life. Throughout the four years at the high school, students work towards a comprehensive portfolio of projects, with each required to give an oral and written defense of their learning experience at the end. Eventually, students achieve the goals set by the school: *know*, *do*, and *reflect*. First, students grasp the basics as defined in the local state by passing the exit exam, demonstrating proficiency postulated in the California state standards tests, and performing well on college entrance exams. Second, students complete a workplace internship and demonstrate the ability to use the core competencies essential for success in college. Third, students reflect on their accomplishments and successes and revise work accordingly. Lenz et al. (2015) offer examples to demonstrate how to blend with Common Core-aligned performance assessment for deeper learning via PBL. Gleason and Link (2019) proposed a Technology-Enhanced Form-Function Project-Based Language Learning (TEFF PBLL) curriculum, which integrates content, language, technology, and standards to develop students' multiliteracies and world and career readiness. The standards here included "CCSS and WIDA Standards (WIDA, 2012) for Grade 3" for students and "TESOL Tech Goal 3, Standard 5 (TESOL, 2008)" for teachers (p. 212). To that end, the authors illustrated a third-grade TEFF PBLL learning segment that organized instructional activities around a project, whose goal was for the third graders to develop their own fictional narratives based on *Pepita and the Bully* and publish them on the class webpage. This storytelling project that incorporated video, audio, and image, as well as writing, engaged students with authentic real-world content, building their confidence, expertise, and skills.

As noted by Beckett et al. (2019), PBL has been adopted as the preferred approach for implementing state-level 21st century curricular goals in U.S. general education. Likewise, federal institutions like the National Science Foundation have also funded various PBL initiatives, aimed at fostering 21st century curricular innovations and providing necessary teacher training. Being versatile and powerful, PBL presents a strong promise for language education. I will, in the next section, propose a hybrid DH and CALL with PBLL to further empower teaching foreign or second languages, in general, and Chinese, in particular.

4.6 Integrating CALL and DH via PBL to Address Standards

As discussed in Chapters 2 and 3, CALL and DH, which are both derived from computing technology, have become two separate robust disciplines, each with its own objectives and characteristics. CALL is mostly to enhance teaching and learning of languages so as to make both more effective and efficient than otherwise, while DH aims to elevate research and teaching of humanities topics and culture studies through technology. DH offers an approach with its digital pedagogy, which highlights building, collaborating, playing, and sharing through engagement with projects by means of digital tools, whereas CALL has little pedagogy to offer. On this notion, DH contributes to language education with its invaluable pedagogical perspectives. It is shown in Chapter 2 that CALL offers a tangible tool as well as opportunities to foster teaching and learning. It is also shown in Chapter 3 that creatively incorporating technologies as well as digital pedagogy not only allowed learners to experience the authenticity of languages and cultures but also fostered their development of information, digital, and media literacies, which are crucial in the modern world of learning. As such, DH and CALL should be incorporated to capitalize on each of their functions. In the following, I will argue that combining CALL and DH is a direction for foreign and second language study in the digital age. I will further contend that for the effectiveness of PBLL in facilitating educators' efforts to nurture learners' 21st century skills, as well as their language skills, PBLL should be used to reconcile CALL and DH. The rationale to harmonize CALL and DH via PBLL will be explained next in more detail.

First, the nature of CALL and DH determines the two to have a relationship like Figure 4.1. In this diagram, superficially, DH is a superset that compasses CALL. However, as pointed out before, DH provides digital pedagogy as an approach, whereas CALL has no pedagogy to offer, suggesting that DH is at an advantageous status as compared to CALL. Despite the fact that CALL lacks pedagogy, the use of technology has been thoroughly explored, with pedagogical benefits revealed by numerous empirical studies conducted across languages. Meanwhile, although DH is also studied extensively, its application of digital pedagogy is either little known to language educators or least explored in the context of foreign and second language acquisition. Since digital pedagogy in DH is a teaching approach with its broader objectives and robust methodology, work should be done to examine how

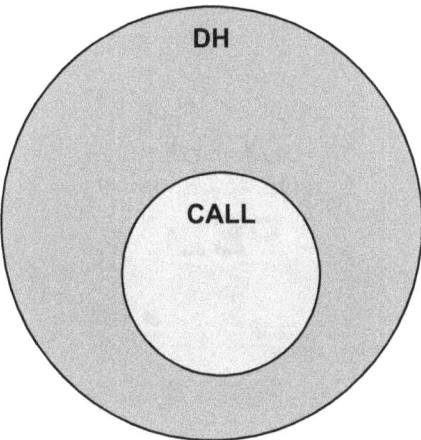

Figure 4.1 Relationship Between DH and CALL

digital pedagogy informs and guides language instruction. Furthermore, DH advocates the ideas to engage students to make things while learning content and share with the public the final product when it is produced. As such, DH should be explored with respect to its function on teaching a given foreign language, as shown in Cro (2020) and Oskoz (2020). Such an investigation, which is urgently needed, should be insightful and implicational to both language teaching practitioners as well as second language researchers.

Second, while the scenario in Figure 4.1 suggests that CALL is only a part of DH in scope, the two are mutually interrelated when it comes to language education. On the one hand, CALL needs to depend on DH's digital pedagogy so that it can play an instrumental role for the right purposes. In other words, CALL is less significant or powerful if there is no support from DH to guide it pedagogically. On the other hand, DH relies on CALL to manifest its methodological insights. Put another way, DH will not maximize its function unless CALL is in place. Therefore, given their mutually complementary nature, the underlying interdependence between CALL and DH implies the necessity of their integration.

Third, to bring the two together to enhance each other and reinforce PBLL, I propose a DH-Augmented Technology-Enhanced PBLL (DATEPBLL) approach, as shown in Figure 4.2. The justification for the model works as follows. Today's global world is well connected through information technology. As technology is becoming ubiquitous, CALL should be infused with PBLL to make the latter more powerful. The potential of combining technology with PBLL for language instruction has been noted and applied in different settings, as in Debski and Gruba's (1999) Project-Based Computing in second language study; Howard's (2002) Technology-Enhanced Project-Based Learning to train student teachers; and Dooly and Sadler's (2016) Technology-Enhanced Project-Based Language Learning (or TEPBLL) to integrate project content, materials, resources, technology, teaching strategies, and human interaction. Recently, more attention is on the studies about

Figure 4.2 The DATEPBLL Approach

Technology-Mediated Project-Based Language Learning (e.g., Thomas' (2017) PBLL with technology in the Japanese context and Beckett and Slater's (2018) research on technology-integrated PBLL). In the collection of Beckett and Slater (2019), a number of works examine the topic, resulting in a creative use of terms, one of which is "technology-enhanced form-function project-based language learning" (TEFF PBLL) by Gleason and Link (2019). Condliffe et al. (2017) observe that "recent innovations in educational technology could enhance the implementation and effectiveness of PBL and may contribute to its appeal" (p. 3). Thomas and Yamazaki's (2021) edited volume is another excellent example to show the prospects of CALL-mediated projects for language development.

No doubt, all the aforementioned scholars share the same view that the use of technology can foster PBL/PBLL implementation and effectiveness. It is worth pointing out that although some scholars recognized the significance of attaching technology to PBLL/PBLL, their integration of the two is for the purposes of enhancing CALL skills. This is evidenced in the terms or phrases that they used, for example, Debski and Gruba's (1999) "project-based CALL" or "PBCALL," or Jeon-Ellis et al.'s (2005) "PrOCALL" (i.e., Project-Oriented Computer-Assisted Language Learning), or Tseng and Yeh's (2019) "using PBL to develop teachers' CALL competencies." No matter whether technology is applied to foster PBL or promote CALL, the incorporation of PBLL and CALL should be a new normal practice for PBLL. In fact, Beckett et al.'s (2019) collection offers not only theoretical frameworks but also empirical studies on the application of technology-mediated PBLL. Some examples include Dooly and Masats' ethnographic studies of technology-enhanced PBLL in primary and middle school contexts, Casal and Bikowsky's theoretical model of learning with digital resources for PBLL in first-year university writing course at an American university, and Slater's knowledge framework as an organizational tool for highlighting the "LL" (i.e., language learning) in a technology-integrated project-based intensive English exit program. The studies, as collected in Thomas and Yamazaki's (2021) volume, explore theoretical insights and practical application of PBLL and CALL from multidisciplinary perspectives.

I have argued for the fusion of CALL with PBLL to maximize the latter's capabilities. What about the potential of linking DH with PBLL? Since DH provides digital pedagogy, which serves as a teaching approach, we should connect DH with PBLL as well to strengthen the latter's power methodologically. PBLL stands as a potent educational instrument. With DH pedagogy further fortified, a DH-augmented PBLL is formed. This synergy amplifies the effectiveness and empowers the approach of PBLL. Up to now, incorporating DH into second language instruction has been rarely examined except for two works. Cro (2020) proposed a "DH-inflected second language (DHL2) pedagogy" (p. 5), with an acknowledgment of the commonalities between DH and L2 learning that both advocate the collaborative and cooperative practice. Appreciating DH's "focus on the pedagogical aspect of second language learning acquisition" (p. 16), Cro implemented the DHL2 pedagogy in her French language classroom to develop students' digital and linguistic proficiency. Oskoz (2020) presented a number of examples that explored the use of digital tools in L2 classrooms in the framework of DH methodology. My proposal to link DH to PBLL resonates with the essence of both works, consequently augmenting PBLL.

Finally, combining DH-empowered PBLL with technology-enabled PBLL leads to the DH-Augmented Technology-Enhanced PBLL (DATEPBLL). By amalgamating DH, CALL, and PBLL, their individual strengths converge. In harmonizing DH with PBLL, instructors are enabled to offer a pedagogically supportive context to further enhance the attainment of curricular goals—building learners' linguistic and cultural competence while cultivating their comprehensive social capabilities. In applying technology-infused PBLL, instructors are empowered to create a favorable learning environment, where individual learners are engaged in projects to develop skills in information, media, and technology literacy in addition to language skills. This powerful approach helps educators to address foreign language learning standards and 21st century skills.

4.7 Conclusion

In this chapter, I examined the fundamentals of PBL/PBLL and the reported studies of the application of PBLL and its benefits for the teaching and learning of foreign and second languages. After a review of language learning standards and the 21st century skills, which language educators are required to address, I proposed a DH–Augmented Technology-Enhanced Project-Based Language Learning (DATEPBLL) approach, which synthesizes the potential of DH pedagogy, CALL technology, and project work to transform language learning. It is argued that this integrated approach will address language learning standards and the 21st century skills. In the next chapter, cases studies will be presented to demonstrate how the DATEPBLL approach is adopted to guide instructors to enhance student learning while developing their critical skills sets.

References

ACTFL. (1999). *Standards for foreign language learning in the 21st century* (Chinese & other languages added). Yonkers. https://eric.ed.gov/?id=ED438726

ACTFL. (2006). *Standards for foreign language learning in the 21st century*. Allen Press.

Alan, B., & Stoller, F. L. (2005). Maximizing the benefits of project work in foreign language classrooms. *English Teaching Forum, 43*(4), 10–21.

Allison, J. M. (2018). *Project based learning to promote 21st century skills: An action research study* [Doctoral Dissertation, William & Mary]. http://dx.doi.org/10.25774/w4-m5xm-wc95

American Council on the Teaching of Foreign Languages (ACTFL). (1996). *Standards for foreign language learning: Preparing for the 21st century*. ACTFL.

American Council on the Teaching of Foreign Languages (ACTFL). (2015). *World-readiness standards for learning languages*. ACTFL.

Beckett, G. H. (1999). *Project-based instruction in a Canadian secondary school's ESL classes: Goals and evaluations*. [Unpublished doctoral dissertation, University of British Columbia]. https://open.library.ubc.ca/soa/cIRcle/collections/ubctheses/831/items/1.0078180

Beckett, G. H. (2002). Teacher and student evaluations of project-based instruction. *TESL Canada Journal, 19*(2), 52–66. https://doi.org/10.18806/tesl.v19i2.929

Beckett, G. H., & Miller, P. C. (Eds.). (2006). *Project-based second and foreign language education: Past, present, and future*. Information Age Publishing.

Beckett, G. H., & Slater, T. (2018). Technology-integrated project-based language learning. In C. A. Chapelle (Ed.), *The encyclopedia of applied linguistics*. John Wiley & Sons. https://onlinelibrary.wiley.com/doi/10.1002/9781405198431.wbeal1487

Beckett, G. H., & Slater, T. (Eds.). (2019). *Global perspectives on project-based language learning, teaching, and assessment: Key approaches, technology tools, and frameworks*. Routledge. https://doi.org/10.4324/9780429435096

Beckett, G. H., Slater, T., & Mohan, B. A. (2019). Philosophical foundation, theoretical approaches and gaps in the literature. In G. H. Beckett & T. Slater (Eds.), *Global perspectives on project-based language learning, teaching and assessment: Key approaches, technology tools and frameworks* (pp. 3–22). Routledge. https://doi.org/10.4324/9780429435096-1

Bellanca, J., & Brandt, R. (2010). *21st century skills: Rethinking how students learn*. Solution Tree Press.

Bender, W. N. (2012). *Project-based learning: Differentiating instruction for the 21st century*. Corwin Press. www.perlego.com/book/1485079/projectbased-learning-differentiating-instruction-for-the-21st-century-pdf

Boardman, A. G., Garcia, A., Dalton, B., & Polman, J. L. (2021). *Compose our world: Project-based learning in secondary English language arts*. Language and Literacy.

Boss, S., & Larmer, J. (2018). *Project based teaching: How to create rigorous and engaging learning experiences*. ASCD.

Brumfit, C. (1984). *Communicative methodology in language teaching*. Cambridge University Press.

Capraro, R. M., Capraro, M. M., & Morgan, J. R. (Eds.). (2013). *STEM project-based learning: An integrated science, technology, engineering, and mathematics (STEM) approach*. Springer Science & Business Media.

Chen, C., & Du, X. (2022). Teaching and learning Chinese as a foreign language through intercultural online collaborative projects. *Asia-Pacific Education Researcher, 31*(2), 123–135. https://doi.org/10.1007/s40299-020-00543-9

Common Core State Standards (CCSS). (2012). *Common core state standards for English language arts & literacy in history/social studies, science, and technical subjects*. National Governors Association Center for Best Practices & Council of Chief State School Officers.

Condliffe, B., Quint, J., Visher, M. G., Bangser, M. R., Drohojowska, S., Saco, L., & Nelson, E. (2017). Project-based learning. *MDRC*. www.mdrc.org/sites/default/files/Project-Based_Learning-LitRev_Final.pdf

Council of Europe. (2001). *Common European framework of reference for languages: Learning, teaching, assessment*. Cambridge University Press. https://rm.coe.int/16802fc1bf

Cro, M. A. (2020). *Integrating the digital humanities into the second language classroom: A practical guide*. Georgetown University Press. https://doi.org/10.2307/j.ctv19vbgjv

Debski, R., & Gruba, P. (1999). A qualitative survey of tertiary instructor attitudes towards project-based CALL. *Computer Assisted Language Learning, 12*(3), 219–239.

Dewey, J. (1916). *Democracy and education: An introduction to the philosophy of education*. The Macmillan Company.

Dewey, J., & Dewey, E. (1915). *Schools of tomorrow*. Dutton. www.gutenberg.org/ebooks/48906

Dooly, M., & Sadler, R. (2016). Becoming little scientists: Technologically-enhanced project- based language learning. *Language Learning & Technology, 20*(1), 54–78. http://llt.msu.edu/issues/february2016/doolysadler.pdf.

Du, X., & Kirkebæk, M. J. (Eds.). (2012). *Exploring task-based PBL in Chinese teaching and learning*. Cambridge Scholars Publishing.

Ellis, R. (2003). *Task-based language learning*. Oxford University Press.

Eyring, J. L. (1989). *Teacher experience and student responses in ESL project work instruction: A case study* [Unpublished doctoral dissertation, University of California]. www.proquest.com/docview/303738761?pq-origsite=gscholar&fromopenview=true

Fried-Booth, D. L. (1982). Project work with advanced classes. *English Language Teaching Journal, 36*(2), 98–103. https://doi.org/10.1093/elt/36.2.98

Fried-Booth, D. L. (1986). *Project work*. Oxford University Press.

Gleason, J., & Link, S. (2019). Using the knowledge framework and genre pedagogy for technology-enhanced form-function project-based language learning. In G. H. Beckett & T. Slater (Eds.), *Global perspectives on project-based language learning, teaching and assessment: Key approaches, technology tools and frameworks* (pp. 204–223). Routledge. https://doi.org/10.4324/9780429435096-1

Grant, S. (2017). Implementing project-based language teaching in an Asian context: A University EAP writing course case study from Macau. *Asian-Pacific Journal of Second and Foreign Language Education, 2*(4), 1–13. https://doi.org/10.1186/s40862-017-0027-x

Gras-Velázquez, A. (Ed.). (2019). *Project-based learning in second language acquisition: Building communities of practice in higher education*. Routledge. https://doi.org/10.4324/9780429457432

Greenier, V. T. (2020). The 10Cs of project-based learning TESOL curriculum. *Innovation in Language Learning and Teaching, 14*(1), 27–36. https://doi.org/10.1080/17501229.2018.1473405

Halliday, M. A. K. (1975). *Learning how to mean: Explorations in the development of language*. Hodder Arnold.

Hedge, T. (1993). Key concepts in ELT. *ELT Journal, 47*(3), 275–277.

Howard, J. (2002). Technology-enhanced project-based learning in teacher education: Addressing the goals of transfer. *Journal of Technology and Teacher Education, 10*(3), 343–364.

Jeon-Ellis, G., Debski, R., & Wigglesworth, G. (2005). Oral interaction around computers in the project-oriented CALL classroom. *Language Learning & Technology, 9*(3), 121–145. http://llt.msu.edu/vol9num3/jeon/.

Kilpatrick, W. (1918). The project method. *The Teachers College Record, 19*(4), 319–335.

Krashen, S. (1982). *Principles and practice in second language acquisition*. Pergamon Press.

Krauss, J., & Boss, S. (2013). *Thinking through project-based learning: Guiding deeper inquiry*. Corwin Press.

Larmer, J., Mergendoller, J., & Boss, S. (2015). *Setting the standard for project based learning: A proven approach to rigorous classroom instruction*. ASCD.

Larsen-Freeman, D., & Anderson, M. (2013). *Techniques and principles in language teaching* (3rd ed.). Oxford University Press.

Laverick, E. K. (2018). *Project-based learning. ELT development series*. TESOL Press.

Legutke, M., & Thomas, H. (1991/1999). *Process and experience in the language classroom*. Longman.

Lenz, B., Wells, J., & Kingston, S. (2015). *Transforming schools using project-based learning, performance assessment, and common core standards*. John Wiley & Sons.

Lewin, C., & McNicol, S. (2015). The impact and potential of iTEC: Evidence from large-scale validation in school classrooms. In F. van Assche, L. Anido-Rifon, D. Griffiths, C. Lewin, & S. McNicol (Eds.), *Re-engineering the uptake of ICT in schools* (pp. 163–186). SpringerOpen. https://doi.org/10.1007/978-3-319-19366-3_9

Long, M. H. (1983). Native speaker/non-native speaker conversation and the negotiation of comprehensible input. *Applied Linguistics*, *4*(2), 126–141.

Long, M. H. (1996). The role of the linguistic environment in second language acquisition. In W. Ritchie & T. Bhatia (Eds.), *Handbook of second language acquisition* (pp. 413–468). Academic Press.

MEN [Ministerstwo Edukacji Narodowej] (2009). *Podstawa Programowa z komentarzami (t. 3. Języki obce w szkole podstawowej, gimnazjum i liceum)*. Ministerstwo Edukacji Narodowej.

Miller, P. C. (2006). Integrating second language standards into project-based instruction. In. G. H. Beckett & P. C. Miller (Eds.), *Project-based second and foreign language education: Past, present, and future* (pp. 225–240). Information Age.

Mohan, B. A. (1986). *Language and content*. Addison-Wesley.

Moss, D., & Van Duzer, C. (1998). *Project-based learning for adult English language learners*. National Center for ESL Literacy Education. ERIC Digest.

Oskoz, A. (2020). Language learning. In R. F. Davis, M. K. Gold, K. D. Harris, & J. Sayers (Eds.), *Digital pedagogy in the humanities: Concepts, models, and experiments*. Modern Language Association. https://digitalpedagogy.hcommons.org/keyword/Language-Learning

Partnership for 21st Century Learning. (2009). *P21 Framework Definitions. (ED519462)*. ERIC.

Pitura, J., & Berlińska-Kopeć, M. (2018). Learning English while exploring the national cultural heritage: Technology-assisted project-based language learning in an upper-secondary school. *Teaching English with Technology*, *18*(1), 37–52. www.tewtjournal.org.

Richards, J., & Rodgers, T. (2014). *Approaches and methods in language teaching* (3rd ed.). Cambridge University Press. https://doi.org/10.1017/9781009024532

Schieffelin, B. B., & Ochs, E. (Eds.). (1986). *Language socialization across cultures*. Cambridge University Press. https://doi.org/10.1017/cbo9780511620898

Schmidt, R. (1990). The role of consciousness in second language learning. *Applied Linguistics*, *11*(2), 129–158. https://doi.org/10.1093/applin/11.2.129

Schmidt, R. (2001). Attention. In P. Robinson (Ed.), *Cognition and second language instruction* (pp. 3–32). Cambridge University Press. https://doi.org/10.1017/cbo9781139524780.003

Stoller, F. (2006). Establishing a theoretical foundation for project-based learning in second and foreign language contexts. In G. H. Beckett & P. C. Miller (Eds.), *Project-based second and foreign language education: Past, present, and future* (pp. 19–40). Information Age.

Swain, M. (1985). Communicative competence: Some roles of comprehensible input and comprehensible output in its development. In S. Gass & C. Madden (Eds.), *Input in second language acquisition* (pp. 235–253). Newbury House.

Teachers of English to Speakers of Other Languages (TESOL). (2008). *TESOL technology standards framework*. TESOL.

Thomas, M. (2017). *Project-based language learning with technology: Learner collaboration in an EFL classroom in Japan*. Routledge. https://doi.org/10.4324/9781315225418

Thomas, M., & Yamazaki, K. (Eds.). (2021). *Project-based language learning and CALL: From virtual exchange to social justice*. Equinox Publishing Limited. https://api.equinoxpub.com/books/3034

Tseng, S.-S., & Yeh, H.-C. (2019). Fostering EFL teachers CALL competencies through project-based learning. *Educational Technology & Society*, *22*(1), 94–105.

Vygotsky, L. S. (1978). Interaction between learning and development. In M. Lopez-Morillas (Trans.) & M. Cole, V. John-Steiner, S. Scribner, & E. Souberman (Eds.), *Mind in society: The development of higher psychological processes* (pp. 79–91). Harvard University Press.

Wang, S. (2019). Project-based language learning: Email exchanges between non-native English speakers. *Theory and Practice in Language Studies*, *9*(8), 941–945. http://dx.doi.org/10.17507/tpls.0908.07

World-Class Instruction, Design, and Assessment Consortium (WIDA). (2012). *Amplification of the English language development standards: Kindergarten- Grade 12*. Madison, Board of Regents of the University of Wisconsin System.

Zhao, J. (2015). Project-based instruction in teaching Chinese as a foreign language. In T. Hansson (Ed.), *Contemporary approaches to activity theory: Interdisciplinary perspectives on human behavior* (pp. 108–127). IGI Global.

Zhao, J. (2019). Bridging cross-cultural teaching practices with technology-enriched PBLL in Chinese as a foreign language education. In G. H. Beckett & T. Slater (Eds.), *Global perspectives on project-based language learning, teaching, and assessment: Key approaches, technology tools, and frameworks* (pp. 146–163). Routledge.

Zhao, J., & Beckett, G. H. (2014). Project-based Chinese as a foreign language instruction-A teacher research approach. *Journal of the Chinese Language Teachers Association*, *49*(2), 45–73.

5 Case Studies

5.1 Introduction

In this chapter, I will present three case studies of my three projects implemented in a university context: gaming, podcasting, and creating e-portfolios. The first two projects are for Chinese language learners, and the third one is for preservice teachers of Chinese, all exemplifying an integration of the Digital Humanities–Augmented Technology-Enhanced Project-Based Language Learning (DATEPBLL) approach proposed in Chapter 4. For each of the case studies, I will demonstrate the characteristics of the project, including the roles of the instructor and students throughout the process, the specific technologies used to complete projects, and the end product. I will also show how the process of the projects transformed student learning.

How can an instructor design, plan, and execute a project for a Chinese language classroom? What kind of projects are appropriate to be integrated in class? What steps should an instructor take to ensure that engaging students in project work contributes to a desired learning outcome? These are the questions that I constantly ponder as I have been testing out and improving the DATEPBLL practices in my classrooms over the past years. My first attempt of applying PBL in 2004 centered on a video production project, which required students who took different levels of Chinese courses in a Chinese program to produce video skits outside of class. Students ranged from beginners to learners of advanced Chinese. Working in groups formed by students themselves on topics of their own choice, they produced situational dialogues, which were filmed by a media professional working for the university's technology center. This video production was a collaboration between students, instructor, teaching assistants, and a media technology expert. While the project was managed by the instructor, in particular, to coordinate students and the technology staff in terms of schedule, students were responsible at each stage, including forming the working group, assigning different roles, writing and revising scripts, and rehearsing. The project provided a natural context for meaningful language use, while the specific responsibilities taken on by the students motivated them to learn the language more effectively (Chen, 2008). Based on this experience, in 2005, I recruited students for different roles of the characters in *Integrated Chinese Level 1 Part 1* (2nd edition) and produced 22 situational dialogues (https://

DOI: 10.4324/9781003292081-5

tltc.shu.edu/chen/multimedia_output.php). Among other projects that I completed (i.e., Chen, 2012, 2017a, 2017b, 2019, 2021a, 2021b) is a study that examined the effectiveness of eTandem English-Chinese exchange with respect to Chinese learning by beginners through a *Skype*-based Computer-Mediated Communication (CMC) project (Chen, 2017a). Twenty-six English-speaking learners of Chinese were assigned to exchange languages with a group of Chinese-speaking learners of English for one hour each week throughout the entire semester. While the exposure to the target language was limited, learners of Chinese benefited from the exchange experience, as evidenced in students' oral interviews with a native speaker at the end of the semester. The scores of fluency, accuracy, and general performance by students in the experimental group were much higher than those of the control group, whose Chinese learning took one year more than the former. Although the differences between the two groups were not statistically significant in learning outcome, there was a greater variation in the control group in terms of standard deviation, suggesting the impact of eTandem language exchange for learners of Chinese.

Some of the projects that I completed are successful in terms of learning outcome, while others are not as expected due to various reasons. For example, the instructor's project design and planning need to be improved. Learners' level of proficiency in the target language may have played a role in the execution of a project. Complexity in technology involved could also affect students' motivation to participate in a project (Chen, 2010). Through years of experiments with PBLL, I have observed that, among many other factors, following a project framework is crucial for the success of PBLL teaching. A rich and solid project model not only guides teachers in designing and planning a project but also offers clear instructions on what and how both instructors and students should do throughout each stage of the project. To that end, in the next section, I will introduce the project model established by Stoller and colleagues (e.g., Sheppard and Stoller (1995), Alan and Stoller (2005), Stoller (1997, 2002, 2006, 2012) and Stoller and Myers (2019)), which I have adopted as a foundation for my exploration of the three projects to be presented. I will then demonstrate the three case studies in the subsequent sections and, finally, provide a summary of the projects.

5.2 Project Framework

Stoller (2006) identified ten conditions for effective project-based learning to take place. That is, PBL must

- orient students to both process and product;
- promote student ownership in the project;
- expand over a set of classes;
- involve different skills;
- be committed to both language and content learning;
- oblige students to work both collaboratively and individually;
- hold students responsible for their own learning;

- assign new roles to students and teacher;
- result in an end product; and
- have students reflect on the project.

These characteristics, which make the PBL approach distinct from what regular non-project-based language instruction can offer, provide a working guide for the instructor to design, plan, and implement a project in a classroom.

With respect to projects, there are a variety of configurations (e.g., Stoller, 2006, 2012; Stoller & Myers, 2019). From the roles assumed by the teacher and students throughout the process, projects span the spectrum from highly structured to minimally structured, with various degrees in between. In the most structured scenario, the instructor is in charge of, for example, designing the project, deciding the theme of the project, and determining the format of the end project. In this scenario, students are usually left with less control, either because they are new to this kind of learning activity or less proficient in the target language. However, students have the freedom to choose the topic and the direction of their project. In the case of the least structured PBL, the teacher lets students explore and develop the project to a maximal extent, as they have experience with the PBL methodology as well as language skills or other strategies to advance learning. In between the two lies semi-structured PBL, wherein both the teacher and students will share the work and responsibilities, including the project design, development, and evaluation. In terms of the nature of a project, it can be linked to a real-world problem, which requires a resolution, or a simulation of some events that relate to the real world. Regardless, the project should be appealing to students in topics and fitting for their proficiency. As for the time required for a project, it may vary from a couple of days, or one week, or one month, to one semester or one academic year.

How is a project implemented in a language classroom? Beckett and Slater (2005) proposed a framework that consists of two parts: the planning graphic and the project diary. The former is created by the teacher before the project, who subsequently guides the students to develop their own project-specific graphics, which include learning goals in the target language, content, and skills. The project diary is a weekly summary that students complete to show the status of their work. These two components work together to ensure students and teachers that the project work will foster the integrated development of language, content, and skills.

Alan and Stoller (2005) proposed ten steps for ESL teachers to maximize potential benefits of project work in the language classroom (pp. 12–13). This is a modification from the original work by Sheppard and Stoller (1995), Stoller (1997), and Stoller (2002):

Step 1: Students and teacher agree on a theme for the project.
Step 2: Students and teacher determine the final outcome of the project.
Step 3: Students and teacher structure the project.
Step 4: Teacher prepares students for the demands of information gathering.
Step 5: Students gather information.
Step 6: Teacher prepares students to compile and analyze data.

Step 7: Students compile and analyze information.
Step 8: Teacher prepares students for the language demands of the final activity.
Step 9: Students present the final product.
Step 10: Students evaluate the project.

These ten steps can be grouped into four stages. The first is the planning stage, which includes the first three steps (Steps 1–3). Basically, teacher and students work together to plan and determine the details of the project, including the theme, the structure, and the configuration. The second is the project production stage, including the next five steps (Steps 4–8), during which students work on the project based on the requirements with scaffolding from the teacher. The third stage entails project completion, Step 9, where students share with others their end product. It is crucial that students, before presenting the final product, revise their work based on the feedback from the teacher as well as their peers. The fourth stage, Step 10, is evaluation, during which students reflect on the language and the content acquired throughout the process of the project.

This four-stage model differs from Hoyt's (2013) in that it requires students to reflect on the project, which Stoller considered as a *must* in PBL. A few years later, Stoller (2012) reduced the ten steps into seven and cut four stages into three. The first is the preliminary stage (Steps 1–3), the same as the prior model, at which both the teacher and students must reach a consensus on the project's theme (Step 1), define the ultimate tangible outcomes (Step 2), and establish a project structure that will lead students to produce a product (Step 3). During the initial phase, it is important that students understand the objectives and requirements as well as their responsibilities. The extent to which students' roles versus teacher's determine the nature of the project and the time of the class used for preparing the project mainly depends on the language proficiency of students and their comfort with project work. Regardless, students should be well informed of details so that they understand the value of doing the project as compared to traditional assignments. The next is the information gathering, compiling and analyzing, and reporting stage (Steps 4–6). During each of these phases, the teacher provides the language needed for students to do the project by combining the original Step 4 with Step 5, Step 6 with Step 7, and Step 8 with Step 9. If, for example, conducting interviews is part of the project, the teacher should guide students how to raise questions in the target language and how to carry over the conversation with language gambits. Students then learn and practice the language, for example, vocabulary, grammar, expressions, skills and strategies, and other necessary content resources. When students run into challenges or problems while analyzing information, the teacher should scaffold with assistance so that students can continue to evaluate, interpret, and finally, present the information. At each of these stages, the teacher places explicit attention on the language in order to empower students as they are exploring and synthesizing the information to report it. The last stage is evaluation of the project (Step 7), that is, the old Step 10, which is crucial for students to evaluate the language acquired, the skills improved, the strategies perfected, the content learned, and the project completed. This stage not only serves as a valuable measure to increase students' motivation, self-esteem, and self-concept but also works as a viable tool for teachers to evaluate their own work, aiding them to improve for future success (pp. 42–44).

As can be seen, the major changes in the new model as compared to the old ten-step model involve the project production stage. Specifically, the three language improvement steps, Steps 4, 6, and 8, were merged into the information gathering, processing, and reporting steps respectively. With teacher's support about language bound with students' engagement with project development (i.e., Steps 4+5, Steps 6+7, Steps 8+9), "attention to language is an integral and iterative component of the model," in the words of Stoller (2012, p. 41). These adjustments, which place more emphasis on the language and the instructor, seem reasonable. Moreover, to implement a project in a real-world classroom, the teacher should have some flexibility, allowing for a reduction or expansion of steps as deemed appropriate, depending on student needs.

This is exactly true. In Stoller and Myers (2019), a new model is proposed. Crucially, the new five-stage framework puts the prior second stage's three subparts (i.e., information gathering, information compiling and analyzing, and information reporting, as in Stoller (2012), into three independent cycles and uses the wording of "Processing" and "Displaying" to replace "Compiling and Analyzing" and "Reporting" respectively. These three separate components are regarded as "student engagement," corresponding to the "scaffolded instruction" offered by the teacher, who guides students at each of the three cycles. Here, "scaffolded instruction" is used instead of "teacher's support about language" to highlight the function of teachers' roles.

Under this new model, the teacher's and students' responsibilities are clearly explained for each cycle. These modifications provide detailed guides for both language teachers and students with respect to each step of the project process. As claimed by the authors, this new five-stage framework, as shown in Table 5.1, a modification from the original framework appearing in Stoller and Myers (Figure 2.1, p. 27) can be adopted for second or foreign language learning contexts; learners of different ages, with various levels of languages proficiency or language-learning skills; learning objectives; and different time frames (pp. 25–26).

In summary, the conditions for effective PBL; the configurations of project work; and the framework for planning, implementing, and evaluating PBL, as discussed in Table 5.1, pave the way for the presentation of the current work. What should be pointed out is that the project framework as postulated by Stoller and colleagues has undergone an evolution from the initial eight-step process (Sheppard & Stoller, 1995) to a subsequent ten-step process (Alan & Stoller, 2005), then developed into a three-stage model (Stoller, 2012), and now an expanded model of "five distinct cycles of student engagement and scaffolded instruction" (Stoller & Myers, 2019, p. 26). Each transition signifies momentum for refining project work based on numerous experiments of projects integrated in language classes in second and foreign language contexts. Over the past decades, this project model in different versions has been used to guide practitioners of PBL in teaching second languages, developing course material, and designing curricula. I

Table 5.1 PBL Five-Stage Framework

Stage	Cycle	Iterative Process for T (Teachers) and S (Students)
1	Preparation Cycle	T & S: Determine project theme/topics
		T & S: Agree on project outcome(s)
		T & S: Plan project
2	Information Gathering Cycle	T: Scaffold instruction
		S: Gather information
3	Information Processing Cycle	T: Scaffold instruction
		S: Organize information
		T: Scaffold instruction
		S: Analyze information
4	Information Display Cycle	T: Scaffold instruction
		S: Display information
5	Reflection Cycle	T & S: Reflect on learning (content, language skills, academic skills, life skills, strategies, technology skills)
		T & S: Reflect on project (process and product)

Source: Stoller and Myers (2019)

will, in the following, demonstrate my three projects in light of this new five-stage model. For each case, I will provide a background, which serves as a rationale for the project with a literature review of the issues in discussion, before presenting details of the project.

5.3 Case 1: Gaming Project

Since the emergence of video games, gaming has become a potential instructional tool for education. According to Pearce (2002), a game is a structured framework containing some components such as "obstacles, resources, rewards, penalties, and information" for a "goal-oriented experience" (p. 22). Similarly, Khine (2011) defines the character of game playing as consisting of "rules, goals, engagement, challenge, feedback, fun, interactive, outcome and immediate reward" (p. 121). A digital game is designed to be played on an electronic device, such as a computer, smartphone, iPad, or videogame console. However, whether they are digital or not, games "embody some specific features that facilitate learning . . . Digital games also provide the learners with a platform that supports interaction" (Khatibi & Cowie, 2013, p. 35).

Games for language learning, as argued by Sykes and Reinhardt (2012), possess some inherently important features. First, games have a learner-directed goal orientation that drives learners towards their own objectives. Second, games provide plenty of opportunities for learners to play and interact with other gamers throughout the play. Third, individualized and timely feedback encourages learners to improve their language skills constantly. Fourth, games create a context that provides a meaningful experience for learners. Finally, learners are motivated to play and enjoy playing because of the engaging experience. These characteristics resemble the attributes promoted by the communicative language teaching (CLT) approach and reflect effective practices in second language teaching and learning. Lee (2016) described the benefits of some game-like learning principles related to gaming. For example, when one is involved in playing games, s/he is a participant and learning happens by acting. The games provide ongoing challenges with constant helpful feedback. If the student fails, the failure is reframed in a new iteration. Thus, learning feels like playing without stress or struggle.

With respect to the learners of the 21st century who are exposed to a wide variety of emerging and evolving technologies, some educators/researchers suggest a change regarding teaching approaches, methods, and strategies. Khatibi and Cowie (2013) pointed out that to help today's students to learn, educators must connect to them by acknowledging that digital games are a significant part of their lives. Godwin-Jones (2014) remarked that integrating gaming into language learning is a "winning situation for both students and educator" (p. 9). Based on the research in the field, Sykes (2018) claimed that the "incorporation of digital games into world language teaching and learning offers interesting and varied possibilities" (p. 220). In a recent article that reviews studies on technology-enhanced language teaching and learning, Shadiev and Yang (2020) found that the technologies that have been used the most in language teaching are games, followed by online videos. Games are not only major recreation for most young adults but also play a crucial role in their learning. This suggests that incorporating games as part of instructional activities should be an important issue for educators to explore.

5.3.1 Background

Numerous theoretical and empirical studies have been conducted on digital gaming and language development (e.g., Pomerantz & Bell, 2007; Thorne, 2008; Thorne et al., 2009; Talak-Kiryk, 2010; Benson & Chik, 2011; Reinders, 2012; Reinders & Wattana, 2012; Peterson, 2013; Khatibi & Cowie, 2013; Vandercruysse et al., 2013; Godwin-Jones, 2014; Lan et al., 2015; Ketterlinus, 2017; Sykes, 2018). A number of pedagogical advantages have been reported for language teaching and learning. Pomerantz and Bell (2007), for instance, observed that gaming introduces "fun" and "creativity" to the language classroom. Gameplay motivates learner autonomy, which, in turn, leads to the retention of what is being learned. Prensky (2001b) argued that the reasons why a digital game facilitates learning are its features of engagement, interactivity, and the combination of the two aspects. Sylvén and Sundqvist (2012), in a study of young Swedish subjects, discovered that frequent gamers (those playing games five or more hours a week) achieved the highest scores on English proficiency tests, followed by moderate gamers and non-gamers, thereby suggesting a positive correlation between L2 gaming and L2 learning. Godwin-Jones (2014) highlighted three benefits of gaming in language learning. First, while participating in a "massively multiplayer online game," gamers are inspired to use the target language actively in a socially appropriate context. Second, as the gaming system provides continuous feedback, players are encouraged to repeat, revise, and reproduce constantly. Finally, players enjoy the play because of a sense of accomplishment.

Despite the extensive literature of gaming and world language education, few studies focus on the examination of language learning in the Chinese context. In 2006, the International Edutainment (i.e., *education* and *entertainment*) Conference was initiated in China and has been held there a few times since. However, scant research has been published on game-supported learning with respect to teaching Chinese as a second language or teaching English to Chinese students. Of the limited research on the topic, Lan et al. (2015) conducted a study that investigated how the virtual environment (VE) impacted the L2 acquisition of Chinese vocabulary. They found that the VE was able to accelerate the learning of vocabulary. In Chik's (2012) study, which examined the perspectives of students and teachers in Hong Kong about digital gameplay for autonomous English language learning, the author found that teachers considered gameplay as an independent activity but not connected with language learning and use in gamers' personal and social worlds. Most of the teachers in the study thought that English learning through gaming was not possible for most gamers. Some teachers disapproved of gaming as it was a waste of time.

The teachers' mixed feelings about the use of games for education as reported in Chik (2012) may reflect some Chinese cultural sentiments towards the word *game*. When the sense of *game* in the context of learning is translated into Chinese, it is *yóuxì* 游戏 meaning *play*. Chinese renditions for *play, pastime, and play games* are all *yóuxì* 游戏. In the sixth edition of *Modern Chinese Dictionary* (2012), *yóuxì* 游戏, when used as a noun, means *entertainment* and refers to *play* when it is a verb. The English phrase *play games* is translated as *wán yóuxì* 玩游戏. To many Chinese parents, *xuéxí* 学习 *learn* or *yánjiū* 研究 *study* is serious and painstaking work, while *yóuxì* 游戏 is not. Furthermore, the word *yóuxì* 游戏 contains some derogative connotations. Playing games in kindergarten is fine, but pupils would be discouraged or criticized for doing so in elementary school. In fact, buried among tons of homework and assignments in preparation for numerous tests, Chinese kids have little time to "play." Before entering colleges, students are expected to work diligently on various school subjects, while instructors must "teach" wholeheartedly. As such, serious teachers would require students to spend all their school time and beyond "studying" rather than "playing."

The controversy surrounding the use of games for educational purposes is not only exclusive to instructors in the Chinese context. Duggan (2015), for example, noted that public attitudes towards games are complex and uncertain. On the other hand, Guy Cook, an applied linguist, distinguished *game* from *play* by stating that "'game' is used to describe a range of activities" referring to "intricate, rule-governed, and culturally variable competitive activities" (Cook, 2000, p. 127), while "play" is a "free activity," "rule-governed," but "not serious" (p. 112). However, in his observation, as structured activities, both *game* and *play* can engage learners to study. In 2007, I conducted a study on the perception of classroom activities by college learners of Chinese. Surprisingly, most of the surveyed participants regarded games as more effective and enjoyable than quizzes and homework (Chen, 2007). This aligns with the claims and suggestions put forth by the language educators who advocate for the use of educational games, as reviewed earlier. In the following, I will argue that there is a rationale for integrating games in teaching Chinese as a foreign language. With that critical argumentation laid out, I will describe how I developed a matching game, which paved the way for a student gaming project.

5.3.2 Developing a Game for the Chinese Language Classroom

The reasons why games should be incorporated in a Chinese classroom are related to two linguistic phenomena, which constitute two obstacles for learners, in particular, English-speaking students of Chinese at the initial learning stage. Mandarin Chinese possesses four distinct tones, which are four different pitch patterns: the level tone (1st tone), the rising tone (2nd tone), the dipping tone (3rd tone), and the falling tone (4th tone). Learners must perceive the subtle nuance of each tone. In addition to learning to identify the four tonal differences, students must discern the four tonal representations coded in pinyin, a Chinese romanization system that beginners usually start with. Marked by four dialectics, ‾, ╱, ⌄, ╲, placed on the top of the primary final (i.e., vowel), these tone graphs, which may look simple, actually appear counter-intuitive to learners (Bar-Lev, 1991). According to Bar-Lev (1991), the conventional method to represent Chinese tones not only fails to alert the learner to the distinctive role each tone accent plays but also lacks sufficient meaningful cues to remind the learner that each syllable that bears a unique tone is an individual sound. Furthermore, there are special cases with tones, one of which is known as "Tone Sandhi" or "tonal alternations when syllables are connected in natural speech" (Sun, 2006, p. 40). For example, the original dipping pitch of a third-tone syllable is changed to a rising pitch when followed by another third-tone syllable. Such similar tone changes also occur with some words in a given context. The other unusual case refers to the various scenarios in which the second syllable of a compounding word or grammatical particles may lose its original tones, becoming toneless. Navigating Chinese tones, in general, and taking care of special tone changes will present a straightforward challenge for English speakers of Chinese because all these features are absent in the English language. While English incorporates "intonation" at the sentence level, for example, holding a rising tone when posing a question or a falling tone when making a statement, the Chinese tone is lexically localized. Thus, when speaking Chinese, one must apply a specific tone to nearly every syllable, a skill that requires extensive practice for memorization.

DeFrancis (1984) noted the English-speaking learners' difficulty with the Chinese writing system. Among many others, the difficulty includes (i) a requirement to learn logographic radicals, which are the building blocks of Chinese characters; (ii) a lack of direct association between a writing image that one sees and how it is pronounced; (iii) a need to memorize three elements, that is, image, pronunciation, and meaning, simultaneously for each given character; and (iv) an understanding of differences between a character and a word. This means that grasping Chinese writing requires huge effort, such as handwriting each character countless times or typing a character in a computer while memorizing its pronunciation and meaning in order to build a connection of these elements.

As is evident, mastering either tones or radicals necessitates extensive repetition and rote learning. The question at hand is whether the current "digital natives" or "games generations" (Prensky, 2001a, 2001b) are equipped to withstand such a monotonous process. The repetitive nature of the learning journey may intimidate and scare the students away unless they are extremely motivated or determined. However, digital games provide a solution to these challenges. When immersed in gameplay, learners actively pursue goals without consciously grappling with the manual and mental repetitions, reducing boredom and monotony while enhancing overall effectiveness and efficiency. Building upon Godwin-Jones's (2014) insights, which emphasize the careful consideration of practical, pedagogical, and personal aspects when introducing gameplay into language classrooms (p. 14), I assert that the challenges associated with learning Chinese tones and characters underscore the rationale for integrating games into the teaching process.

Bilbrough (2011) claimed, "There is no learning without remembering. And language learning—perhaps more than most forms of learning—places huge demands on memory" (p. 1). Remembering language involves encoding, storage, and retrieval, supported by certain parts of the brain. Bilbrough considered the memory skill as the fifth skill of language learning, which is vital for the development of other skills like listening, speaking, reading, and writing. As such, it may be hypothesized that developing games to facilitate students' memory skills should improve their language learning skills. This assumption is also supported by Khatibi and Cowie's (2013) research, which, based on neuroscientific studies, shows that some brain structures are involved in both language learning and gaming. The authors deduced that "in both processes of learning a language and playing a video game, memory of previously encountered situations facilitate both processes since what we remember serves as a foundation for learning new information simultaneously" (p. 26). Given that learning Chinese implies a transformation from struggling with tones and characters to being able to use them comfortably, the key is to help learners establish memory skills, which will further foster learning of the language. This suggests that a game for building memory through matching exercises to reinforce the associations among different elements of a character, that is, its pronunciation with a correct tone, its meaning, and its image, will benefit the learning of Chinese tones and characters. With that understanding, I decided to create a matching game with the following eight matching pairs in Table 5.2.

All eight categories have one thing in common: enabling learners to build an association between two components. Repeated exposure to these elements throughout matching games will help learners retain these connections, which eventually become a part of their own mental repertoires. The last pair is a combination of two radicals to form a single character, for which there are two models: either a semantic-semantic compound or a semantic-phonetic compound, representing two productive ways to form Chinese characters (e.g., Sun, 2006).

Table 5.2 Eight Matching Pairs

Pairs	Categories	Examples
1	Matching Pinyin to English	rén ⟷ person
2	Matching Character to English	人 ⟷ person
3	Matching Pinyin to Character	rén ⟷ 人
4	Matching Pinyin to Sound	rén ⟷ 🔊
5	Matching Character to Sound	人 ⟷ 🔊
6	Matching Pinyin to Tone Graph	rén ⟷ ↗(35)
7	Matching Character to Tone Graph	人 ⟷ ↗(35)
8	Matching Radical to Radical	人 ⟷ 人

The practice of the eight matching pairs will push learners to develop their memory skills, which will help them recognize, store, retrieve, and produce tones and characters.

To implement the eight pairs in a game, a commercial product, Puppeteer's (Abdulqadir, 2017) *Matching Game Template*, was purchased at the advice of an instructional designer of the university. This shortcut not only saved tons of time but also assured a good quality of the game, regarded as an effective practice (Reinders & Wattana, 2012; Whitton, 2012). Using *Unity* (www.unity.com), which is open source and a leader among the global game industry, as the building tool, I created two versions of matching games, with one version consisting of four modules, whose interface is shown in Figure 5.1 (see Chen (2019) for each step of the game's development).

Playing the matching game is straightforward. To start, the player clicks any of the four modules, as shown in Figure 5.1. Clicking "Character & English," for example, the user will be presented to two pairs of characters and English words, as shown in Figure 5.2. If the matching of the first pair is correct, that pair will disappear, and 100 points will be awarded, showing on the top middle of the interface. If not, the two items remain on the screen. When the two pairs are finally matched, the player advances to the next level with three pairs. For each subsequent level, more pairs are added, while the time is reduced one second after another, as shown by the timer on the top right corner. As more pairs pop up, creating complexity and confusion, so do the awarding credits, which doubles the basic 100 points for each matched pair. When the player matches all the pairs within the given time, s/he wins the game!

This matching game, simple as it may be, fully reflects the major characteristics that a game should have, as defined by Pearce (2002). Winning the game is the goal. When extra pairs are added to be matched, more time is needed. As no additional time is provided, this causes an obstacle, preventing the player from reaching the goal. When a pair is matched, the player receives a reward with a score of 100 points. That further motivates the player to move on so as to achieve the ultimate victory. When the given time runs out while there are still pairs to match, the game is over, resulting in penalties. Most players will likely repeat the game in hopes of

Case Studies 103

Figure 5.1 Interface of the Matching Game with Four Modules

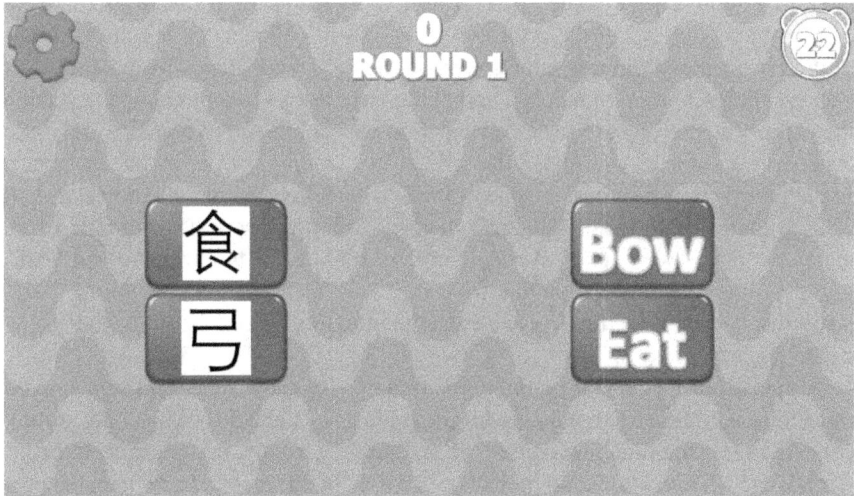

Figure 5.2 Interface of Matching Character to English

performing better next time. Each match, whether correct or incorrect, makes an informative and meaningful learning experience, thus helping the player to build and strengthen the association between two related items.

Note that the ultimate goal of the project is to engage learners of Chinese to create more matching games. The concept of having students build games conforms to Whitton's (2012) perspective that "giving learners agency as game creators rather than simply players" directs their focus towards the process instead of the product, thereby enhancing the learning experience (p. 249). I will next describe how students created matching games.

5.3.3 Engaging Students to Create Matching Games

The gaming project was purposely designed for students who enroll in the second part of the Introductory Chinese course. There are four primary objectives for this project. First, students are required to interact with peers while studying Chinese so that they can learn from and help each other. Second, students are given an opportunity to develop some digital literacy through creating games, which will be useful for future careers. Third, in developing a game, students are challenged to learn how to solve a real-world problem. Fourth, the final products that students complete can be games played by other learners of Chinese, benefiting the TCFL community. Therefore, in Spring 2018, the project was assigned to ten students of Introductory Chinese II. In teams of two students, each team was required to produce one set of matching games with four modules, each of which incorporated the vocabulary from a chapter in *Integrated Chinese Level 1 Part 1* (Liu et al., 2018). As a mandatory assignment of the course, the project contributed 10% to the total of their course grade. As a result, five matching games were successfully completed by the end of the semester. In Fall 2018, students taking the first part of the Introductory Chinese course were invited to create games for bonus points because their Chinese knowledge and skills were not sufficient enough to handle the complicated project. As the participation was completely voluntary, only one team of two students completed the project by creating a set of matching games. In the following two semesters, one of the two students who did the project in Fall 2018 volunteered to single-handedly develop four more sets. Thus, a total of 10 matching games were made available online, serving for the teaching and learning of Chinese. In the section that follows, I will, using the case of Spring 2018, detail the steps that the teacher and students took throughout the process of game development.

Preparation Cycle During the preparation cycle, the teacher and students did three things: (i) agreed on a theme for the project (i.e., creating a matching game); (ii) determined the final outcome of the project (i.e., a game that can run on the internet); and (iii) structured the project (i.e., who will do what and how long the process lasts). Detailed requirements were included in the syllabus and made available to students before the start of the semester. On the first day of class, the instructor assigned the project, explaining the learning goals and pedagogical benefits of doing this project. Students were given time to play the games and ask questions, including how a game would be created and how they would be assessed for the completion of the project.

A project orientation was held in the following class, when the instructional designer of the university, with whom I worked together to create the games, was invited to class to talk about the significance of doing this project. She also guided students to download *Unity* and install it on their school-provided laptop. As a structured project, the instructor created a game template, a gaming user menu, a time schedule, and a rubric, which were posted online for students to access. At the orientation, students formed their own teams of two partners and selected a chapter from the textbook (i.e., *Integrated Chinese*) to create a matching game, with the vocabulary of the chapter serving as the content. Students were assigned to complete the games by the last day of the semester when each team was to showcase its game in class. The students appeared excited about having a hands-on gaming creation assignment.

Information Gathering Cycle Since the purpose of the project was to enhance students' learning of the language through game creation, the teacher provided students with the gaming template. This template is an action-packed game that contains all the key assets such as graphics, sounds, and the source code, ready to be customized by students to insert a list of vocabulary that they selected. Supplying students with such a template helped them concentrate on the subject matter—the vocabulary—rather than the technology. In addition, the instructor created a 10-page step-by-step user manual for building the game, which was to guide students from beginning to completion. The game template was posted on the *OneDrive* of the school, which each student was able to access and download, while other documents, such as the user manual and rubric, were posted on *Blackboard*, the course management system used at the university.

With the help of the instructor's scaffolding instructions, students' engagements included familiarizing themselves with the *Unity* system by watching video tutorials about *Unity*, which were provided by the instructor. In addition, students needed to read through the user manual to gain an understanding of the mechanism for the matching game. With respect to the content of the game, students needed to learn how to key into the computer a Chinese character as well as its pinyin form with a correct tone. Second, students needed to produce an individual sound file for each item in the vocabulary list via the text-to-speech technology, which required their knowledge of a character, pinyin, and pronunciation for accuracy. In sum, students had to prepare themselves from technology to language through watching videos, reading documents, doing research, and learning basics about inputting Chinese characters. These steps were done either working on their own, collaborating with a team partner, or discussing with the instructor for the purposes of making a good preparation for the next stage.

Information Processing Cycle Creating a game with matching pairs in the four modules was technologically demanding for students enrolled in a Chinese class. While no coding was involved, students needed to be fluent with each of the components of *Unity*, its function, and how each interacts with one another in order to produce a game. Each of the components functions as a library that needs to be called out to work with others. This concept may appear counterintuitive for students without training in programming. However, if one puts in time to study the *Unity* tutorials and user manual, it was doable. In this case, since students worked in pairs, they could study together, discuss the problem, and talk about the solutions. For example, one team of students were stuck at one step, unable to perform a required procedure as documented in the provided user manual. When they came to the instructor for help, the latter troubleshot the problem together with students by going through each step. It was through joint troubleshooting that the students finally determined the cause of the problem and worked out a solution.

Other than technology, language is another major aspect that the instructor should pay special attention to. First, students were helped with keying in Chinese characters and presenting each pinyin with a correct tone graph. Second, for the sound file, students were guided in determining the correct pronunciation generated by the text-to-speech technology. The scaffolding assisted students in becoming skillful in making the computer display Chinese characters and pinyin and generating sounds for each word. In the end, it was ultimately anticipated that students would be able to achieve a full grasp of the vocabulary in different aspects, that is, able to pronounce each item, identify and write each image, and be ready to tease apart one from another in meaning.

Information Display Cycle In the last class of the semester, the students in separate teams showcased their products respectively by demonstrating each of the four different modules of the game that they had created. In addition, students of each team shared their experiences in doing the project, such as what problems they encountered, how they solved the problems, and what they learned linguistically and technologically through completing this project. After all presentations, students completed a questionnaire of eight questions, three of which involved the game development project. Except for one multiple-choice question, the other two are open-ended questions: What three keywords would you highlight if your friend asked about your experience of doing the project? What have you learned by doing this matching game project? Finally, each group submitted its final executable files, which were then uploaded onto a university server and linked to the site of a web-based Chinese program (https://tltc.shu.edu/chen/).

Reflections Cycle In terms of the post-project survey, for the question that solicited students' perceptions (in three keywords) about their own experience with the project, students' answers were mostly positive, ranging from *"educational"* to *"triumph,"* from *"exciting"* to *"rewarding."* Four students considered the project *"educational,"* and another four *"challenging."* While three students regarded the experience as *"frustrating"* and two as *"confusing,"* there were another three students who found it *"interesting"* or *"helpful,"* and two students found it *"fun."* Some students responded with *"perseverance,"* *"hard work,"* and *"slight accomplishment,"* suggesting that the project was hard, but manageable. Only three students regarded the experience as either *"tedious,"* *"time-consuming,"* or *"stressful."* It was evident that except for a couple of students, all others reported a positive learning experience, which was further supported by their reflections quoted in Table 5.3.

From teaching perspectives, some lessons have been learned from this project. First, creating a game can be a truly student-centered task that promotes active learning. The project offered valuable experiences that students would hardly achieve from a traditional classroom without PBL. For example, the game development presented a real learning opportunity with a focus on meaningful content, through which students were challenged for their creative analysis, decision-making, and

Table 5.3 Student Reflections on the Matching Game Project

Students	Reflections
S1	"Technology is harder than what it seems."
S2	"I learned a little about game development and how to use Unity."
S3	"Troubleshooting is necessary, and computers do not always work the way we want."
S4	"I was able to truly know the vocabulary. How to use Unity."
S5	"Review Chinese and some computing skills."
S6	"I have picked up basic understanding of coding and further assimilated the Chinese words I interacted with."
S7	"Seek help when necessary."
S8	"I am not too good at programing."
S9	"Follow the directions instead of trying to figure it out."
S10	"It would be a good method for others to learn Chinese words and their English meanings."

problem-solving by working collaboratively. Because the gaming development depends on the successful operation of each prior move, students were cultivated to focus on each step of the process rather than the final product, and they learned to constantly assess their own work to ensure that things were on the right track. All these steps contributed to the cultivation of students' linguistic skills, meaningful engagement, authentic learning, and technology skills, as observed by Tavares and Potter (2018). Second, while the majority of students presented positive perceptions about gaming, there were some who needed a lot of help with technology. This observation aligns with what has been reported in the literature. For example, Hill and Cook (2011) found that just as there were students who were "technophiles," comfortable with using different tech products, some were "technophobes" (p. 37). In the same vein, Oskoz (2020) noted that many students were savvy users of some recreational tools, but they were not competent to avail themselves of the tools for academic learning.

As such, it is suggested that there is an urgent need to engage students in more technology-supported projects in the sense of DATEPBLL. The more students are involved in playing with tools while studying the subject matter, the stronger their abilities to use technology for learning purposes. Third, having one deadline for a semester-long project may cause excessive stress for students. It would be helpful if several separate dates were set in order to engage students more effectively. An alternative is to give some time in class for one team to report on their progress and ask other teams if they have any questions that need discussion. In so doing, students' anxiety would be reduced or lowered and more meaningful interactions among students be assured. Finally, for the effective administration of a gaming project on this scale, the instructor should be capable of troubleshooting issues and ready to fix them. Since most language instructors are already overloaded with heavy teaching responsibilities, I propose a more practical solution: engaging students to develop games based on the existent game-based learning platforms such as Quizlet and Kahoot!, which are free, but fully developed with plenty of open resources. In taking advantage of these tools, students could concentrate on the language elements (i.e., vocabulary, expressions, grammar structures, or discourses). When encountering any issues, students can easily get support by searching online. A gaming project that utilizes existing open resources would be more manageable from the teacher's point of view.

5.3.4 Summary

Engaging students to create a game as they learn Chinese is an innovative application of the DATEPBLL approach to a Chinese language classroom. Such practice provides a transformative learning experience. In developing a game, students not only learn and use the language in an effective fashion but also experience gaming technology and develop creative analysis and collaborative skills, which are part of 21st century skills. A more sustainable way to engage students with a gaming project is to take advantage of ready-made games or to modify commercial games in accordance with pedagogical objectives.

5.4 Case 2: Podcast Project

According to Drew (2017), podcasts emerged after the boom of Web 2.0 technologies in the early 2000s. *Merriam Webster Dictionary* defines *podcast* as "a program (as of music or talk) made available in digital format for automatic download over the Internet" (www.merriam-webster.com/dictionary/podcast). Phillips (2017) refers to *podcast* as "a digital audio (or video) file that is created and then uploaded to an online platform to share with others" (p. 159). These two definitions suggest that a digital recording cannot be long in order to achieve "automatic download" and "sharing" purposes. While podcasts are usually short, they must be stimulating in content, audibly interesting, with content-appropriate music and/or sound effects, and even be entertaining when done well. As podcasts contain materials rich in genres and topics and are convenient to listen to and replay, they present potential as an ideal pedagogical tool for instructional purposes.

As podcasts become a popular tool for language education, podcasting, or the creation of podcasts by students to fulfill course requirements, has also grown into a novel instrument among innovative educators (e.g., Abelmann, 2014; Green et al., 2014; Phillips, 2017; Smith et al., 2019). In Phillips (2017), two different student cohorts of the English for Health Professionals course were required to create two digital recordings. After the completion of the work, the learners were questioned about their perceptions of the podcasting assignments by a survey and an interview. It was found that the majority of students enjoyed developing podcasts and responded with positive comments about the activities. The experience made the students, including those who were shy, feel more confident about speaking English and using technologies. Phillips concluded that podcasting supported language teaching, as it (i) increased learner confidence, (ii) supported collaborative learning, (iii) improved language production skills, and (iv) built transferable skills.

5.4.1 Background

Language educators are among the pioneers to embrace the use of podcasts in a classroom (e.g., McCarty, 2005; O'Bryan & Hegelheimer, 2007; Salmon & Nie, 2008; Ducate & Lomicka, 2009; Kim & King, 2011). Lomicka and Lord (2011) observed three goals for utilizing podcasts inside or outside the language classroom: developing learners' listening abilities, building their speaking skills, and improving pronunciation. Hasan and Hoon (2013) gathered 60 articles that addressed the advantages of integrating podcasts into ESL teaching and learning, 20 of which were carefully reviewed, as they were "original and empirical" studies about the effects of podcasts on students' achievements and learning attitudes. The authors found that having students access podcasts not only improved learners' functional skills in listening and speaking but also concomitantly developed their positive perceptions about the use of podcast pedagogy.

Subsequent research by other scholars continues to focus on either the impact of podcasts on student learning outcomes or the change on student perspectives, or a combination of both (e.g., Ghee et al., 2012; Basaran & Cabaroglu, 2014; Thomas & Toland, 2015; Soerjowardhana & Nugroho, 2017). Empirical investigations have also been conducted to determine if there is quantitative evidence regarding the effects of podcasts with respect to the acquisition of various languages (e.g., Hirzinger-Unterrainer, 2012; Ghee et al., 2012; Kelly & Klein, 2016; Abdulrahman et al., 2018). For example, Ghee et al. (2012), an examination of the perception of learners of Chinese towards podcast content and design, involved Malaysian university students of elementary Chinese who were required to listen to 5-to-10-minute podcasts posted on a website for 12 weeks. The results of the research showed that students regarded the use of podcasts as a good learning tool. Kelly and Klein (2016) investigated whether listening to supplementary Chinese podcasts would improve students' listening and speaking skills of the target language and learning confidence for the university beginners of Chinese. Their results showed that listening to supplementary Chinese grammar podcasts significantly improved learners' speaking skills and confidence but not listening skills; visual learners did not benefit from audio podcasts when learning the language.

Lomicka and Lord (2011) claimed, "Podcasting has several theoretical underpinnings in Second Language Acquisition (SLA) research, especially in the areas of input, output, and motivation" (p. 16). Input refers to learners' exposure to the language while output to their production of the language, both directly resulting in the acquisition of a second language, as contended by Krashen (1982) in his comprehensive language input theory and Swain (1985) in her output model. In creating a podcast, students read and listen to the language and speak and write in the language. The more input that students can absorb, the more output they would generate. As students make progress in receiving and producing the target language, their motivation in learning arises accordingly. Thus, learners' active language engagement enables them to further enjoy learning. That is why Willis (1996) considered input, output, and motivation as three essential conditions for successful language learning.

5.4.2 Engaging Students to Develop Podcasts

Over the past few years, I assigned students taking the second part of the Introductory Chinese course to interview, in Chinese, a classmate about his/her experience of learning Chinese as part of course assessments. Students were required to submit a videotape of the interview, which fulfilled the course requirement. However, students did not have a chance to view each other's work after it was done. Furthermore, the assignment did not require much higher-order thinking, in-depth analysis, extended preparation, repeated practice, or complicated digital techniques. Intrigued by the value of "making," "collaborating," and "sharing," with the DH pedagogy, and inspired by a colleague's presentation on integrating podcasting into a social work undergraduate course, I wanted to expand this interview assignment into a term-long podcasting project, which I describe next in more detail.

Preparation Cycle Before the project was assigned, the following questions were examined as part of teacher preparation. What are the objectives of doing the project? If an interview is involved, what will the topic be? What logistic support is needed? Determining the objective of the project was the first priority. According to the principles of Backward Design (Wiggins & McTighe, 2005), "desired results"—what the instructor hopes the students to achieve from the project—should be identified before planning the other details of implementation. In my understanding, the essential curricular goals of this project were to motivate students with more meaningful interactions, through which students would build communication skills in the target language while also acquiring podcasting techniques. Topics for the interview should be relevant to students' interests as well as the target language proficiency. The end product would be placed on a discussion board in *Blackboard*, where students could visit and make comments. Having worked out the answers to these questions, I decided to create this project as my action research. My goal was to engage students to work with other peers in learning Chinese and to enhance their higher-order thinking, in-depth analysis, and digital literacy skills.

Participating in this project were 23 students in 2 separate sections of the Introductory Chinese II course, including 10 females and 13 males, with an age range of 19 to 22 years old. Fourteen students were freshmen, seven sophomores, and two juniors, pursuing a variety of majors. All the students successfully completed their first part of Introductory Chinese in the preceding semester except one student who studied on her own and passed an interview with the instructor. Consequently, these students were able to respond to simple direct questions or requests for information related to greetings, introducing themselves and family members, describing their hobbies, and telling time. Based on the results of a mock HSK Test Level 1 (i.e., a proficiency test of Chinese as a foreign language), of the students who participated in the test, all except one passed. In terms of speaking, their oral proficiency was generally rated as Novice Mid, with some who would fall in between Novice Mid to Novice High in accordance with the ACTFL proficiency guidelines (ACTFL, 1987) because their conversation consisted of mostly formulaic expressions and memorized structures. As most students were only able to carry guided conversations due to a limited vocabulary and restricted grammar, it was crucial to provide an appropriate topic that was neither too challenging nor too dull so that it sustained students' interests. With these criteria in mind, "language learning experience" and "school life" were designated as topics, which were relatable to students' lives and moderate in complexity regarding words and structures.

During this cycle, while the instructor designed and prepared the project by deciding the format of the podcast, determining the project theme, making timelines, and sorting out logistic needs, students needed to agree on the project theme and were given freedom to express their voice by choosing a topic of their own liking. Moreover, students were allowed to find their own partner to discuss the topic. Finally, students agreed on the project outcome: creating a podcast and posting it on the *Blackboard—Discussions* page for the class community.

Information Gathering Cycle For this project, technology was a major concern centered on issues captured by questions such as these: What tools could be used for recording? What apps are available to turn the recording into a podcast? What is the platform that can be used to host the podcasts? Who would be the support personnel that students could go to when help is needed? Fortunately, a discussion with the faculty member who had succeeded in completing his student-generated podcast project in his social work course shed some light on the answers to these questions, which equipped me to proceed with the project. The information gathering phase kicked off when the project was assigned to students in the first-day class of Spring 2020. The project outlined in the syllabus was posted on *Blackboard*. The requirements included the following: (i) the podcast must be in the target language; (ii) it should be around three minutes long; and (iii) it should contain three components: an introduction highlighting the purpose of the conversation, an interview of a self-selected partner on one of the two assigned topics, and a conclusion summarizing the interview. The project constituted 10% of the course grade. The textbook adopted for the course contained relevant vocabulary and grammar for the two topics, which students learned at a planned pace in accordance with the syllabus. These linguistic elements could serve as building blocks for students to develop their scripts for either of the two topics. For students to undertake this project, the teacher's scaffolding centered on two primary aspects: the content and the technology.

Regarding the content, after the students had a grasp of essential vocabulary, the instructor organized the students to brainstorm what questions would be appropriate to raise for a conversation on the topic of language learning experience. To that end, a group activity was organized in class. Each of the students was provided with a list of 20 questions in English related to the learning of Chinese, such as "How long have you been learning Chinese?," "Do you often practice speaking Chinese?," "How often do you write Chinese characters?," "With whom do you usually practice speaking Chinese?" Randomly placed in a group of three or four and assigned five questions, students in each group were given ten minutes to discuss how to express themselves in the target language by translating the questions from English into Chinese and how to answer the questions. After that was done, each group took turns sharing its work with the class. This activity guided students to think about how to develop their own interview questions and answers if they decided to select the topic of language learning experience. For the topic of school life, a list of 12 questions in English was posted on *Blackboard* for students to work on individually. These preparations were made to ensure that students would be able to start in the right way as they began to write their scripts. In addition to the preparatory activity, students were also instructed on how to start and end an interview by including an introduction and a conclusion. For the introduction, students were advised to include a prologue introducing who s/he was, whom s/he was to interview, and what they were going to talk about. For the conclusion, students were guided to summarize in one or two sentences what they learned from their conversation partner. Two Chinese samples of the introduction and conclusion were provided for both topics, serving as models for students.

Regarding technology, two steps were taken. First, the instructor consulted an instructional designer of the university, seeking advice and resources for podcast creation. Second, the instructor reached out to the university student-run radio station in hopes for students to access its expertise and/or equipment. The manager of the station sent a media specialist to assist the instructor with this project. The specialist provided helpful instructions with respect to the following: (i) the structure of the video in terms of the length of time, (ii) the required preparation before recording, and (iii) the special recording instructions with *Skype* or *FaceTime*. She also generously offered to edit students' recordings and publish them. This technical assistance not only tremendously helped students complete the project on time but also assured that the final products were published.

During the information gathering cycle, along with the teacher's support, students' engagement contained three parts. First, they selected a topic from the given options based on their own interests and ability to handle the topic. Second, they decided whom to interview regarding the topic. Third, they needed to work on the language, which was the main focus for this project.

Information Processing Cycle A large part of the designing and planning of the project took place before the start of the semester because the instructor had to evaluate in advance the pros and cons of doing the project from both teaching and learning perspectives. After the project was assigned, the instructor endeavored to ensure that each stage would be executed on the right track. However, it was beyond anyone's control when the pandemic broke out in the middle of semester, which forced the in-person class to switch to an online mode abruptly. With little preparation either pedagogically or psychologically, normal teaching and learning was disrupted. As the instructor was desperately hoping for rescue regarding the project, the media specialist came to help. Acting as a reliable consultant, the specialist provided a list of useful resources and offered to work with both the instructor and students on any technology issues. With her assistance, the initial work plan was modified for a smooth continuation of the project.

Throughout the entire process, students were the sole actors responsible for their own project. With the technology resources provided and the editing taken care of by the media specialist due to the unpredicted circumstances, students could focus mostly on the language. During this information processing cycle, the following major tasks were completed by the students: (i) writing and revising their script,

(ii) practicing reading their script aloud both on their own and also by working with the partner until they both felt ready for recording, and (iii) selecting a tool to conduct the interview. It was imperative that their recording contained the three pieces: an introduction, an interview, and a conclusion. Although the students did not edit their own work as initially planned, they experienced the challenges and fun of interviewing their partners.

Information Display Cycle Due to the outbreak of COVID-19, students were not able to display their end products directly to classmates. However, all works were posted on *Blackboard* for students to listen to and comment on.

Reflection Cycle Everyone completed the project on time. All students except 2 (21 out of 23) selected "language learning experience" as the topic, with the other 2 choosing "school life" as the topic for the interview. The reason for this imbalance was probably that by the middle of March, students had left the school to study remotely due to the pandemic. As there were only remote classes to attend, with neither extracurricular activities nor in-person interaction outside the class, there was little interesting campus life to talk about. Apart from that, it was also hard for students to describe in the target language their school life, which was largely disrupted by COVID-19. On the topic of language learning experience, of the 21 students, 18 focused on learning Chinese as a foreign language and three on learning English as a foreign language. As far as the conversation partner was concerned, most of the students (20) turned to their peers in the same class for the interview. This again might be related to the pandemic, which had posed challenges for students to reach out to others beyond their own classroom. However, five students were among the exceptions. Two talked with their family members (i.e., mother and sister respectively), two with their friends from other schools, and one with his friend from the same school. Out of these five students, four served as interviewers only. It is worth pointing out that one student interviewed her language partner, who was a Chinese-speaking university student in China, on the topic of the experience of learning English. In the meantime, this student was interviewed by her classmate who was interested in knowing her experience with learning Chinese. Since most students worked with their classmates, each of the 18 students ended up acting as both interviewer and interviewee. This is good as well as bad. The good part was that students, working in pairs, were able to prepare and practice together. In so doing, the students doubled their meaningful interactions and gained a truly collaborative experience as they learned from and helped each other, thereby increasing the opportunity to use the language. The drawback was that students would tend to ask similar questions and answer in the same manner. Anticipating this possible issue, the instructor reminded students to be creative by adding their own characteristics to both questions and answers. Some students handled the challenges very well.

After the products were posted online, students listened to the podcasts, celebrated their own accomplishments, and reflected upon their work, while the instructor started to analyze what had worked and what had not, in addition to assessing the performance of each student. As can be seen, throughout the whole process of the project implementation, the students, assisted by the instructor and

114 *Case Studies*

the media specialist from the radio station, were fully involved in the creation of their products. They endeavored to do all the work as required either individually (e.g., deciding the topic, looking for a partner, writing up the script, and practicing) or collaboratively (e.g., determining a time for the interview rehearsal and a time for the interview recording). If the quality was not to their satisfaction, they would do it again. In the process, students dove into deep learning and built teamwork and self-management skills. It was certain that students needed to take over the complete ownership of the project from the time they started it until they were done; otherwise, they would not be able to finish the work.

The pandemic made the post-project survey impossible. However, some students shared their thoughts in blog posts submitted to the Digital Humanities project website of the university. Their perceptions, though limited, provided a look at the educational benefits of podcasting from learning perspectives. For example, one student who interviewed a native Chinese speaker about the latter's English learning experience and was, at the same time, interviewed by a classmate regarding her own learning of Chinese, stated that the project was "*such an enjoyable learning experience.*" She "*discovered*" the secret of successful language learning through participating in the project—learning a foreign language, regardless of Chinese or English, required "*studying methods and motivation for learning.*" The conversation with a Chinese learner of English and an English learner of Chinese allowed the student to appreciate both the hardship and fun of learning a language firsthand. This reflection proved inspiring because the student came to understand what it meant to be an effective and efficient language learner. This will likely remain a valuable asset for her lifelong journey of learning Chinese. For another student, the podcasting project appeared daunting at the beginning. The difficulty increased after the campus was closed due to the pandemic. However, as time passed, with the support of the media specialist, the student began to enjoy creating his podcast and was able to "*truly dive into the language.*" In his blog submission, the student pointed out that he and his partner created two presentations of which they were "*both sincerely proud.*" The student even mentioned "*If I ever have to make another podcast in my future . . ., I now know that it is an assignment to look forward to.*" This testimony provides evidence of a transformative learning experience. Acting as both an interviewer and an interviewee on the same topic, the student had the opportunity to carry two parallel conversations but from different points of view. This helped him improve his Chinese conversational skills. It is particularly refreshing to note some exemplary aspects of his language in the two interviews. For example, he provided an engaging introduction to set a stage for his interview and an incisive conclusion following the interview, and he spoke fluently with clear pronunciation and intonation. Additionally, he appropriately used filler words or language gambits like *ò* (*oh*) and *èn* (*okay*) to keep the conversation flowing naturally. He politely responded with remarks like *Hěn yǒu yìsi* (*Very interesting*) or *Wǒ yě juéde shēngdiào hěn nán* (*I also found the tones very difficult*) to give his listener feedback. He even followed the Chinese verbal behavior to repeat the word *Shì* (*Yes*) and the phrase like *Hěn kù* (*It's cool*) to express his agreement. Injecting filler words, giving the right feedback with encouraging expressions, and repeating certain words to make his responses more relevant and emphatic showed that the student was aware of applying communicative strategies in his Chinese conversation. These kinds of authentic skills would rarely be acquired in a regular classroom. The authenticity was further reinforced by the fact that students' final products were posted online, which, in turn, made students more serious about "producing high-quality work" for the "public audience" (Boss & Larmer, 2018, p. 48).

Burdick et al. (2012) regarded PBL as a "complement to classroom-based learning" by engaging students with real-world projects (e.g., Larmer et al., 2015; Boss & Larmer, 2018). The current project created a real-world scenario in which students of Chinese were able to converse meaningfully with other interlocutors. As students prepared for the assignment, they had to consider such questions as who would serve as an ideal partner for the interview, what to ask to facilitate an engaging conversation, and how to communicate in the target language. After students determined who would be their partner, they began writing their individual scripts. They also needed to rehearse until they both felt comfortable and ready for recording. To achieve an ideal effect in both content and technology, students recorded their work several times. The entire process, which lasted around three months, served as an ideal formative assessment—the assessments for learning—through which students self-monitored their own learning and progress. These characteristics align with the work by Du (2012), Zhao and Beckett (2014), Pitura and Berlińska-Kopeć (2018), and Tavares and Potter (2018). The first two examined the application of PBL in the acquisition of Chinese, while Pitura and Berlińska-Kopeć (2018) and Tavares and Potter (2018) explored PBL in the acquisition of English. Like the previous studies, the current work demonstrated that students improved linguistic skills, developed meaningful engagement with the language, and gained authentic learning experiences.

From the instructor's point of view, a number of valuable observations were obtained. First, the podcasting assignment was an effective learner-centered work, which allowed students to provide their "voice and choice" (e.g., Morrison, 2008; Larmer et al., 2015) with the right to select a partner to talk about a topic that interested them. Although students were not able to meet each other in person starting from the middle of the semester, their interest in and enthusiasm about achieving an ultimate goal drove them to work hard. The fact that students were motivated to pursue and perform both individually and collaboratively promoted learner autonomy, the "ability to take charge of one's own learning" (Holec, 1981, p. 3). Second, students were aware that the podcast, once produced, would be "published" for other peers to listen to or download. This might have encouraged students to make greater efforts, as the majority would want their final product to be regarded as good work. Many students felt proud of their achievements when their work was showcased on the discussion board of the class community, which greatly built up their confidence. Third, the meaningful interaction and communication throughout the process enabled the students to get to know one another, which further developed their social, emotional, and collaborative skills, or how to work with others in order to achieve their joint goal. Autonomous learning, high-level motivation and confidence, and the development of lifelong skills to understand and to connect to the subject matter are part of 21st century skills (Nazikian & Park, 2016). The results show that not only was the curricular goal of this project met, namely, enhancing student interaction so as to build communication skills and developing podcasting literacy, additional benefits were also achieved, for example, learner autonomy, motivation and confidence, and social skills, some of which are in alignment with what was reported by Phillips (2017).

The instructor learned good lessons from overseeing the project. First, a rubric that details project requirements should be supplied to students in advance. In so doing, students would become well-informed as to what exactly they are expected to do and what efforts they need to make to achieve the highest goal. This way, students strive for academic excellence. Such a rubric would also guide the instructor in assessing students' work objectively. Second, students should be encouraged to exchange the script with their partner if the latter is their classmate. Requiring students to review each other's scripts and provide feedback would further strengthen meaningful interactions among students and reinforce their learning as well. Peers' feedback would serve as a helpful formative assessment to ensure that students work towards the learning goal. Third, students should be required to hand in their scripts to the instructor for final checking. This requirement would remind students to pay careful attention to linguistic elements. From a learning point of view, a meeting with the instructor to go over the script or co-edit the language would help students understand why certain words are not ideal and why some structures would be more appropriate. Such a process would assist students to learn effectively. Fourth, it would be more beneficial if students were required to edit their own recordings and publish them by themselves. While this requirement is demanding, it would certainly afford a greater learning experience. In editing recordings, students would listen to their own readings many times, enhancing practice. In addition, students would learn how to handle copyright issues regarding the use of music or sound effects. By experiencing the entire process, students would acquire a complete set of podcasting skills, which could be transferrable to the learning of other subject matter and future careers. Finally, it would be helpful if students were asked to write journals detailing their experience. Having students reflect on the process would enhance their learning and reinforce skills.

5.4.3 Summary

This project engaged learners taking the Introductory Chinese II course to create a podcast in the form of an interview. Promoting this kind of meaningful assignment as an interactive exchange between the creator and listener demonstrated potential in advancing student learning in the following ways: (i) elevating listening, speaking, and writing to the level of effective and interactive communication with others; (ii) fostering autonomous learning; (iii) boosting learning motivation and confidence; and (iv) cultivating social, emotional, and collaborative skills. The hands-on project enabled students to improve critical analysis, creativity, collaboration, and communication, as well as some digital literacy. Although their recordings were edited by a media specialist, students had an opportunity to make a podcast from scratch. They explored how to express themselves in the target language authentically. The project enables students to improve their 21st century skills, which are crucial for students to survive and thrive in a increasingly competitive society. For this project, as a vital part of scaffolding instruction, the teacher served as architect, organizer, cheerleader, coach, model, supporter, and evaluator. Nevertheless, students took on an instrumental role throughout the entire process.

Since this first experiment with podcasting in a Chinese language class, I have continued the project with students at each level of proficiency in the target language. No matter whether they are learners of the first part of Introductory Chinese, Advanced Chinese, or Modern Readings of Chinese, students create their podcasts either by working on their own or collaborating with peers or native speakers, in different project configurations, with different requirements. For true beginners, "my family" or "my friend" would be a good topic for them to talk about. The students who have studied the language for a semester are encouraged to carry on a conversation with their self-selected partner about "language learning experience," "school life," or "daily schedule." Those in the higher-level Chinese course have an option to determine their own topic and the freedom to decide to work independently or interactively with others. Some topics that students selected include their academic journey and growing up bicultural. Some students talked about a Chinese historical figure, a city in China, or Chinese cuisine. Three students took on the challenges to introduce a Chinese/American Exhibition: Matter and Sprit, held on campus, by describing some artifacts that impressed themselves or by interviewing the director of the gallery about the stories related to the exhibition. Some good products from the past experiments are featured on the following website (https://shulearnerschinese.podbean.com/). Having worked with students over the past three years, I believe integrating podcast production into a Chinese curriculum is a sustainable project that students of any proficiency level can handle. This is contingent on explicitly defining curricular goals with a robust work plan and ensuring students understand from the outset the project's relevance to them and how to execute it. It is incumbent on the teacher to scaffold instruction and make rubrics available to students.

5.5 Case 3: e-Portfolio Project

In 2002, the American Council on the Teaching of Foreign Languages (ACTFL) proposed program standards for the preparation of foreign language teachers (ACTFL, 2002), which were first endorsed by the National Council for Accreditation of Teacher Education and then approved by the Council for Accreditation of Educator Preparation State Partnerships and Content Areas Committee in 2013. These standards mandate that preservice teachers be knowledgeable and skillful in six areas. Specifically, preservice teachers must, first of all, know the target language, linguistic structures, and the similarities and differences between the target language and other languages. In addition, they must be familiar with the cultures and the literature of the language taught and understand cross-disciplinary concepts. Moreover, they should be familiar with language acquisition theories and instructional practices. They should also be able to integrate standards into curriculum design and classroom instruction and understand various methods for assessing language proficiency and cultures. Finally, the preservice teachers should engage in professional development and serve as advocates for the value of foreign language learning.

In order for preservice teachers to attain the knowledge, skills, and dispositions described in these standards, teacher preparation programs must not only include the required components in their curriculum but, more importantly, should be able to demonstrate that their students have achieved these goals. For those involved in teacher training on the front end, the question is how to assess preservice teachers. In other words, what are the effective methods that assure us that our teacher candidates achieve the ideal objectives by the end of their training? One valuable tool that has been utilized in teacher education is having students create teaching portfolios (e.g., Jarvinen & Kohonen, 1995; Shulman, 1998; Martin-Kniep, 1999; Bullock & Hawk, 2001; Fasanella, 2002; Kilbane & Milman, 2003; McColgan & Blackwood, 2009; Struyven et al., 2014; Ogan-Bekiroglu, 2014; Kim & Yazdian, 2014; Demirel & Duman, 2015).

Advanced technology has made it easier and more effective for preservice teachers to produce dynamic portfolios in the format of individual websites. This kind of electronic portfolio (henceforth, e-portfolios), which usually contains a variety of material, can be accessed by all stakeholders involved in teacher education, including preservice teachers, teacher-trainers, mentors, and potential employers. As an instructor of a graduate course that covered methods of teaching Chinese, I worked with our graduate students in the teaching track (preservice teachers), who were cultivated to be Chinese language teachers in K–12 settings, to build teaching portfolios. Having experimented with paper-based portfolios with two groups of cohorts, I wanted preservice teachers to create e-portfolios in hopes that their end products could be shared with other interested parties. This wish was made possible by the availability of *WordPress*, an open-source tool that can be used to build a website to "hold" one's portfolio. Stoller (2002) claimed that "project-based learning should be viewed as a versatile vehicle for fully integrated language and content learning, making it a viable option for language educators working in a variety of instructional settings . . . including general English, English for academic purposes (EAP), English for specific purposes (ESP), and English for occupational/vocational/professional purposes, **in addition to preservice and in-service teacher training**" (p. 109, emphasis mine). With an interest in whether the technology-enhanced teaching portfolio application will enable preservice teachers to advance academically and professionally, I tried the e-portfolio project for the Supervised Teaching of Chinese course in Spring 2016, details of which are provided in the sections that follow.

5.5.1 Background

A teaching portfolio, as defined by Armstrong et al. (2005), "includes evidence a teacher gathers to document what he or she has accomplished with a given group of learners over a period of time" (pp. 416–417). The concept of using portfolios in teaching and teacher education dates back to the 1980s, and it has now become common in teacher education programs in the US (e.g., Worf, 1996; Wolf & Dietz, 1998; Zeichner & Wray, 2001; Foote & Vermette, 2001). According to Bal (2012), a portfolio is a collection of a learner's work over a specific period, showcasing her or his knowledge and development through different stages of education and training. The items in the compilation reveal the learner's development and achievements, as well as experience, and self-evaluation represented either by his or her own writings or by artifacts. Portfolio applications offer the potential to document each student's learning journey, thereby serving as an effective tool for individual learning (e.g., Imhof & Picard, 2009; Gibson & Barrett, 2002). The core of the portfolio is the systematic evaluation of the learner's performance and work as argued by Moya and O'Malley (1994). Barrett (2010) emphasized that the real value of portfolios is their ability to promote students' reflection and learning.

Portfolios used to be collections of work assembled in "boxes" or "three-ring binders," but a new container emerged with the advent of information technology, resulting in what is known as e-portfolios, "stored in digital form" (Gibson & Barrett, 2002, p. 556). Kilbane and Milman (2003) noted that the terms such as *digital portfolios, multimedia portfolios, e-folios, webfolios, and electronically-augmented portfolios* contain the same basic content as traditional teaching portfolios but presented in digital format. In the early days, e-portfolios were created through generic and/or customized tools such as HTML editors, multimedia authoring software, programming, and databases (Gibson & Barrett, 2002). Now e-portfolios can be efficiently made through much more sophisticated technology, such as *Adobe Express* tools. Regardless of the format, paper-based or web-based, portfolios have become an established practice to achieve different purposes. Bal (2012) claimed that portfolios serve as "an essential evaluation tool revealing descriptive, formative and summative information about students and their products, as well as suggesting the information about students' strengths and weaknesses in line with the organization of the education" (p. 88). Tucker et al. (2002) suggested that portfolios have a dual goal: evaluating and developing professionalism. McColgan and Blackwood (2009) noted the two functions that portfolios fulfill: encouraging students to engage in producing evidence of their competency and personal development and providing employers with a tool to evaluate their staff. Wolf and Dietz (1998) proposed a threefold model based on the authorship of the portfolio and the roles that the portfolio can play. That is, a *learning portfolio* created by preservice teachers for self-assessment; an *assessment portfolio* developed by in-service teachers for their professional growth; and an *employment portfolio* presented by individuals to prospective employers for career development. Therefore, the function of a portfolio can span a student teacher's entire academic career.

There has been a myriad of research on portfolios/e-portfolios since the concept was incorporated into teacher education. Many studies explored their benefits, including student learning (Zou, 2003), quality teaching (Kim & Yazdian, 2014), or assessment (Fasanella, 2002; Price, 2013). Some looked at training teacher candidates in separate disciplines, such as mathematics (Birgin, 2011; Bal, 2012), physics (Ogan-Bekiroglu, 2014), ESL (Kim & Yazdian, 2014), and foreign language learning (Demirel & Duman, 2015). Others examined their use in K–12 education (Kim & Yazdian, 2014), in higher education (McColgan & Blackwood, 2009), or for distance English language teachers (Kecik et al., 2012).

With respect to the research that examined preservice teachers' perceptions of e-portfolios, Cakir and Balcikanli (2012) examined the perspectives of ELT student teachers and teacher-trainers on the use of the portfolio in preservice language teacher education. The results suggested that both student teachers and teacher-trainers found that portfolios were beneficial in reflection, self-assessment, and awareness. Based on their findings, the authors proposed integrating the European Portfolio for Student Teachers of Languages as part of teacher education program and further converting it into an online format to make it more convenient for the student teachers. In the same vein, Kecik et al. (2012) conducted a survey of the needs of preservice teachers in order to determine whether the portfolios would satisfy the requirements of distance teaching practice courses. Comparing and analyzing the quantitative and qualitative data from university supervisors, teacher candidates, and cooperating teachers on the feasibility of the e-portfolio application, they found that all three groups agreed about the needs of preservice teachers (i.e., planning, teaching, and reflection in the teaching process). While there were some minor variances in the perspectives of each group, they found that the e-portfolio application can meet most of the requirements. Ogan-Bekiroglu (2014) measured preservice teachers' reflections using targeted qualitative research, such as participants' portfolios and interviews. The findings showed that most of the preservice teachers gained expertise in reflecting upon their teaching skills.

5.5.2 Engaging Preservice Teachers to Produce e-Portfolios

In view of integrating e-portfolios in Chinese language teacher education, Chen (2017b) reported on her experiment and the effects of utilizing e-portfolio in a Chinese-language teacher preparation program in order to evaluate students' academic and personal development. In presenting the project that integrated the development of e-portfolios in a graduate-level teacher preparation curriculum with the goal of gaining insights for improving Chinese-language teacher education, two research questions were examined: (i) whether the e-portfolio development serves as a learning tool as well as a means of assessment for Chinese teacher education and (ii) whether applying technology to portfolio construction adds value. It was hypothesized that building e-portfolios is a dynamic learning process towards learning objectives, while the end product provides evidence for evaluating student learning. As preservice teachers develop the content of their portfolios, they would learn to formulate teaching beliefs, design instructional activities, create lesson plans, and prepare teaching demonstrations. All of these should contribute to the cultivation of competence, knowledge, critical thinking, reflections, experience, skills, and professionalism required for a qualified Chinese-language teacher (ACTFL, 2002; Everson, 2009). I will next demonstrate the five stages of this e-portfolio development project.

Preparation Cycle The ten graduate students participating in this project were undergoing training in the Asian Studies program at my home university to become Chinese teachers in K–12 settings in the US. All except one had completed the course Methods of Teaching Chinese before they undertook the project. All of them had some experience tutoring or teaching American students as a guest teacher, a student teacher, or a teaching assistant. Some were working part-time in private schools or weekend heritage Chinese schools. It is worth mentioning that of the ten students, six had either completed one-year study in the graduate program Teaching Chinese to Speakers of Other Languages at a Chinese university in China or had already earned an MA degree from that program. Demographically, one was from Taiwan, and nine were from mainland China, with two male students and eight female students, ranging from mid to high 20s in age.

All the participants registered in Supervised Teaching of Chinese, a core course specially designed to help preservice teachers acquire skills and techniques required to teach Chinese language and culture. Foreign language education standards (ACTFL, 1996, 1999, 2006, 2015) were re-visited and major principles of second language acquisition (e.g., Lee & VanPatten, 2003; Lightbown & Spada, 2013) were re-examined in the class. However, the focus of the course was to cultivate preservice teachers' ability to apply standards to teaching, thereby gaining a better understanding of the requirements and developing teaching skills. To that end, students were required to explore the teaching of the Chinese language in a real-world setting. To meet the requirements, the students needed to teach at a self-selected school for at least a month or co-teach four to six classes under the supervision of the instructor in conjunction with their mentors in the school. For each class, students were expected to hand in a lesson plan, including the objectives to be achieved, the materials to be taught, the methods or techniques to be applied, and the activities to be used. To prepare in that regard, students were required to observe classes and to compile five separate journals that recorded their experiences. Each journal should include their reflections about the instructor's lesson plan, teaching methods, student reactions, student performance, and any other relevant issues if observed. For class teaching, participants also needed to design five teaching activities with respect to a given aspect of the Chinese language or culture. Finally, students submitted a paper reflecting on what they learned throughout the project as well as the course as a whole. All these activities—the teaching, journal writing, activities designing, and reflection paper—were purposely assigned to prepare the preservice teachers to build their own portfolios.

The instructor assigned the project of building an e-portfolio at the beginning of this course, which students agreed to complete. Students also agreed to publish their finished e-portfolio. As required, the e-portfolio must have a complete profile, containing a minimum of the following: resume, introduction of oneself, teaching philosophy, lesson plans, instructional activities, video-taped teaching demonstrations, and student work. The project was evaluated based on a rubric, contributing 10% to the total grade of the course.

Information Gathering Cycle To build an e-portfolio, students needed a technology tool, for which the instructor did research in advance during the preparation cycle. *WordPress*.com (henceforth *WordPress*), one of the most popular online publishing platforms, was selected. As open-source software, *WordPress* has two types of platforms: *WordPress*.com and *WordPress*.org. The former has both free and paid options, both running on the servers of *WordPress*.com, and the latter requires the user to download and install the *WordPress* software script on a local server (e.g., Jones & Farrington, 2011; O'Neill, 2017). The primary rationale for choosing *WordPress*.com is its popularity and the fact that it is free of charge. In addition, *WordPress* is flexible, enabling one to build a blog, a full website, a combo, a portfolio, or a business site. For this project, the blogging function was not utilized. The third reason was that *WordPress* offers professional-looking templates but allows for individual customization. The fourth reason for selecting the tool to host the preservice teachers' portfolios is that the platform provides universal access by any interested party on a wide range of devices. During this information gathering cycle, it is important for preservice teachers to understand the two different tools. In addition, while *WordPress* "is the easiest place to get started," as boasted by *WordPress*.com, it still presents difficulty or complexity to new users who have little technical knowledge or skill (e.g., Kilbane & Milman, 2003; Avila et al., 2016). Aware of the challenges of building a website, I invited a senior instructional designer from the university's technology center to the class to lecture on the fundamentals of developing a website by using *WordPress*. Not only did the instructional designer show the class how to create a website from scratch, but she also offered advice on some practical issues such as how to handle online media files and also how to get started. Apart from this guidance, she provided some useful resources as to how to build a website via *WordPress*. All this, as part of scaffolding instruction, was made available in the middle of the semester when preservice teachers were ready to put their content materials up online. Students then had three weeks to focus on developing the website. Thus, sufficient time was guaranteed for each one to create the content, modify it after receiving feedback, and resubmit it.

Other than receiving the crucial assistance in technology from the instructional designer, students were assisted with the content by the instructor. For example, developing a powerful teaching statement and creating effective teaching activities can be challenging for preservice teachers. To that end, samples of teaching statements were presented to students, followed by analysis and discussion in class. With those steps completed, students brainstormed what should be included in order to develop a reflective teaching philosophy. Students were also guided on how to develop engaging instructional activities by watching videos of teaching activities and teaching demonstrations. Class discussions were planned afterwards so that students could learn to create their teaching statements and activities.

Information Processing Cycle In accordance with the requirements established by the graduate program for the teaching track, preservice teachers were expected to become competent in teaching Chinese as a foreign language in the K–12 setting by the end of the program. In other words, the preservice teachers in this e-portfolio project should showcase, on their self-built website, their knowledge and skills about teaching Chinese as a foreign language in the US. Specifically, they should be able to (i) develop their teaching philosophy, (ii) produce a professional resume and provide an appealing introduction about themselves, (iii) design solid lesson plans, and (iv) present a teaching demonstration. As such, during this information processing cycle, preservice teachers must focus on working in these four aspects. While all required effort and hard work, showcasing their teaching demonstration was the most difficult undertaking because it involved working with the teacher mentor of the school in terms of when to teach, what to teach, and how to teach in addition to designing the lesson plan and teaching in class. Thus, preservice teachers should focus on working out those details first. After they completed the teaching and generated the video of their teaching, they could then post materials on their website. With that done, by now the preservice teachers developed a draft of their e-portfolios, which they sent to the instructor for feedback for them to improve. They also shared their work with other peers for comments. At this stage, preservice teachers and the instructor worked very closely.

Information Display Cycle The final products were submitted to the instructor. In order for preservice teachers to evaluate their e-portfolio, their performance in the four aspects should be measured based on the rubric. For that purpose, a scoring system was developed, as follows. First, if a preservice teacher developed a profound teaching philosophy with deep thinking and reflections, the individual would receive a full score of 7.5 points. Second, if the preservice teacher produced a strong resume with an introduction highlighting his or her career objectives, credentials, experience, and skills, the individual was awarded a perfect score of 7.5 points. Third, if the preservice teacher presented well-prepared lesson plans, engaging activities, and a solid teaching demonstration, s/he garnered a score of 7.5 points. Finally, a score of 2.5 points was given if the website exhibited a professional look and was easy to navigate. Thus, a total of 25 points indicated "excellent" work, a score of 20 points was considered "good", and 15 points was "fair." The scores of preservice teachers' e-portfolios appear in Table 5.4. As can be seen, two of the ten participants achieved an excellent performance, and two were almost perfect (24.5

Table 5.4 Scores of Preservice Teachers' e-Portfolios

Students	Teaching Philosophy	Professional Resume & Background	Lesson Plan & Teaching	Navigation With No Error	Total Points (25 points)
S1	7.5	7.5	7	2.5	24.5
S2	7	6.5	6.5	1.5	21
S3	7.5	7.5	7.5	1.5	24
S4	7.5	7.5	7.5	2.5	25
S5	7.5	7.5	7	2.5	24.5
S6	7	6.5	6.5	1.5	21
S7	7.5	7.5	7.5	2.5	25
S8	7.5	7.5	4.5	2.5	22
S9	7	6.5	7	1.5	22
S10	7	6	6	1.5	20

points), with one approaching the excellent (24 points). Four participants scored between excellent and good (achieving 21 and 22 points, respectively), and one received a good performance (20 points).

As part of the information display, preservice teachers' perceptions about the e-portfolio creation were surveyed through a questionnaire administered in the beginning of the following semester. The survey consisted of four multiple-choice questions and three open-ended questions. The first two questions solicited preservice teachers' thoughts about their own learning on the whole. The third survey question requested them to reflect on their achievements throughout the project. The fourth question asked whether they found it difficult to develop an e-portfolio, and the seventh question required them to spell out the challenges if there were any. The fifth and sixth questions targeted their views about the benefits of the e-portfolio production and their use of it in job searches, if applicable. The preservice teachers' answers to these questions also displayed their learning outcomes through this project, that is, the understanding of some issues involved in the teaching and learning of Chinese in the US and their attitudes towards teaching professionalism.

Reflections Cycle All the participants completed the survey. As the answers that students provided to the first and the fifth questions overlapped, their responses are summarized in Table 5.5. The left column of the table presents the six key phrases generated out of the commonalities of the students' writings with respect to their perceptions of the learning through the e-portfolio application and of the benefits from such a project. The right column indicates how many participants had expressed that idea and who the participants were, along with sample quotes. Table 5.5 shows that nine out of the ten participants explicitly remarked that they had learned how to build an e-portfolio in the form of a website. The know-how on website development represents advanced technology skills, including information, media, and technology skills, which are a crucial part of a variety of skill sets required for students of the 21st century (Partnership for 21st Century Learning, 2009). It is significant that preservice teachers acquire these skills and take advantage of technology throughout their careers. The remarks by S4, *"The technology, which I learned helps me a lot for my current Chinese teaching"* indicates the student's satisfaction with the experience. It is also interesting to note that seven participants felt that they had greatly benefited from the opportunity to promote themselves via the website, suggesting progress in transforming from "modesty" (a virtue of traditional Chinese culture) to "expressive" (an attribute of an effective teacher). Furthermore, six participants noted the significance of reflection in the learning process. The following quotes, *"This project gives me an opportunity to let me think what I already did and what I should have done but I didn't in the past"* (S1); *"Because I need to make the profile look abundant, I would push myself to . . . record more teaching activities"* (S3); and *"Thinking more about how to become better Chinese teacher"* (S9), evidently demonstrated that these individuals had a clear goal in mind and that they were constantly pursuing that objective. We can also see from Table 5.5 that roughly half of the participants felt the project improved their understanding of the requirements of the teaching professional and English writing skills. Half of the participants found

Table 5.5 Perceptions of Preservice Teachers on Learning and Viewpoints About Benefits

Preservice Teachers' Reflections	Number of Preservice Teachers Who Had Similar Thoughts, With Sample Quotes
a. Building a website	**9 Preservice Teachers: S1, S2, S4, S5, S6, S7, S8, S9, S10** S1: *"I learned how to build a useful website"* S4: *"I learned some technology about building the personal website, which is useful for me . . . The technology which I learned helps me a lot for my current Chinese teaching."* S7: *"I have learnt the basic skill to create the e-portfolio"* S9: *"How to design my website"*
b. Promoting oneself	**7 Preservice Teachers: S2, S3, S4, S5, S6 S8, S10** S2: *"It is like a window which parents and employer could understand me deeply. Also, I could share my teaching inspiration and welcome to suggestions from my colleagues"* S3: *"I learned how to promote myself and show my teaching experience and products which is very helpful for interviews . . . it's a great platform to demonstrate my teaching philosophy; teaching methods, activities, and students' works."* S5: *"that I can present the qualifications on what makes me a good language teacher"* S6: *"It's an effective method to show my Chinese class directly. It's a better way to show my resume directly and it's also convenient for people who want to learn Chinese to check some course they really want."* S8: *"How to promote myself using website"*
c. Reflecting on learning	**6 Preservice Teachers: S1, S3, S4, S7, S8, S9** S1: *"this project gives me an opportunity to let me think what I already did and what I should have done but I didn't in the past as a Chinese language teacher or a student who wants to be a Chinese language teacher."* S4: *"It gives me an opportunity to know more about myself and summarize the teaching materials. I appreciate the feedback, and learned a lot from the other classmates. Without these, I may be stuck and cannot improve myself."* S8: *"It helped me review what I learned about teaching theory"* S9: *"Thinking more about how to become a better Chinese teacher."*

(Continued)

Table 5.5 (Continued)

Preservice Teachers' Reflections	Number of Preservice Teachers Who Had Similar Thoughts, With Sample Quotes
d. Understanding requirements	**5 Preservice Teachers: S1, S4, S5, S9, S10** **S4:** "*after I finished the project, I have a logical and clear understanding of my teaching target, what are the requirements of an effective Chinese teacher and my teaching philosophy*" **S9:** "*Understanding the requirements of Chinese teacher . . . Understanding more about the qualities of Chinese teacher*" **S10.** "*Understanding the requirements*"
e. Improving English writing skills	**4 Preservice Teachers: S1, S2, S8, S9** **S1:** "*this project also improves my writing skills in English, since I have to write my resume, teaching philosophy and introductions of my teaching program in English.*" **S8:** "*how to write teaching philosophy and introduction in an appropriate way.*" **S2:** "*improving my English*"
f. Searching for jobs	**5 Preservice Teachers: S3, S4, S5, S7, S9** **S4:** "*Above all, the e-portfolio helped me find a job and gave me a fully prepared interview.*" **S5:** "*It is very helpful when looking for the job*" **S7:** "*Useful when I search for a job*"

that the e-portfolios were useful for job searches. The four participants, S1, S3, S4, and S5, who scored high in portfolio performance, felt they had made greater achievements. They were also the ones who reflected the most about their progress. While S10 scored the lowest and S8 also lower, both believed that they had progressed in different areas.

In terms of the second survey question, *Did the project enable you to become a serious learner about the K–12 Chinese language teaching?* all the participants answered YES, suggesting that the e-portfolio application has made them become more reflective about teaching Chinese in the K–12 setting. The third question, *During the process of developing your e-portfolio, did you achieve any progress in the following aspects?* allowed each individual to select as many as six given statements, as presented in Table 5.6, which they believed best described their personal growth.

It is clear from the table that almost all the participants thought that they had obtained a better understanding of requirements for Chinese-language teachers in the real world. Most of them became more committed to pursuing a Chinese teaching career in the K–12 setting. Again, many believed that they had improved English writing skills. Half of them felt that their sense of responsibility was raised and their high-level critical and reflective thinking skills were improved as well. Four of the ten participants indicated that they had strived for professionalism. The self-evaluation from the preservice teachers as shown in Table 5.6 suggested that the project experience enhanced their academic progress and personal growth. Those who scored high in terms of e-portfolio (S1, S3, S5, and S7) had made significant progress, as shown by their selection of four statements in Table 5.6. What is worth noting is that S9 seems to be a rising star among this group. As evident in her/his reflections, *"Thinking more about how to become better Chinese teacher"* shown in Table 5.5, S9 felt s/he had progressed in all the six areas. Even S10, who scored the lowest in Table 5.4, believed that s/he had also made good progress in three areas.

Table 5.6 Perceptions of Preservice Teachers About Accomplishments Obtained

Statements of Six Accomplishments	Number of Preservice Teachers Selecting the Statement
a. Gained a better understanding of requirements for Chinese-language teachers in the real world	9: S1, S3, S4, S5, S6, S7, S8, S9, S10
b. Became more committed to, and serious about pursuing a teaching career in the K–12 setting	8: S2, S3, S4, S5, S6, S7, S8, S9
c. Improved high-level critical and reflective thinking skills about teaching and learning	5: S3, S5, S8, S9, S10
d. Increased the sense of responsibility	6: S1, S3, S4, S6, S7, S9
e. Improved English writing skills	7: S1, S2, S3, S6, S8, S9, S10
f. Strived for professionalism	4: S1, S5, S7, S9

As for the fourth question, *Is it difficult to complete the project?*, only two students gave comments, which will be discussed when the seventh question is addressed. Regarding the sixth question, *Since you completed your website, have you ever used it for your job search?*, seven students answered YES. Two mentioned that they used their websites as a sample in a summer STARTALK (a federal-sponsored language program) Teaching Training session, receiving good feedback. This positive attitude towards their own e-portfolios was correlated with the perceptions that they provided when answering the fifth question regarding the benefits of the project.

For the seventh survey question that asked in what way the project was difficult, two students made comments. Participant S4 said, "*My answer to Question 4 is (b)(not difficult), but I remember that I need a lot of time. It is not difficult, but it needs time and patience.*" The other preservice teacher, S10, expressed the opinion in Chinese, which I translated as follows:

> *The portfolio requires many teaching plans and teaching materials, which may not be difficult for those with some teaching experience. It is very time-consuming as well as stressful for inexperienced students. From the perspective of future career development, e-portfolio is very useful. But as a classroom assignment, it added additional pressure to some inexperienced students.*

The successful creation of an e-portfolio and the preservice teachers' reflections on their experiences suggested a positive answer to the first research question, that is, the e-portfolio development serves as a learning tool for preservice teacher training. The entire process offered a valuable opportunity for students not only to work hard towards their learning objectives but also to help them plan their learning journey. In order to complete the requirements of the portfolio, preservice teachers needed to establish learning goals, organizing their self-regulated and self-directed learning, thereby building their autonomous learning (e.g., Gibson & Barrett, 2002; Cakir & Balcikanli, 2012). While they were developing their profiles, the preservice teachers constantly reflected upon their goals, their progress, and the challenges associated with their learning. The e-portfolio application provided a supportive context in which each individual was able to take responsibility for one's own learning (i.e., controlling, monitoring, and self-evaluating their progress). At the same time, the preservice teachers also had the freedom to discuss issues with their peers, the instructor, and, sometimes, mentors and receive feedback and support on a regular basis during the portfolio construction process. Such a learner-centered environment further facilitated learning autonomy, which led to teacher autonomy, an attribute necessary for teachers. The entire project stimulated learning and growth. Consequently, preservice teachers obtained a better appreciation of foreign language education standards and the qualifications necessary for teachers, formulated their own teaching style and personality, and developed their professionalism. The observations indicate that the participants in the e-portfolio project raised their competency and skills, enhancing student learning (e.g., Campbell et al., 2004; Imhof & Picard, 2009; Kecik et al., 2012) and reinforcing their dedication to lifelong learning (e.g., Frey, 2008).

The project also suggests that the e-portfolio creation, at the same time, served as a method to evaluate the performance of each individual, informing the instructor whether a preservice teacher had achieved the course goals, and in which areas the instructor should further guide and coach her or him. The data presented in Table 5.4 shows that all preservice teachers produced satisfactory work, with some exceeding expectations. As discussed before, even for those who did not achieve excellent scores, their self-evaluation in the post-project survey, as shown in Tables 5.5 and 5.6, reveal that they had also made good progress in various areas. Involving a process as well as a product, the e-portfolio fulfills the respective roles as specified by formative and summative assessments (Middle States Commission on Higher Education, 2007). The process of developing e-portfolios satisfactorily offered continuing feedback not only to the instructor for adjusting and improving instruction quality but also to the preservice teachers for self-monitoring and planning their learning. Such a formative assessment that informed and guided both parties proved to be constructive in the ongoing teaching and learning context. Because the preservice teachers took entire ownership of e-portfolio development and they were informed in advance of what they were expected to produce, this assessment practice was particularly helpful to them. When the e-portfolios were completed, the final learning outcomes enabled the instructor to evaluate each preservice teacher by reviewing her or his performance and comparing it against the standards or benchmarks outlined in the rubric. The current findings that the e-portfolio project was able to motivate and evaluate student learning simultaneously support the argument for the dual-goal of portfolios in education, as postulated by Zeichner and Wray (2001), Tucker et al. (2002), and Struyven et al. (2014). That is, the e-portfolio is a useful instrument for evaluating as well as developing teacher competencies.

Regarding the research question of whether there is any added value of technology associated with portfolio creation, some findings are noteworthy. First, the e-portfolio construction enabled all the participants to succeed in developing a professional-looking website, which advanced their multimedia and information technology skills in addition to their creative thinking and problem-solving skills. This set of digital skills will be helpful to preservice teachers when they educate their future tech-savvy students, or "digital natives" in the sense of Prensky (2001a). Second, *WordPress*, which provided flexibility in how materials could be organized and displayed, enabled the participants to think more logically when laying out their profiles, helping to expand web design skills. This kind of experience is captured in the participant S4's reflections:

I have to summarize the teaching materials and then upload to the website. Before that, I did not sort [any] of these materials . . . This project made me [think] more clearly about what kind of the materials I need to use.

Third, the nature of e-portfolios—being accessible to anyone—pushed the preservice teachers to be conscientious about the process as well as the product. As compared with my previous two experiments with the paper-based portfolio application, the enthusiasm of the preservice teachers, the quality of portfolios, the student learning experience, and their final accomplishments for the current project were all superior. Some preservice teachers expressed that they specifically benefited a great deal from the digital format of the portfolios by remarking on the value that technology added to their work. For example, references to *"multi-media,"* as highlighted by participant S9, and the comment by S6, who noted how e-portfolios can *"combine teacher's resume with their Chinese courses together,"* illustrate the versatility of the technology used in creating e-portfolios. Knowing that their portfolios were to be posted online in the public domain, all the preservice teachers strived to make their profiles look as professional as possible by reviewing and revising each item of content several times before uploading them so as to ensure that they were accurate and appropriate. For the participants for whom English was not their native language, such a process offered them an opportunity to improve their writing skills, which is absolutely necessary for a qualified Chinese-language teacher in the K–12 setting. Finally, unlike the paper-based portfolio, which has to be mailed to potential employers, the e-profile is available online and, therefore, easy to share with potential employers. The finding that the majority of the participants used their e-portfolio as part of their job searches suggests another advantage, which emerged from this technology, as illustrated by the following reflections from the participant S5:

The e-portfolio arranges all the information together which helps the interviewer find everything they want to know about a candidate. Compared with a normal paper resume, it actually shows the candidate in a teaching demo. This is important because the employer can see if the qualifications in the resume are reflected in the candidate's demo. One of the interviewers told me that he was very impressed with my e-portfolio because he said that I clearly demonstrated my skills to him.

Were all the accomplishments discussed here attributed to the mere completion of the e-portfolios? Could it be possible that the practicum experience also contributed to the learning progress? It is difficult to tease out the practicum experience or exclude other factors. However, it is clear that it was through engaging in this project that the preservice teachers were encouraged to participate in practicum training that, in turn, resulted in the enhancement of learning. In addition, while the study has lent support in validating *WordPress* as a powerful platform for hosting portfolios or using *WordPress* as a content management system (e.g., Jones & Farrington, 2011; Avila et al., 2016; O'Neill, 2017), little was done on its effectiveness as a learning tool. Particularly, it is unknown what role *WordPress* holds in facilitating preservice teachers' learning through exchanges with the instructor and peers via its blogging mechanism.

5.5.3 *Summary*

This project demonstrated that engaging preservice teachers in the development of e-portfolios can place them in a supportive contextualized position to start their learning journey and advance academically and professionally. In building portfolios digitally on an independent website via WordPress, preservice teachers developed their multimedia and information technology, critical thinking, and creative skills. Simultaneously, they made achievements in six areas through reflection upon their learning objectives, the course material, and their professional career development. By reflection and practice, the would-be teachers have achieved a better understanding and appreciation of professional requirements, teaching methods, and instructional skills. Such a project provides a means for the teacher or even prospective employers to evaluate the teaching credentials and skills of preservice teachers.

5.6 Conclusion

As outlined in Table 5.7, the first two projects were incorporated in an Introductory Chinese classroom and the third one in a Chinese language teacher education course. All the projects involve technology, including *Unity* for developing games; *Skype*, *FaceTime*, and *Teams* for creating podcasts; and *WordPress* for producing e-portfolios, without which these projects would not have been possible. As demonstrated, the gaming technology, podcasting tools, and *WordPress* add evidence of support to the "published research on how projects that implement technology explicitly facilitate the learning of language in general and language form in particular" (Beckett et al., 2019, p. 8). The first two projects engaged students to work collaboratively to achieve language learning goals, while the third one encouraged preservice teachers to strive for success by working with the teacher trainer, peers, and mentor, as well as their own students, towards their career objectives as Chinese language educators. These projects, which support the claim that PBLL is a powerful tool for language, content, and skills integration (Stoller, 2002; Beckett & Slater, 2005), speak of the value of the DATEPBLL approach in language education.

The gaming project consisted of two parts, involving the development of the matching game template by the instructor and the creation of matching games by three student cohorts. The project enabled students to experience how a game could be built and acquire some gaming technology literacy as well as methodology while studying Chinese in an engaging fashion. Through the joint efforts of the instructor

Table 5.7 A Summary of Three Projects

Projects	Configurations	Participants	Goals	Technology	Products
Gaming	Structured	Learners of Introductory Chinese II	Learn Chinese	*Unity*	Matching games
Podcasting	Structured	Learners of Introductory Chinese II	Learn Chinese	*Skype*, *Teams* *FaceTime*	Podcasts
Creating e-portfolio	Semi-structured	Preservice teachers	Learn to teach	*WordPress*	Web-based e-portfolios

and students, ten matching games were eventually developed using the vocabulary of the ten chapters of the popular Chinese textbook *Integrated Chinese Level 1 Part 1* (Liu et al., 2018). One of the significant implications gleaned from this project is that gaming should be incorporated in the Chinese language classroom, but an easy and more effective practice is to involve students in developing games based on existing platforms such as *Quizlet* and *Kahoot!*. During the COVID-19 pandemic, when the class was forced to be held online, my students of Chinese was able to create a *Quizlet* instead of doing a daily quiz.

The experiment with podcasting was completed on time thanks to the assistance of a media specialist despite many challenges related to the pandemic. This project provided a number of insights, which inform the instructor that podcasting is a manageable and sustainable task that can be adapted to students learning any language at all different levels of proficiency. As more advanced technologies are available with regard to recording, editing, and publishing, podcasting can now be done in a much more effective fashion. By immersing students in the process of making and sharing podcasts, the instructor can encourage and enable students to develop lifetime learning skills, which "help students thrive in today's digitally and globally interconnected world" (Howlett & Waemusa, 2019, p. 74).

The e-portfolios project completed by graduate students in a teaching track showed the potential of e-portfolio development for language teacher education. When creating their own e-portfolios, preservice teachers, by working together with other peers, teaching mentors, and the instructor, developed their teaching skills, technology literacy, and professionalism. Since the e-portfolio project was applied in Spring 2016, it was repeated three times with different cohorts in the same graduate program. Based on these experiments, I suggest teacher training programs develop a framework that specifies the content as required in the e-portfolios (see Snyder et al., 1998 for an example of a portfolio framework). Teacher-trainers should help preservice teachers to determine the content in accordance with various courses at different learning stages. If the e-portfolio project is incorporated in a theory-oriented course such as applied linguistics, students can develop a presentation on their understanding of how languages are acquired, that is, what theories explain first language acquisition and second language learning. If it is involved in a teaching methods course, preservice teachers can add lesson plans and teaching activities to their portfolios. As part of scaffolding instruction, teaching faculty must provide the content, knowledge, and technical assistance as needed for students. In this way, students will be equipped to examine, hypothesize, and reflect upon what they are learning professionally and technologically. In this way, students' portfolios are ensured to be of high quality and the students will fulfill their learning goals. It is ideal to start the project as soon as students enroll in the program because it takes time to construct a meaningful, functional, and professional portfolio (Wolf & Dietz, 1998). In building their e-portfolios, preservice teachers learn and grow simultaneously. Finally, faculty of the education program should endeavor to collaborate with the mentors and administrators in the K–12 setting as much as possible. As noted by Zeichner and Wray (2001), incorporating the assistance of teachers from the K–12 setting into the portfolio development process will help preservice teachers to reflect upon and evaluate their learning effectively. Preservice teachers will learn from experienced teachers in the real world while being able to network with the teaching community.

In Lam's (2023) recent review of the e-portfolios scholarship on L2 and EFL classroom contexts spanning from 1999 to 2019, he concludes that "e-Portfolio is an alternative approach to advancing language teaching and learning" (p. 214). Chism and Faidley (2021), who look at the implementation of e-portfolios in an intermediate French language course, show that students appreciate the experience of generating e-portfolios via *Weebly*, as compared to the use of a traditional textbook. The collaborative group work strengthened students' sense of community, social interaction skills, and intercultural awareness. With the e-portfolio becoming commonplace in language education, it is the time to try e-portfolios with learners of Chinese so as to explore its potential on the development of students' linguistic and cultural skills.

The case studies illustrate the effectiveness of Stoller and Myers' (2019) project framework in PBLL instruction. As compared to Alan and Stoller's (2005) 10 steps, Greenier's (2020) 10Cs (10 stages starting with "C"), Stoller's (2012) 3 stages with 7 steps, Hoyt's (2013) 3 steps, and Meng's (2022) 3 stages in 7 steps, this 5-cycle framework has the appropriate number of steps, neither more nor less. It precisely directs both the teacher and students to engage in their projects from start to completion. In particular, each cycle specifies the roles of stakeholders involved, thereby helping the teacher to oversee the project and informing the students of their responsibilities. While the five cycles are crucial for orchestrating successful classroom projects, the teacher may not always follow its rigid sequential order, as suggested by Stoller and Myers. For example, based on my own observations, the information gathering and information processing cycles may intermittently go hand in hand because gathering and processing information is an intertwined continuum of engagement. Normally, students first collect information and then process it accordingly. However, sometimes, while processing certain information, students may feel the need to gather additional information about a given content area or some linguistic and cultural elements, thus returning to the information gathering cycle again for more details. Likewise, the reflection cycle may not only occur at the end of the information display cycle. In fact, all the involved parties may start reflecting, more or less, on the project work right after the project is assigned. Regular reflection on the project work by the teacher and students is a necessary and crucial component of the entire project process. The possible variations between reflections at the end and reflections in the middle of process may focus on different perspectives or different emphases. When the project is completed, everyone feels relieved, excited, and accomplished, thus tending to concentrate more on the positive side of the end product. When the project is in progress, in particular, after some unexpected occurrences, students may feel anxious because of stress, hence, reflecting more on the challenges of the assignment. It is my experience that to motivate each student to participate in and complete a project, adjustments to the project cycles should be allowed in order to achieve desired learning outcomes.

References

Abdulqadir, M. (2017). *Matching game template* (A digital game template).
Abdulrahman, T., Basalama, N., & Widodo, M. R. (2018). The impact of podcasts on EFL students' listening comprehension. *International Journal of Language Education, 2*(2), 23–33. https://eric.ed.gov/?id=EJ1245044
Abelmann, N. (2014). The intimate university: "We are all in this together." In M. Winkelmes, M. A. Burton, & K. Mays (Eds.), *An Illinois sampler: Teaching and research on the prairie* (pp. 14–20). University of Illinois Press.
ACTFL. (1987). ACTFL Chinese proficiency guidelines. *Foreign Language Annals, 20*(5), 471–487.
ACTFL. (1996). *National standards for foreign language learning: Preparing for the 21st century.* ACTFL.
ACTFL. (1999). *Standards for foreign language learning in the 21st century* (Chinese & other languages added). Yonkers. https://eric.ed.gov/?id=ED438726
ACTFL. (2002). *Program standards for the preparation of foreign language teachers.* www.american.edu/cas/education/pdf/upload/actfl2002.pdf
ACTFL. (2006). *Standards for foreign language learning in the 21st century.* Allen Press.
ACTFL. (2015). *World-readiness standards for learning languages.* ACTFL.
Alan, B., & Stoller, F. L. (2005). Maximizing the benefits of project work in foreign language classrooms. *English Teaching Forum, 43*(4), 10–21. http://exchanges.state.gov/englishteaching/forum/archives/docs/05-43-4-c.pdf
Armstrong, D. G., Henson, K. T., & Savage, T. (2005). *Teaching today: An introduction to education.* Pearson.
Avila, J., Sostmann, K., Breckwoldt, J., & Peters, H. (2016). Evaluation of the free, open source software WordPress as electronic portfolio system in undergraduate medical education. *BMC Medical Education, 16*(157), 1–10. https://bmcmededuc.biomedcentral.com/articles/10.1186/s12909-016-0678-1
Bal, A. P. (2012). Teacher candidates' point of views about portfolio preparation (Turkey setting). *Cukurova University Faculty of Education Journal, 41*(2), 87–102. https://dergipark.org.tr/en/download/article-file/46491
Bar-Lev, Z. (1991). Two innovations for teaching tones. *Journal of Chinese Language Teachers Association, 26*(3), 1–24.
Barrett, H. (2010). Balancing the two faces of e-portfolios. *Educação, Formação & Tecnologias, 3*(1), 6–14. http://educa.fcc.org.br/pdf/eduform/v03n01/v03n01a02.pdf
Basaran, S., & Cabaroglu, N. (2014). Language learning podcasts and learners' belief change. *The Electronic Journal for English as a Second Language, 17*(4), 1–32.
Beckett, G. H., & Slater, T. (2005). The project framework: A tool for language, content, and skills integration. *ELT Journal, 59*(2), 108–116. https://doi.org/10.1093/eltj/cci024
Beckett, G. H., Slater, T., & Mohan, B. A. (2019). Philosophical foundation, theoretical approaches and gaps in the literature. In G. H. Beckett & T. Slater (Eds.), *Global perspectives on project-based language learning, teaching and assessment: Key approaches, technology tools and frameworks* (pp. 3–22). Routledge. https://doi.org/10.4324/9780429435096-1
Benson, P., & Chik, A. (2011). Towards a more naturalistic CALL: Video gaming and language learning. *International Journal of Computer-Assisted Language Learning and Teaching, 1*, 1–13.
Bilbrough, N. (2011). *Memory activities for language learning, memory activities for language learning.* Cambridge University Press.
Birgin, O. (2011). Pre-service mathematics teachers' views on the use of portfolios in their education as an alternative assessment method. *Educational Research and Reviews, 6*(11), 710–721.
Boss, S., & Larmer, J. (2018). *Project based teaching: How to create rigorous and engaging learning experiences.* ASCD.

Bullock, A. A., & Hawk, P. P. (2001). *A guide for preservice and practicing teachers*. Merrill Prentice Hall.

Burdick, A., Drucker, J., Lunenfeld, P., Presner, T., & Schnapp, J. (2012). *Digital humanities*. The MIT Press. https://direct.mit.edu/books/book/5346/Digital-Humanities

Cakir, A., & Balcikanli, C. (2012). The use of the European portfolio for student teachers of languages (EPOSTL) to foster teacher autonomy: English language teaching (ELT) student teachers' and teacher trainers' views. *Australian Journal of Teacher Education, 37*(3), 1–16.

Campbell, D. M., Cignetti, P. B., Melenyzer, B. J., Nettles, D. H., & Wyman, R. M. (2004). *How to develop a professional portfolio. A manual for teachers*. Pearson.

Chen, D. (2007). Games: Why are they popular among CFL students? In Y. Zhu & T. Yao (Eds.), *Proceedings of the 5th international conference on Chinese language pedagogy* (pp. 262–269). World Publishing Corporation Press.

Chen, D. (2008). Student-produced video clips in Chinese: A learner-centered task. *Journal of Chinese Language Teachers Association, 43*(1), 59–71.

Chen, D. (2010). Enhancing the learning of Chinese with second life. *Journal of Technology and Chinese Language Teaching, 1*(1), 14–30. http://www.tclt.us/journal/2010v1n1/chen.pdf

Chen, D. (2012). Digital storytelling in Chinese: A technology-assisted project. *Journal of Chinese Language Teaching and Research in the U.S, 5*, 150–157.

Chen, D. (2017a). Can language exchange help beginners develop Chinese proficiency? *Journal of Chinese Teaching and Research in the U.S, 10*, 1–11.

Chen, D. (2017b). Developing electronic teaching portfolios: A way to success for preservice teachers. *Journal of Technology and Chinese Language Teaching, 8*(1), 66–85. http://tclt.us/journal/2017v8n1/chen.pdf

Chen, D. (2019). Developing Chinese matching games: From inception to completion. *Journal of Technology and Chinese Language Teaching, 10*(1), 57–72. http://tclt.us/journal/2019v10n1/chen.pdf

Chen, D. (2021a). To game or not to game, that is not the question. In S. Jiang, N. Liang, J. Da, & S. Liu (Eds.), *Proceedings of the 11th international conference and workshops on technology and Chinese language teaching* (pp. 7–12). www.tclt.us/tclt11/proceedings.php

Chen, D. (2021b). Producing podcasts in a Chinese classroom: A digital humanities project. *Chinese Language Teaching Methodology and Technology, 4*(1), 27–43. https://engagedscholarship.csuohio.edu/cltmt/vol4/iss1/

Chik, A. (2012). Digital gameplay for autonomous foreign language learning: Gamers' and language teachers' perspectives. In H. Reinders (Ed.), *Digital games in language learning and teaching* (pp. 95–114). Palgrave Macmillan.

Chism, R., & Faidley, E. (2021). Project-based learning via ePortfolios: Integrating Web 2.0 tools into higher education world language classes. In M. Thomas & K. Yamazaki (Eds.), *Project-based language learning and CALL: From virtual exchange to social justice* (pp. 171–198). Equinox eBooks Publishing. www.equinoxpub.com/home/project-based-language

Cook, G. (2000). *Language play, language learning*. Oxford University Press.

DeFrancis, J. (1984). *The Chinese language: Fact and fantasy*. University of Hawaii Press.

Demirel, M., & Duman, H. (2015). The use of portfolio in English language teaching and its effects on achievement and attitude. *Procedia—Social and Behavioral Sciences, 191*(2), 2634–2640. https://doi.org/10.1016/j.sbspro.2015.04.598

Drew, C. (2017). Edutaining audio: An exploration of education podcast design possibilities. *Educational Media International, 54*(1), 48–62. https://doi.org/10.1080/09523987.2017.1324360

Du, X. Y. (2012). A proposal of task-based PBL in Chinese teaching and learning. In X. Y. Du & M. J. Kirkebk (Eds.), *Exploring task-based PBL in Chinese teaching and learning* (pp. 37–61). Cambridge Scholars Publishing.

Ducate, L., & Lomicka, L. (2009). Podcasting: An effective tool for honing language students' pronunciation. *Language Learning & Technology*, *13*(3), 66–86. www.lltjournal.org/item/10125-44192/

Duggan, M. (2015). *Games and gamers*. Pew Research Center—Internet and Technology. www.pewinternet.org/2015/12/15/gaming-and-gamers/

Everson, M. (2009). The importance of standards. In M. Everson & Y. Xiao (Eds.), *Teaching Chinese as a Foreign language: Theories and applications* (pp. 3–17). Cheng & Tsui Company.

Fasanella, K. (2002). *The professional teaching portfolio as a tool for formative evaluation: A case study* [Doctoral dissertation, Seton Hall University]. eRepository @ Seton Hall. https://scholarship.shu.edu/cgi/viewcontent.cgi?article=2660&context=dissertations

Foote, C. J., & Vermette, P. J. (2001). Teaching portfolio 101: Implementing the teaching portfolio in introductory courses. *Journal of Instructional Psychology*, *28*(1), 31–37.

Frey, T. (2008). Determining the impact of online practicum facilitation for in-service teachers. *Journal of Technology and Teacher Education*, *16*(2), 181–210.

Ghee, T. T., Heng, L. T., & Shuang, G. C. (2012). Students' perception on using podcast in learning Mandarin. *International Conference on Education and e-Learning Innovations*, 1–6. https://doi.org/10.1109/ICEELI.2012.6360574

Gibson, D., & Barrett, H. (2002). Directions in electronic portfolio development. *Contemporary Issues in Technology and Teacher Education*, *2*(4), 556–573. https://citejournal.org/volume-2/issue-4-02/general/directions-in-electronic-portfolio-development/

Godwin-Jones, R. (2014). Emerging technologies games in language learning: Opportunities and challenges. *Language Learning & Technology*, *18*(2), 9–19. http://llt.msu.edu/issues/juné014/emerging.pdf

Green, L. S., Inan, F. A., & Maushak, N. J. (2014). A case study: The role of student-generated vidcasts in K–12 language learner academic language and content acquisition. *Journal of Research on Technology in Education*, *46*(3), 297–324. https://doi.org/10.1080/15391523.2014.888295

Greenier, V. T. (2020). The 10Cs of project-based learning TESOL curriculum. *Innovation in Language Learning and Teaching*, *14*(1), 27–36. https://doi.org/10.1080/17501229.2018.1473405

Hasan, Md. M., & Hoon, T. B. (2013). Podcast applications in language learning: A review of recent studies. *English Language Teaching*, *6*(2), 128–135. https://ccsenet.org/journal/index.php/elt/article/view/23820

Hill, J., & Cook, P. (2011). First-year seminar blogs. *Library Technology Reports*, *47*(3), 36–39. https://link.gale.com/apps/doc/A255559915/AONE?u=anon~cb785336&sid=googleScholar&xid=b1bd9f04

Hirzinger-Unterrainer, E. M. (2012). Mobile learning in foreign language learning: Podcasts and lexicon acquisition in the elementary instruction of Italian. *CALL: Using, learning, knowing, EUROCALL conference, Gothenburg, Sweden, 22–25 August 2012, proceedings*. http://dx.doi.org/10.14705/rpnet.2012.000070

Holec, H. (1981). *Autonomy and foreign language learning*. Pergamon Press. 41. https://eric.ed.gov/?id=ed192557

Howlett, G., & Waemusa, Z. (2019). 21st century learning skills and autonomy: Students' perceptions of mobile devices in the Thai EFL context. *Teaching English with Technology*, *19*(1), 72–85.

Hoyt, S. (2013, January 11). Project based learning: Freedom and excitement in the classroom [Webinar]. *TESOL Virtual Seminars*. https://www.tesol.org/

Imhof, M., & Picard, C. (2009). Views on using e-portfolios in teacher education. *Teaching and Teacher Education*, *25*, 149–154. https://doi.org/10.1016/j.tate.2008.08.001

Jarvinen, A., & Kohonen, V. (1995). Promoting professional development in higher education through portfolio assessment. *Assessment & Evaluation in Higher Education*, *20*(1), 25–36. https://doi.org/10.1080/0260293950200104

Jones, K. M. L., & Farrington, P. (Eds.). (2011). *Using WordPress as a library content management system*. ALA Editions of the American Library Association.

Kecik, I., Aydin, B., Sakar, N., Dikdere, M., Aydin, S., Yuksel, I., & Caner, M. (2012). Determining the feasibility of an e-portfolio application in a distance education teaching practice course. *The International Review of Research in Open and Distance Learning*, *13*(2), 160–180. www.erudit.org/en/journals/irrodl/1900-ū-n1-irrodl05114/1067249ar.pdf

Kelly, W. Q., & Klein, J. (2016). The effect of type of podcasts and learning styles on language proficiency and confidence. *Journal of Educational Technology Systems*, *44*(4), 421–429. https://journals.sagepub.com/doi/10.1177/0047239515617159

Ketterlinus, L. (2017). Using games in teaching foreign languages [MA Thesis]. United States Military Academy. https://www.usma.edu/cfe/Literature/Ketterlinus_17.pdf

Khatibi, E., & Cowie, E. (2013). *Language learning through interactive games* [Student thesis, Malmo University, Malmo University Productions]. http://muep.mau.se/handle/2043/16116.

Khine, M. S. (Ed.). (2011). *Playful teaching, learning games: New tool for digital classrooms*. Sense Publishers. https://doi.org/10.1007/978-94-6091-460-7

Kilbane, C. R., & Milman, N. B. (2003). *The digital teaching portfolio handbook: A how-to guide for educators*. Allyn and Bacon.

Kim, D., & King, K. (2011). Implementing podcasts with ESOL teacher candidates' preparation: Interpretations and implication. *International Forum of Teaching and Studies*, *7*(2), 5–19.

Kim, Y., & Yazdian, L. S. (2014). Portfolio assessment and quality teaching. *Theory Into Practice*, *53*(3), 220–227. https://doi.org/10.1080/00405841.2014.916965

Krashen, S. (1982). *Principles and practice in second language acquisition*. Pergamon Press.

Lam, R. (2023). E-Portfolios: What we know, what we don't, and what we need to know. *RELC Journal*, *54*(1), 208–215. https://doi.org/10.1177/0033688220974102

Lan, Y., Fang, S., Legault, J., & Li, P. (2015). Second language acquisition of Mandarin Chinese vocabulary: Context of learning effects. *Education Tech Research Development*, *63*, 671–690. https://doi.org/10.1007/s11423-015-9380-y

Larmer, J., Mergendoller, J., & Boss, S. (2015). *Setting the standard for project based learning: A proven approach to rigorous classroom instruction*. ASCD.

Lee, J., & Vanpatten, B. (2003). *Making communicative language teaching happen* (2nd ed.). McGraw-Hill.

Lee, J. L. (2016, March). *Games for social and educational impact: Lessons learned and what's next?* [Gamification Symposium], Rutgers University Press.

Lightbown, L., & Spada, N. (2013). *How languages are learned*. Oxford University Press.

Liu, Y., Yao, T. C., Bi, N., Ge, L., & Shi, Y. (2018). *Integrated Chinese level 1 Part 1* (3rd ed.). Cheng & Tsui Company.

Lomicka, L., & Lord, G. (2011). Podcasting—past, present, and future: Applications of academic podcasting in and out of the language classroom. In B. R. Facer & M. Abdous (Eds.), *Academic podcasting and mobile assisted language learning: Applications and outcomes* (pp. 15–44). IGI Global. https://people.clas.ufl.edu/glord/files/LordLomicka-PodcastingVolume.pdf

Martin-Kniep, G. (1999). *Capturing the wisdom of practice*. ASCD. https://eric.ed.gov/?id=ED434884

McCarty, S. (2005). Spoken internet to go: Popularization through podcasting. *JALT CALL*, *1*(2), 67–74. https://doi.org/10.29140/jaltcall.ūn2.11

McColgan, K., & Blackwood, B. (2009). A systematic review protocol on the use of teaching portfolios for educators in further and higher education. *Journal of Advanced Nursing*, *65*(12), 2500–2507. https://doi.org/10.1111/j.1365-2648.2009.05189.x

Meng, L. (2022, February). *Multi-dimensional use of PBL in teaching Chinese*. Chinese Language Teachers Association of Greater New York (CLTA-GNY) Online Lecture, Zoom.

Middle States Commission on Higher Education. (2007). *Student learning assessment: Options and resources*. www.academia.edu/22956955/Middle_States_Commission_on_Higher_Education

Morrison, K. A. (2008). Democratic classrooms: Promises and challenges of student voice and choice, part one. *Educational Horizons*, *87*(1), 50–60. https://files.eric.ed.gov/fulltext/EJ815371.pdf

Moya, S. S., & O'Malley, J. M. (1994). Portfolio assessment model for ESL. *Journal of Educational Issues of Language Minority Students*, *13*, 13–36. https://eric.ed.gov/?id=EJ489574

Nazikian, F., & Park, J. (2016). How to develop "21st Century Skills" in foreign language education. *Japanese Language and Literature*, *50*(2), 347–373. www.jstor.com/stable/24892016

O'Bryan, A., & Hegelheimer, V. (2007). Integrating CALL into the classroom: The role of podcasting in an ESL listening strategies course. *ReCALL*, *19*(2), 162–180. http://dx.doi.org/10.1017/S0958344007000523

Ogan-Bekiroglu, F. (2014). Quality of preservice physics teachers' reflections in their teaching portfolios and their perceived reflections: Do they intersect? *Action in Teacher Education*, *36*(2), 157–170. https://doi.org/10.1080/01626620.2014.901197

O'Neill, J. L. (2017). Deploying a WordPress-based learning object repository to scale up instruction and effect a culture of sharing. *Reference Services Review*, *45*(1), 131–140. https://doi.org/10.1108/rsr-10-2016-0059

Oskoz, A. (2020). Language learning. In R. F. Davis, M. K. Gold, K. D. Harris, & J. Sayers (Eds.), *Digital pedagogy in the humanities: Concepts, models, and experiments*. Modern Language Association. https://digitalpedagogy.hcommons.org/keyword/Language-Learning

Partnership for 21st Century Skills. (2009). *P21 framework definitions*. ERIC. https://eric.ed.gov/?id=ED519462

Pearce, C. (2002). Emergent authorship: The next interactive revolution. *Computers & graphics*, *26*(1), 21–29.

Peterson, M. (2013). *Computer games and language learning*. Palgrave Macmillan. https://link.springer.com/book/10.1057/9781137005175

Phillips, B. (2017). Student-produced podcasts in language learning—Exploring student perceptions of podcast activities. *IAFOR Journal of Education*, *5*(3), 157–171. https://doi.org/10.22492/ije.5.3.08

Pitura, J., & Berlińska-Kopeć, M. (2018). Learning English while exploring the national cultural heritage: Technology-assisted project-based language learning in an upper-secondary school. *English with Technology*, *18*(1), 37–52. https://eric.ed.gov/?id=EJ1170629

Pomerantz, A., & Bell, N. (2007). Learning to play, playing to learn: FL learners as multicompetent language users. *Applied Linguistics*, *28*(4), 556–578. https://doi.org/10.1093/applin/amm044

Prensky, M. (2001a). Digital natives, digital immigrants. *On the Horizon*, *9*(5), 1–4.

Prensky, M. (2001b). *Digital game-based learning*. McGraw-Hill.

Price, K. (2013). Using the teaching portfolio to anticipate programmatic assessment. *Business Communication Quarterly*, *76*(2), 207–215. https://doi.org/10.1177/1080569912470488

Reinders, H. (Ed.). (2012). *Digital games in language learning and teaching*. Palgrave MacMillan.

Reinders, H., & Wattana, S. (2012). Talk to me! Games and students willingness to communicate. In H. Reinders (Ed.), *Digital games in language learning and teaching* (pp. 156–188). Palgrave Macmillan. https://doi.org/10.1057/9781137005267_9

Salmon, G., & Nie, M. (2008). Doubling the life in iPods. In G. Salmon & P. Edirisingha (Eds.), *Podcasting for learning in universities*. McGraw-Hill.

Shadiev, R., & Yang, M. (2020). Review of studies on technology-enhanced language learning and teaching. *Sustainability*, *12*(524), 1–22. https://doi.org/10.3390/sū2020524

Sheppard, K., & Stoller, F. L. (1995). Guidelines for the integration of student projects in ESP classrooms. *English Teaching Forum*, *33*(2), 10–15.

Shulman, L. (1998). Theory, practice, and the education of professionals. *Elementary School Journal*, *98*(5), 511–526. www.journals.uchicago.edu/doi/10.1086/461912

Smith, C., Frick, G., & Siebel, P. (2019). Student voice: Podcasting and protocols: An approach to writing about writing through sound. In B. Bird, D. Downs, I. Mccracken, & J. Rieman (Eds.), *Next steps: New directions for/in writing about writing* (pp. 252–260). University Press of Colorado. https://upcolorado.com/utah-state-university-press/item/3588-next-steps

Snyder, J., Lippincott, A., & Bower, D. (1998). The inherent tensions in the multiple uses of portfolios in teacher education. *Teacher Education Quarterly, 25*(1), 45–60.

Soerjowardhana, A., & Nugroho, R. A. (2017). Developing English job interview skill by self- access language learning through audio podcast-based learning media. *Celt: A Journal of Culture, English Language Teaching & Literature, 17*(2), 178–195. https://doi.org/10.24167/celt.ü7í.1115

Stoller, F. L. (1997). Project work: A means to promote language and content. *English Teaching Forum, 35*(4), 2–9. https://eric.ed.gov/?id=EJ653896

Stoller, F. L. (2002). Project work: A means to promote language and content. In J. C., Richards & W. A. Renandya (Eds.), *Methodology in language teaching: An anthology of current practice* (pp. 107–119). Cambridge University Press.

Stoller, F. L. (2006). Establishing a theoretical foundation for project-based learning in second and foreign language contexts. In G. H. Beckett & P. C. Miller (Eds.), *Project-based second and foreign language education: Past, present, and future* (pp. 19–40). Information Age Publishing.

Stoller, F. L. (2012). Project-based learning: A viable option for second and foreign language classrooms. In *Perfect score: Methodologies, technologies, & communities of practice* (pp. 37–47). Proceedings of the 20th Annual KOTESOL International Conference, Seoul, October 20–21, 2012.

Stoller, F. L., & Myers, C. C. (2019). A Five-stage framework to guide language teachers. In A. Gras-Velázquez. (Ed.), *Project-based learning in second language acquisition: Building communities of practice in higher education* (pp. 24–47). Routledge. https://doi.org/10.4324/9780429457432-3

Struyven, K., Blieck, Y., & De. Roeck, V. (2014). The electronic portfolio as a tool to develop and assess preservice student teaching competences: Challenge for quality. *Studies in Educational Evaluation, 43*, 40–54. https://doi.org/10.1016/j.stueduc.2014.06.001

Sun, C. (2006). *Chinese: A linguistic introduction*. Cambridge University Press.

Swain, M. (1985). Communicative competence: Some roles of comprehensible input and comprehensible output in its development. In S. Gass & C. Madden (Eds.), *Input in second language acquisition* (pp. 235–253). Newbury House.

Sykes, J. (2018). Digital games and language teaching and learning. *Foreign Language Annals, 51*(1), 219–224. https://eric.ed.gov/?id=EJ1172877

Sykes, J., & Reinhardt, J. (2012). Language at play: Digital games in second and foreign language teaching and learning. In J. Liskin-Gasparro & M. Lacorte (Eds.), *Theory and practice in second language classroom instruction* (pp. 1–157). Pearson-Prentice Hall.

Sylvén, L. K., & Sundqvist, P. (2012). Gaming as extramural English L2 learning and L2 proficiency among young learners. *ReCALL, 24*(3), 302–321. https://doi.org/10.1017/s095834401200016x

Talak-Kiryk, A. (2010). *Using games in a foreign language classroom, MA TESOL collection.* [MA thesis, SIT Graduate Institute]. https://digitalcollections.sit.edu/ipp_collection/484

Tavares, J. F., & Potter, L. E. (2018). *Project based learning applied to the language classroom*. Teach-in Education.

Thomas, S., & Toland, S. (2015). Imitating podcasts by providing audio content to support and enhance language learning. *The JALT CALL Journal, 11*(1), 3–17. https://doi.org/10.29140/jaltcall.ü1n1.181

Thorne, S. L. (2008). Transcultural communication in open Internet environments and massively multiplayer online games. In S. Magnan (Ed.), *Mediating discourse online* (pp. 305–327). John Benjamins. https://doi.org/10.1075/aals.3.17tho

Thorne, S. L., Black, R. W., & Sykes, J. (2009). Second language use, socialization, and learning in internet interest communities and online games. *Modern Language Journal*, *93*, 802–821. https://doi.org/10.1111/j.1540-4781.2009.00974.x

Tucker, P., Stronge, J., & Gareis, C. (2002). *Handbook on teacher portfolios for evaluation and professional development*. Routledge. https://doi.org/10.4324/9781315853703

Vandercruysse, S., Vandewaetere, M., Cornillie, F., & Clarebout, G. (2013). Competition and students' perceptions in a game-based language learning environment. *Education Tech Research*, *61*, 927–950. https://link.springer.com/article/10.1007/s11423-013-9314-5

Whitton, N. (2012). The place of game-based learning in an age of austerity. *Electronic Journal of e-Learning*, *10*(2), 249–256. https://files.eric.ed.gov/fulltext/EJ985426.pdf

Wiggins, G., & McTighe, J. (2005). *Understanding by design, expanded 2nd Edition*. Association for Supervision and Curriculum Development.

Willis, J. (1996). *A framework for task-based learning*. Longman.

Wolf, K., & Dietz, M. (1998). Teaching portfolios: Purposes and possibilities. *Teacher Education Quarterly*, *25*(1), 9–22. www.jstor.org/stable/23478104

Worf, K. (1996). Developing an effective teaching portfolio. *Educational Leadership*, *53*, 34–37.

Zeichner, K., & Wray, S. (2001). The teaching portfolio in US teacher education programs: What we know and what we need to know. *Teaching and Teacher Education*, *17*, 613–621. https://doi.org/10.1016/S0742-051X(01)00017-8

Zhao, J., & Beckett, G. H. (2014). Project-based Chinese as a foreign language instruction: A teacher research approach. *Journal of the Chinese Language Teachers Association*, *49*(2), 45–73. https://works.bepress.com/gulbahar-beckett/14/

Zou, M. (2003). Organizing instructional practice around the assessment portfolio: The gains and losses. *The Professional Educator*, *26*(1), 73–81. https://eric.ed.gov/?id=ED469469

6 Best Practices in PBLL From Other Chinese Language Teachers

6.1 Introduction

In the field of teaching Chinese as foreign language (TCFL), there is no shortage of Chinese language educators who are constantly searching for effective pedagogy. Numerous instructors have explored the Project-Based Language Learning (PBLL) instructional approaches in Chinese classrooms either in secondary schools or at institutions of higher education (e.g., Zhao & Beckett, 2014; Chen et al, 2016; and Zhao, 2019; Hegedus, 2020a; Meng, 2022, Lee et al., 2022). Some teachers are advanced enough to embrace the use of PBL in class without using any textbooks, while others expand their teaching curriculum by adding the assignment of a project in the sense of PBLL. In this chapter, I introduce six best practices in PBL that deserve a special mention, not only because the teachers have made great efforts in testing the approach but also because students achieve satisfactory learning outcomes and hold positive perceptions towards this kind of pedagogy. Three projects took place in the K–12 setting with two in high schools, and one in a middle school. For those in the former setting, one project engaged students to conduct research comparing Chinese and American sports culture and one enlisted students to explore how to tackle racial bias. The project involving middle school students was about learning the subject of Asian Americans and Pacific Islanders (AAPI). Of the three PBLL practices in a university context, the first project required students to produce a video of their own design and creation about Chinese calligraphy. The second project charged students to develop a survival guide website for prospective Chinese-speaking international students. The third one obliged students to deliver written and oral presentations on Chinese music and culture. I will start with the projects in second schools, followed by those in universities.

6.2 Exemplary Projects in K–12 Settings

In 2015, I collaborated with Ms. Liping Meng and Mr. Michael Hegedus, both Chinese language teachers in New Jersey (USA) high schools, to form a dedicated panel on the topic of "Applying Project-Based Language Learning in the Chinese Classroom." We subsequently presented our findings at the 2016 American Council on the Teaching of Foreign Languages (ACTFL) annual meeting held in Boston (Chen et al., 2016). Ms. Liping Meng and Mr. Michael Hegedus have integrated

PBLL in their Chinese classrooms for years, and both presented their innovative application of the approach at different conferences (e.g., Hegedus, 2016, 2019, 2020a, 2020b; Meng, 2016, 2022). Ms. Meng won the Best Teaching Activity Award at the 2nd International Symposium of Chinese Language Teachers Association (CLTA) at the University of Maryland in 2016. Trained in music composition, Mr. Hegedus conducted his master's research on the preservation of intangible culture among the ethnic minority groups of Guizhou, China. His interest in oral history began with the interviews he completed with the many stakeholders undertaking this cultural preservation, including the marginalized members of various Chinese ethnic minorities. His passion for oral history is also inspired by the work of the Smithsonian Institution archives and the StoryCorps archive housed at the U.S. Library of Congress. He seeks to share the lived experience of the Chinese diaspora and address social injustices as part of his work as a Chinese teacher. In 2019, Mr. Hegedus received the Chinese Language Association of Secondary-Elementary Schools (CLASS) Outstanding Chinese Teacher Award, presented each year to an individual of the Chinese teaching profession who is currently in practice and has demonstrated excellence in teaching Chinese language and culture to students at K–12 schools. I will next describe their works respectively. I will also talk about a work implemented in a public middle school in New Jersey. I will finally summarize the major features of these projects.

In an invited talk, "Multi-dimensional Use of PBL in Teaching Chinese," delivered in 2022 as part of the online workshop series organized by the Chinese Language Teachers Association of Greater New York (CLTA-GNY), Ms. Meng shared her best practice of PBL instruction, using the word "PROJECT," each letter symbolizing some key elements (Meng, 2022), as described in Table 6.1:

Table 6.1 PROJECT

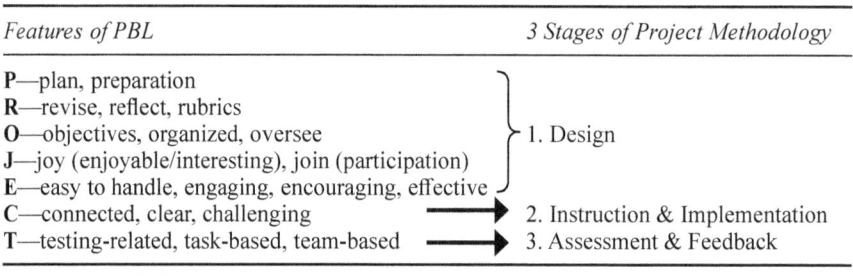

Features of PBL	3 Stages of Project Methodology
P—plan, preparation	
R—revise, reflect, rubrics	
O—objectives, organized, oversee	1. Design
J—joy (enjoyable/interesting), join (participation)	
E—easy to handle, engaging, encouraging, effective	
C—connected, clear, challenging	2. Instruction & Implementation
T—testing-related, task-based, team-based	3. Assessment & Feedback

Source: Meng (2022)

According to Ms. Meng, these procedures of "PROJECT" serve as a 3-stage project methodology, which can effectively guide project designing and execution. I once took our preservice teachers to observe her PBLL Chinese classes, where her students, regardless of proficiency in the target language, were fully engaged with the learning of Chinese in listening, speaking, reading, and writing. Unlike the traditional non-PBL class organized around a textbook, hers was structured around projects with a theme, under which there were some mini tasks on different topics. For each learning activity, the instructor provided students with learning sheets containing vocabulary and sentence structures, which students studied and consulted throughout the process. Each of her PBLL classes that we visited constituted a meaningful social context, in which students learned actively by interacting and communicating with peers in the target language enthusiastically. Some interesting topics that she designed for her students over the years include "My Chinese Language Classroom," "Chinese Food and Cooking," "Comparing Chinese and American Sports Cultures," and "Lifestyle and Health." Of these projects, the research-based project on the comparative examination of Chinese and American sports cultures is particularly commendable. For this project, students working in a team conducted a survey with both Chinese and American speakers soliciting their opinions on some questions about sports. They also interviewed their teachers, administrators, and parents on the topic. Students then analyzed the data collected and provided their conclusion regarding similarities and differences between the two cultures. One of the teams presented their research at a cultural contest in New Jersey. Students spoke in a mixture of native and target languages about their findings, and they sang and rapped in Chinese. Such a multiple-form presentation, delivered in speaking and performing with props, not only empowered students to grasp language and culture in an enjoyable way but also enhanced their skills in teamwork and time planning and management, resulting in a highly effective learning outcome.

In the summer of 2020, Mr. Michael Hegedus was invited by CLTA-GNY to conduct an online workshop "Using Project-Based Learning in the Chinese Classroom to Tackle Racial Bias" for Chinese language teachers. He shared a project, through which he had engaged his students to explore racial bias concerning Chinese immigrants in the USA using the format of interviews. The students were at a high level of Chinese class, yet their Chinese proficiency was not sufficient to communicate in the target language with Chinese native speakers. To help students with the challenges, the instructor used *Quizlet* to introduce the vocabulary to describe bias and discussed issues in class to enhance their understanding. With the scaffolding instruction, the students were able to formulate five interview questions in Chinese and send them to the interviewees (recommended by the instructor), who were Chinese-speaking graduate students studying in the US. Through email correspondence, the high school students not only interacted with native speakers on such a complicated issue but also obtained firsthand, authentic learning experiences (Hegedus, 2020a).

Ms. Jenny Qin is a dynamic and resourceful Chinese language teacher with over ten years of experience. Her project mobilized middle school students to learn the history of Asian Americans, in general, and Chinese Americans, in particular. The project was meticulously planned, involving school administration, library staff, colleagues, and over 200 students studying Chinese. As part of scaffolding instruction, Ms. Qin invited a librarian and an English teacher to lecture on the history of Chinese Americans by telling stories about their journey of immigration to the USA and their outstanding contributions to the country. After the lecture, students had a class discussion and answered questions. Those students in the 7th and 8th grades then conducted research on well-known Asian Americans. Students, either individually or in a team of no more than two peers, had one week to research, design, and create posters on AAPI individuals (the final outcomes of their projects), which were posted on all the bulletin boards and hallways of the school. Students in the 5th and 6th grades had three days to study the posters and select three Asian Americans whom they admired. In addition, each student in this group answered questions on a worksheet prepared by the instructor. Although the two groups were engaged in the same project, each had its own requirements. Hence, the evaluations of the two differ. However, both assessments were objective. For the 7th and 8th grade students, their posters were evaluated by a panel of judges including the principal, world-language supervisor, librarian, and social studies teacher, based on a rubric developed by the Chinese instructor. The scores that students received counted towards their student growth achievements. For the 5th and 6th grade students, their worksheets were reviewed by the instructor using a different rubric, with each score counted as a culture test. Based on the success of Ms. Qin's pioneering work, she repeated the project in 2023 and demonstrated it at the New York International Conference on Teaching Chinese (Qin, 2023). From the pictures displayed, we could see that her students enjoyed learning the history of AAPI via the PBLL approach.

Evidently, these projects possess major characteristics of Stoller's (2006) PBL model, such as focusing on both the process and product, involving individual and collaborative work outside the classroom, and fostering the learning of language and content simultaneously. One element that stands out from the three projects is their engaging students with real-world issues, thereby challenging as well as promoting their high-level thinking, research, and communication skills.

6.3 Exemplary Projects in University Contexts

In this section, I introduce three notable projects that were implemented by Chinese-language instructors at universities. These educators have been practicing the technology-mediated PBLL instruction, which conforms to the Digital Humanities–Augmented and Technology-Enhanced PBLL (DATEPBLL) model that I proposed in Chapter 4. The first is a project, resulting in various interesting videos related to Chinese calligraphy. The second is a website project, leading to survival guide platforms for prospective students. The last one is a mini project about music and culture, ending in written and oral presentations with PPT slides. For each of these projects, I will describe why it was developed and how it was executed, concentrating on teachers' role and students' end project. An analysis of each project will be provided in terms of Stoller's project configuration and conditions (Stoller, 2002, 2006, 2012; Stoller & Myers, 2019).

6.3.1 Calligraphy Project

Starting in early 2018, Prof. Kang Zhou, Chinese lecturer of the Department of Global Languages, Massachusetts Institute of Technology (MIT) launched a Chinese calligraphy course as an introductory Independent Activity Period (IAP) class. Offered during the winter break, spanning three weeks right before the start of the spring semester, the course immediately became a hit on campus, with 17 students registered for it. Since then, the course has continuously sparked such profound interest and enthusiasm among students that enrollment increased every year, totaling to 45 in 2022. In order to ensure an appropriate faculty-student ratio to achieve ideal learning conditions, Prof. Zhou conducted a screening survey to select the most committed learners out of a large pool of applicants. The admission policies granted priority to either those who declared Chinese as a minor or concentration or those who had taken Chinese language courses at MIT. Apart from that, a decision was made in 2023 to run two parallel sections of the course to accommodate growing enrollments. One section targeted the advanced heritage learners of Chinese and, hence, was taught in Chinese. The other welcomed students at lower levels of Chinese proficiency and was conducted in English. Regardless of different teaching language, the learning objectives and requirements were the same. Above all, both required students to complete a video production and presentation project. For illustration purposes, I will use Prof. Zhou's class with heritage learners of Chinese as an example because he initiated, designed, and taught the course for several years. In addition, he presented his project at the New York International Conference on Teaching Chinese in May 2023 (Zhou, 2023).

This IAP 12-credit university course could be taken by students to fulfill the mandatory requirements of the arts. As such, the three-week intensive course, which ran three hours every day, covered four aspects: writing, culture, language, and arts. The five objectives of the course, as outlined in the syllabus (Zhou, 2023), were as follows: first, students will achieve a basic knowledge of Chinese characters and calligraphy, in particular, the origin and evolution of the Chinese writing system and historical developments of calligraphic arts. Second, students will familiarize themselves with different writing scripts of calligraphy and learn how to write the standard script with brush and ink. Third, students will develop an appreciation for the aesthetics of Chinese calligraphy, distinguishing between techniques and styles employed by various schools of calligraphic arts and understanding its role in the Chinese culture. Fourth, students will understand the function of calligraphy in the current era of globalization and also the impact of technological advances for the development of Chinese calligraphy. Finally, through the course, students will be able to showcase their knowledge of calligraphy from disciplinary perspectives and skills of writing calligraphy. As a course that engages both mind and hand, Prof. Zhou included two components for each class meeting: Fact and Act. For the Fact part, the instructor would briefly introduce a topic planned for the class, which could be one from the list that he had developed, such as the evolution of Chinese characters, the history of calligraphy scripts, appreciation of classic calligraphy works, well-known calligraphers, contemporary calligraphy education, calligraphy and the public, and the relationship between calligraphy and other art forms. Following the lecture would be a class discussion, arranged to involve everyone in talking about their understanding of the topic in question. For the Act part, the instructor would expose students to calligraphy by having them learn how to write, from the basic movement of strokes such as dots, horizontal strokes, vertical strokes, etc., to the techniques of different scripts, with a focus on practicing regular script. For this hands-on course, the instructor designed a number of mini projects, for example, creating a hand-made calligraphy greeting card, writing Spring Festival Scrolls for the community on the Chinese New Year occasion, or writing a Chinese proverb or a poem in the calligraphic style of their own choice. In addition to these mini projects, the video production and presentation was the major term-long project.

Contributing 15% to the total grade of the course, the video project was designed to further enhance the learning goals established for the course. In particular, it provided students with an opportunity to express their understanding and appreciation of calligraphy, that is, its function, meaning, and significance. To that end, students could address any theme related to calligraphy, but it should cover interdisciplinary exploration and showcase their own calligraphy, again reflecting the two cores of the course (i.e., Fact and Act). As calligraphy involves arts, literature, history, philosophy, and other cultural aspects in addition to language, students were encouraged to integrate one or many of these elements into their video. Given that students had diverse majors, including computer science, engineering, and math, the instructor emphasized the importance of making their videos interdisciplinary by connecting calligraphy with any other disciplines that were related to their majors or minors or those areas they found interesting to explore (Zhou, 2023). Students had freedom to undertake the project alone or together with no more than two other peers in the class.

The project was assigned on the first day of class, and students were required to present on the last day, with the final products submitted afterwards. For the video presentation, students described why the particular topic was chosen for the project, what inspired them to create the video in this fashion, and what they had learned through the project. A review of the videos displayed on the university website shows that a diverse array of topics was chosen, such as comparing calligraphy with Chinese medicine, comparing calligraphy in Chinese and Western culture, cooking Dongpo rou (a Chinese dish named after Su Dongpo, an accomplished calligrapher during the Song Dynasty), dancing calligraphy, distinguishing fake from true calligraphy work (achieved through generative adversarial network), and making calligraphy fonts. In one project titled "English With a Chinese Twist," a student showcased his calligraphy writing of 100 unique words with his recitation of Robert Frost's poem "The Road Not Taken." Creative, informative, interpretative, and reflective, these videos demonstrated that students combined calligraphy with anything that had captivated them, from those that appeared to be seemingly unrelated subjects like cooking, dancing, and technology, to poem and prose. Such a diverse exploration was appreciated by students, as shown in a reflection from one student (Zhou, 2023).

> *Today we watched the class's video presentations. I was very impressed by how creative everyone was. In particular, the presentations about writing calligraphy using various tools, the ones involving food, the one using an ML [machine learning] model to detect fake characters, and the one involving the creation of a font. I also enjoyed watching the more informational ones that explored certain historical figures! I wish we had more time to continue learning about the history of calligraphy and modern developments in the*

art, but I feel like I've learned a lot in this class, and each lecture also served as a great starting point for my own exploration into various topics.

To give a sense of students' final works, let me elaborate on an end product that impressed me the most. It is a joint work by two students who raised an interesting question, *What can you do about practicing Chinese calligraphy if there is no brush, paper, or ink?* The two students addressed the question by demonstrating that there were as many as 18 possibilities to do so. They first showed how to write calligraphy with the following 12 materials one after another: pencil, ballpoint pen, brush pen, fountain pen, marker, finger, straw, chopstick, rice, whipped milk, hair, and a leek. They then displayed how one could apply calligraphy on materials such as glass, ceramic, fabric, leaf, ice, and lantern. From the video, viewers could see that the two students collaborated very well for their work, with one narrating and the other writing by using one of the above makeshift "brushes" and materials. The narrator informed viewers that the characters being written were taken from a poem and asked for a guess about it. Viewers could see the writing of each character very well. What struck me the most is the beautiful and fluent movement of the "brush" in the hand of the "calligrapher," even though they were just a leek or a grain of rice, suggesting that the student had achieved a good grasp of basic calligraphy writing techniques. When all the writing materials were displayed, students revealed the answer to their question regarding the poem. The 20 characters that they selected to demonstrate were taken from the well-known poem composed by Li Bai, one of the greatest and most important poets of the Tang dynasty.

The screenshot of this "masterpiece" is given in Figure 6.1, which interestingly shows the special effect of the calligraphy produced by non-brush tools and non-paper material. The idea of this video project is simple but creative, with a deep meaning in two respects. As long as there are some makeshift materials, there is a way to practice calligraphy; calligraphy is more a process than an end. It is truly an enjoyable experience to see how the calligraphy can be done with unusual materials. All the videos are featured on (http://calligraphy.mit.edu/class-projects/video-projects).

This video production and presentation has the major characteristics of projects in PBL (Stoller, 2006). First, the focus was placed on the process as well as the products, through which students were engaged to work actively and collaboratively towards the final end product. Second, throughout the process, the instructor provided sufficient coaching, which included, for example, "explicit" and "implicit" scaffolding. According to Prof. Zhou, "explicit" scaffolding refers to the fact that the instructor met with students, individually or in groups, about the project when students were searching for an interesting topic to work on and an appropriate method to present their ideas. Brainstorming together with the students at a one-on-one meeting outside the class guided them to dive in and think hard, which eventually helped them settle on the right track for the project. Such scaffolding also included guiding questions prepared by the instructor for class discussion. In the case of the aforementioned work completed by the two students, when Prof. Zhou conducted his class discussion on different kinds of brushes to practice calligraphy, students' interest in exploring various materials was initially aroused. This project enabled

Figure 6.1 Students' Calligraphy Created with Unusual Materials

the students to explore the ideas that they were fascinated with. Eventually, as illustrated by the description provided, the two students produced a video with their work showing the effect of calligraphy produced by different "brushes" on different objects. "Implicit" scaffolding refers to the fact that the teacher constantly reminded students of the project in class, informally checking their progress status and offering needed help. Third, the video project encouraged students to integrate other disciplines in their work, such as programming in the designing of calligraphy fonts, distinguishing fake from true calligraphy, and dancing with calligraphy, thereby opening up new horizons for them. As students learned to appreciate different scripts of calligraphy and practice writing regular scripts, they, at the same time, improved their skills in Chinese language, culture, communication, and collaboration, which promoted their ownership in the projects. Finally, the end products were made available online for anyone to access, serving the general public as well as those who are learning or are interested in calligraphy within MIT.

Other than the orientation to both process and product and the effective promotion of student ownership in their work, the calligraphy project cultivated students' development of critical thinking skills, analytical and communication skills, decision-making skills, commitment to both language and calligraphy learning, and active and autonomous learning. Furthermore, there were several impressive aspects regarding the project design and implementation, mostly related to the project requirements. First is the requirement of connection, manifested in four ways: (i) relating the learning of calligraphy with that of Chinese writing, language, and culture; (ii) linking the understanding of calligraphy with that of the Chinese history and literature; (iii) associating the study of calligraphy with sciences or engineering disciplines that students major or minor in; and (iv) connecting the appreciation of calligraphy with that of other arts. Second is the emphasis on daily reflections, which entailed 10% of course assessments. By using the tool *Padlet*, students were able to post their thoughts and opinions on anything related to calligraphy that was inspired by the lecture or discussion in class or on any experience related to the projects that they were working on. The reflections could be written in Chinese or in English but had to be shared in class, thereby contributing to an active, friendly, supportive learning environment. Likewise, the instructor also recorded his own understanding of the topic(s) under discussion, which helped him improve his instruction (Zhou, 2023). Third, the requirements for a creative and interdisciplinary video pushed students not only to achieve a good understanding of the significance of calligraphy in the Chinese culture and familiarize themselves with evolving calligraphy scripts and distinctive techniques of different calligraphy schools but also to become competent in writing the regular scripts. A grasp of the basic knowledge of and skills in calligraphy enabled students to produce expressive videos. Thanks to these requirements, some students developed an enduring interest in practicing calligraphy, making it a part of their self-mediation.

In sum, the video project results in an effective learning journey and achievements with regard to calligraphy, as shown by students' excellent videos and their glowing evaluation, available at (http://calligraphy.mit.edu). Due to its success, the calligraphy course will be part of the Spring 2024 offerings, continuing to attract students, not only freshmen and sophomores but also juniors and seniors. An experienced lecturer of Chinese language, as well as a savvy calligrapher practicing calligraphy since a young age, Prof. Zhou is continuing to teach the course with the assignment of an engaging video project. He strives to improve his teaching pedagogy to further advance student learning. The project, which succeeded in engaging students to explore calligraphy in relation to any other disciplines or its relevance to students' lives in a creative format, made the learning goals of calligraphy interesting and enjoyable. While it is not evident exactly how students developed their multimedia videos, it is certain from the end products that different apps were involved in taping and editing. In some cases, students created a computing program to design calligraphy fonts or detect fake calligraphy from original work.

6.3.2 Website Development Project

Dr. Chih-Jen Lee and two colleagues—from the Chinese program in the Department of East Asian Languages and Civilizations at the University of Pennsylvania—initiated a website production project for their Intermediate Chinese curriculum in Fall 2020. The students participating in the project enrolled in three parallel sections of the course. They were required to create a Chinese website that would introduce prospective Chinese-speaking international students to the following four topics: (i) arriving at Philadelphia International Airport and the city of Philadelphia, (ii) living on Penn campus, (iii) a typical U.S. college student's daily life, and (iv) getting around Philadelphia (post office and transportation). The goal of the project was twofold: (i) to create an opportunity for students to apply the acquired Chinese language knowledge and skills to real-world needs of a community and (ii) to empower learners to showcase their achieved skills by writing and speaking through a self-designed website. As such, the website should provide helpful information for those who had chosen to study at the University of Pennsylvania so that they could benefit when preparing for the trip to the US and their life journey at Penn.

In order to help students to start with the building of an informative and functional website with the four topics, the instructors scaffolded instruction in two ways. Linguistically, a list of Chinese language elements, including lexicon and grammar structures, was prepared for students to study and apply. Specifically, students were explicitly instructed to choose five to seven vocabulary items and grammar points respectively from the list when describing the content of each topic. As shown in Table 6.2, an adaption from Lee et al. (2023a), these language requirements serve as guidelines, that is, the vocabulary serving as building blocks and grammar points as structural templates with which students could compose their interesting stories about those four topics.

In terms of technology for building such a navigable website, students were recommended to use tools such as *Google Site*, *Wix*, and *Weebly*. Students were also encouraged to explore and try any other tools that they felt comfortable with. According to Dr. Lee, the *Weebly* tool is not too sophisticated for students to learn. With a team of two or three peers working together, students would be able to collaborate to resolve any technical issues that they encountered. A rubric, as shown in Table 6.3 (Lee et al., 2023b), was specially developed to assure that students were well-informed of the expectations in each of the five areas, including, for example, the use of language in both speaking and writing (i.e., vocabulary and grammar), the presentation of content (i.e., menu and multimedia), and the function of a website (i.e., feature and navigation).

The project was assigned to students after the add/drop deadline and lasted for about 12 weeks. Students were required to work in teams of two or three peers of their own selection to build the website. Students must submit their first script to the instructors for review around the seventh week and showcase their website in class a month later. The final product should be made accessible around two weeks before the end of the semester. For fair assessment purposes, each team's final work was reviewed and scored by the three instructors of the course based on the rubric shown in Table 6.3. The average score of the three assessors is the final credit assigned to each individual producing the website, which constituted 10% of the total course grade.

Table 6.2 Language Requirements for Four Topics

Topics	Choose 5–7 Vocabulary and Grammar Items for Each Topic	
1: Arriving at Philadelphia International Airport and the City of Philadelphia	生词:	降落 国际 机场 接 通过 海关 担心 带 类 杂志 (检)查 严 松 打开 行李 大巴 城里 现代化 古老 印象
	语法:	有点儿 + adj. 根本 据说 给......的印象/对......的印象 对 as a preposition 差不多 A没有B那么adj. 又adj.1又adj.2 因为......的关系 A和B不同/相同
2: Living on Penn campus (facilities)	生词:	顺利 放心vs.担心 单人/双人间 同屋 条件很好/差 整理vs.打扫 简直 旅馆 照顾 惯坏 校园 adj. 得很 adj. 极了 食堂 借口 努力 注意 长途 请{病/事/公}假
	语法:	...... adj. + 是 + degree adverb + adj.，可是/但是/不过...... 不但......, 还...... A比B还adj. Verb + 起来 不太 + adj. (necessary condition) 才 (result) 没Verb好(O) Verb不好 Condition 1,(subject 2)又(condition 2) 倒是 一方面......,(可是)另一方面...... 不大 + VP. ......,结果......(undesirable result) Place word...... 都是Noun 越来越 adj. Verb掉 A被(B)Verb + (Complement) + (了)
3: A typical US college student's daily life	生词:	洗澡 早晨 迟到 一般来说 经常 提供(......)服务 好处 午觉 浪费 坚持 精神 热茶 冰水 凉开水 泡茶 难喝 方式 当地 多半儿(mostly) + Verb vs. 多数(most) + Noun 得......才行
	语法:	就(time is early, short, or fast) vs. 才(time is late, long, or slow) Verb +过来 从来没 + Verb过 从来不 + Verb 对sb.来说 刚 + Verb 可是subj.却Verb Reduplication of adj. 除了A以外, subj.也...... 除了A以外, subj.都 向sb.学习 本来......,后来...... 不得不 连extreme case 都VP. 以为......, 其实...... 另一MW Noun 并不/没(有) 各Noun有各Noun的......
4: Getting around Philadelphia (Post Office & transportation)	生词:	邮局 邮票 附近 公共汽车 地铁 东/南/西/北 前面/后面/左边/右边/对面 往 寄 窗口 办 挂号 填表/填单子 信 明信片 邮票 又 小包 柜台 丢 出租车 司机 公交车 堵得厉害 急 严重
	语法:	比较(relatively) + adj. 多 (how) + adj. 最好 VP. Topic-Comment Sentence Existence 有 把sentence pattern A不如B A不如B + adj. 还不如B + adj.呢。一MW比一MW + adj. 再过 time duration, subj.就要 + Verb 了 像 Noun 这样/那样 + adj./Verb Interrogative pronoun (question word) + 都/也......

Source: Lee et al. (2023a)

Figure 6.2 is a screenshot of a home page created by a team of two students, which I will use to illustrate students' end product. As can be seen, right in the center of the home page is the Chinese heading 宾大留学指南, "Survival Guide for Studying Abroad at Penn." Showcasing a symmetrical view of the Penn Commons as the background, this home page presents a welcoming atmosphere within its aesthetically pleasing design. Featured on the page from left to right on the top are the menus of "Survival Guide" (宾大留学指南), "Home Page" (首页), "Airport & City" (机场和

Table 6.3 Final Project Grading Rubric

Points	Mechanics	Vocabulary	Grammar	Content	Design
9–12	No typos: accurate punctuation: fulfilled required minimum usage of vocabulary and grammatical items	Accurate and abundant usage of appropriate and new words and expressions	Few grammatical errors and no patterned errors	Clear and well-organized: easy to comprehend: contains abundant meaningful and creative information	Website is visually appealing with abundant multimedia content to assist reading, user-friendly, and creative
6–9	Occasional typos: mostly accurate punctuation: fulfilled required minimum usage of vocabulary and grammatical items	Accurate and abundant usage of words and expressions with only occasional errors (3–5)	Some common random or patterned grammatical errors (3–5)	Mostly clear and well-organized: comprehensible with occasional errors; contains various meaningful and creative information	Website is mostly visually appealing with some multimedia content to assist reading, and mostly user-friendly
3–6	Frequent typos: frequent inaccurate punctuation: does not fulfill required minimum usage of vocabulary and grammatical items	Mostly accurate and limited usage of words and expression with frequent or patterned lexical errors (6–9)	Frequent random or patterned grammatical errors (6–9)	Somewhat clear and organized: somewhat comprehensible with frequent errors; contains limited meaningful information	Website is somewhat visually appealing with limited multimedia content to assist reading, and somewhat user-friendly
0–3	Very frequent typos and inaccurate punctuation that interfere with understanding; does not fulfill required minimum usage of vocabulary and grammatical items	Speech filled with random or patterned lexical errors (10 or more) and speech is hard to understand	Speech filled with random or patterned grammatical errors (10 or more)	Unclear and poorly organized: very frequent errors that interfere with comprehensibility, contains very little meaningful information	Website is not visually appealing with very limited multimedia content to assist reading, and not user-friendly

Source: Lee et al. (2023b)

Best Practices in PBLL From Other Chinese Language Teachers 153

Figure 6.2 Home Page of a Website Created by Two Students

城市), "Campus" (宾大校园), "Student Daily Life" (学生的日常生活), and "Post Office & Transportation" (邮局和交通工具) respectively. At the top of the page, there is also an airplane icon and a search icon for website searching purposes. Clicking either the "Survival Guide" menu on the left or the "Home Page" menu in the middle, one will see the red-colored "Congratulations on being admitted to Penn" underneath the objectives of this website and the photos of the two "webmasters" with a brief introduction. Again, the page radiates a warm and friendly welcome. Next, let me take you to each of the four menus one after another to experience this website.

First is "Airport & City." Assuming an international student has just arrived at the International Airport of Philadelphia. The student is greeted by the red-colored sign "Welcome to Philadelphia," with an iconic image of the horse-drawn carriage touring Independence Hall in downtown Philadelphia. This page provides you with a summary of what you need to know when going through American customs. What is eye-catching is an image of a U.S. Customs and Border Protection form, which presents the newcomers who have never been to the US with a visual experience of what needs to be filled out before entering the country. Related to this form is a list of goods that are allowed to be brought into America. Those that are prohibited to bring in are written in big-font characters. This page also offers some useful information, such as how to travel to campus from the airport. Knowing that you might have been exhausted after the long-distance travel, the webmasters gently advise you to get to school by taxi, with a map showing the route and the time that it might take. They also suggest that new students arrive at campus as soon as possible so as to have some time to chat with their roommate(s) or have a quick tour of campus. Another great feature on this page is the inclusion of the video *Travel Guide of Philadelphia* made by Expedia, which offers the city's major sightseeing spots in just five minutes. This page gives one a welcoming vibe, with clear descriptions scattered among lovely graphics, colors, and fonts.

The second menu item, "Campus," centralizes all the 13 dorm buildings that the university offers with details such as who is eligible to live in which dorm, what facilities are inside each building, and what kind of food each provides. This page also features information on student health services for mental health issues. No doubt, such valuable information, which can only be provided by those who have experience living there, is helpful for prospective students when it comes to choosing where to stay. The third menu is about "Student Daily Life," for which a friendly and humorous description of sleeping, showering, eating, and drinking is given under the headings of "Sleeping Habits," "Shower Habits," "Meal Plan," and "Drinking," respectively. Keeping the international Chinese-speaking students in mind, the two webmasters shared their firsthand observations, comments, and suggestions with respect to each of these important aspects that new students crave to know. In particular, for the category of "Drinking," besides listing bubble tea and soda, there is a gentle reminder about the drinking age in the US under the subheading of "Wines," which is again crucial for international students, who may not be familiar with the legal drinking age in America.

The fourth menu of "Post Office & Transportation" introduces the United States Postal Services (USPS), highlighting helpful tips in terms of where to send and pick up international parcels. As for transportation, the best way to get around on campus is either to walk or to ride a scooter. However, if needed, one can rely on school buses, administered by Penn-Rides in two different directions: Penn Bus East and Penn Bus West. In addition, the site showcases Penn Charter Service and Walking Escort for students who want to take a safe ride home (in the campus neighborhood) in the evening. All the bus services are free of charge for students from Penn. For going beyond campus, for example, how to get to downtown Philadelphia, Chinatown, or the airport, taking Septa or Uber is a popular option. A map of the bus and subway is provided with friendly suggestions. This page displays images of various transportation tools and helpful maps, useful for students.

By this point, visitors to this website should have gathered general ideas about those four aspects of student life at Penn. The two webmasters offered genuine opinions from their perspectives on eating, housing, sleeping, drinking, and transportation from the airport to campus as well as around the city. Obviously, the project resulted in a helpful end product. Note that such a functional website was designed and developed in the target language by two learners of Chinese at an intermediate proficiency level. Although one may catch a few typos and some ungrammatical structures here and there, the city introduction, transportation, descriptions of campus life, and services of dorms and the post office read friendly. Language errors do not hinder any comprehension. Welcoming, inviting, and appealing in beautiful graphics with fonts and colors laid out well, this user-friendly website is well-designed and effectively implemented, truly benefiting the community.

It is evident that a website like this is a valuable platform, presenting helpful information not only for prospective international Chinese-speaking students but also for any Chinese-speaking visitors to Penn and the city of Philadelphia. The website is also pedagogically effective for learners of Chinese as well as for Chinese instructors. Other than the functionality in these respects, this project met with most of Stoller's (2006) conditions for effective PBL. Semi-structured in the sense of Stoller (2002, 2006), this website development task is a natural extension of classroom learning, for which students applied what they had achieved into practice. Simulating a real-world issue, such as addressing the needs of a group of potential students who would be preparing for their trip to the USA and their college life at Penn, the instructors involved the students with a goal-oriented project. Therefore, from the outset, students worked towards the building of a functional website. Noticeably, this project promoted student ownership by allowing them to select their own team member(s), decide their own ways of presenting the menus for the website, and implement their ideas in accordance with their own design. Students had clear "voice and choice" (e.g., Morrison, 2008; Larmer et al., 2015) from designing to planning and finalizing their work in view of the graphics to be included and the font or the color to be used. More importantly, they decided what content would be focused on and how to present it. This freedom, furthermore, enhanced their awareness to take responsibility for their own work so as to achieve excellence. Working outside of the class, the assignment encompassed a period of around three months, lengthening the time of study for students and also reinforcing their interaction and collaboration. Speaking of language, which is the goal of the project, in order to vividly describe the campus and the city in the target language, after students gathered correct information from research, they needed to learn some special vocabulary and study some particular sentence structures to put the new words in order. They then needed to prepare their own scripts to tell an engaging story for each topic. To make their site navigable and attractive, a good mastery of web designing technology was needed. Students thus learned the basics of website development, becoming familiar with some know-how principles and developing techniques and strategies to assure that their stories were well-featured on the website. During the process, each student had to work with partner(s) as a collaborative team member and also on their own. As a consequence, students improved a variety of skills, including research, decision-making, collaboration, time management, and technology literacy, as well as the ability to speak and write in Chinese.

This project, which was presented as a panel of the three instructors of the same course at the 2022 ACTFL conference (Lee et al., 2022), has been repeated twice under the administration of the same group of instructors and is currently ongoing with a different cohort of students. Among many excellent features, one notable strength of the project design is its explicit language requirements, such as the mandatory use of vocabulary items and grammar points. These language requirements, as in Table 6.2, effectively served as good scaffolding, directly guiding students to organize their thoughts and transform their ideas into Chinese in terms of the four topics. Students were thus pushed to acquire the necessary linguistic elements in order to develop a functional website. They were also urged to take into consideration the needs of potential users from the perspective of the target culture, hence their product improved both linguistically and culturally. The other aspect that deserves a special mention is collaboration among the three instructors of the course. Their joint efforts in instruction, assessment, and presentation at a conference improve their understanding of the PBL approach, which further enhances student learning. Dr. Lee and associates are now improving the design of the project. For example, they are adding a reflection component at the end of the project so that students will have an opportunity to reflect on their experience engaging in the project. If students could reflect upon the language and technology, as well as the entire project, they would learn a lot more.

6.3.3 Music and Culture Project

During the COVID-19 pandemic, many colleges held hybrid or in-person classes. As such, students suffered from the virus and worried about their loved ones catching it, leading to much anxiety and depression. In order to help students learn actively while staying healthy physically and psychologically, Yale University encouraged faculty to explore instructional approaches to promote students' interaction and engagement. Prof. Peisong Xu, senior lector of Chinese in the Department of East Asian Languages and Literatures, tried out an innovative instructional approach by employing PBLL in her class to encourage student-student interaction for more desirable learning outcomes. Specifically, she engaged her students with some project work. Inspired by her students' positive learning experiences, after the pandemic, Prof. Xu expanded this practice to another Chinese class. Her observation is that a pedagogical modification is needed for the post-COVID in-person class because the teaching methods that used to work well before the pandemic cannot be applied directly without some changes. More details about her curriculum-reform efforts are explained here.

In Spring 2023, Prof. Xu implemented three mini projects and one term-end project in her advanced heritage Chinese class, which ran three times a week, Monday, Wednesday, and Friday, with 50 minutes for each class meeting. Students enrolled in this course through a placement test and earned one credit upon completion. The mini projects required a team of three or four peers to present their joint work on an assigned topic using PowerPoint (PPT) slides. The goal was to empower students to use the target language acquired for effective communication, that is, in the interpersonal and presentational communication mode (ATCFL, 1996, 2015). The instructor usually assigned the mini project on Monday when students would start doing it collaboratively. The students utilized the time outside class to finalize the project and create their Chinese PPT slides, which were required as they gave an oral presentation in class on Friday. Students were required to post their PPT slides on *Canvas* before the designated deadline and be ready for presentation. On Friday, each team member must present for around two minutes, speaking in the target language with correct lexicon and grammar structures rather than reading the words written on the PPT slides aloud. In addition, students, as a team, needed to prepare one or two questions for class discussion after their presentation. Regarded as a homework assignment, the mini projects contributed to the course grade. For the final term project, students, in teams of 2–3 peers, were required to produce a 6-to-8-minute video on a topic of their own choice. Replacing the final exam, this term-end project was to enable students to review what had been covered in class throughout the semester and utilize their acquired skills of the target language in class. Students did not need to present, but they prepared their script, posted the video on *Canvas*, showed the video in class, and conducted the class discussion afterwards. The goal of the mini and term-end projects was for students to "improve language skills through peer learning and collaboration" (Xu, 2023, p.c.).

For this chapter, I introduce one of Prof. Xu's mini projects with a focus on how the instructor helped the students to get started and how students did the project. The theme of the mini project is Chinese music and culture, for which students needed to recommend a song sung in Chinese that they liked the best. Specific details are as follows. Students should (i) introduce the origin of the song (e.g., the style of the singer who sang the song and the major musical instrument(s) involved in playing the song); (ii) outline the major meaning and characteristics of the song lyrics; (iii) explain the reason why they like the song; and (iv) discuss the impact of the song on society in general. To help students meet the requirements, Prof. Xu offered scaffolding support by (i) giving background resources about a singer or a song; (ii) providing lexical and grammar points; and (iii) conducting a class survey. Let me take her class survey as an example to elaborate on her instructional guidance. The survey (shown in Table 6.4) posed questions in four categories. The first category includes two questions: *What kind of music or song do you like? Why?* The questions in the second category are as follows: *What kind of musical instrument are you good at? Do you like it? Why?* The third category has one question: *What kind of traditional Chinese musical instrument do you know?* For the fourth category, the question is open-ended: *Do you often listen to music or songs? Why?* For the first three categories, lexical items are provided for students to choose from, some of which were new words that students must learn. The instructor raised these questions in class, which checked about students' musical talent in a lively atmosphere, on one hand, and familiarized them with musical terms in the target language, on the other hand. In so doing, the students were guided to think about which category of questions to work on for their mini project and how to handle it.

For analysis purposes, the content of one team's PPT work is given in Table 6.5. This group of students had selected the song "Beijing Welcomes You." As shown on their first PPT slide, they introduced the song from the four perspectives: (i) it was composed for the opening event of Beijing 2008 Olympic Games; (ii) the song was initially featured in the Olympic Games Program of Chinese Central Television;

Table 6.4 Class Survey

Survey Questions	Select Answers/Your Answers
1. 你喜欢听哪种音乐/歌曲？ 为什么喜欢？ *What kind of music or song do you like? Why?*	古典音乐/歌曲、传统音乐/歌曲、现代音乐/歌曲、流行音乐/歌曲、交响乐、爵士乐、摇滚乐、R&B 蓝调、说唱乐
2. 你会哪种乐器？喜欢吗？为什么？ *What musical instrument are you good at? Do you like it? Why?*	西洋乐器：小提琴、中提琴、大提琴、钢琴、黑管、长笛、小号
3. 你知道哪些中国传统民族乐器？ *What kind of Chinese musical instrument do you know?*	二胡、古琴、笛子、琵琶、古筝
4. 你常常听音乐或歌曲吗？ 为什么？ *Do you often listen to music or songs? Why?*	

Source: Xu (2023)

Table 6.5 Students' Work

Questions	Students' Answers
你喜欢听哪种音乐/歌曲?为什么喜欢? What kind of music or song do you like to listen to?	由来及特点 (PPT Slide 1) • 为北京2008年奥运会创作的**歌曲**,也**与**开幕式**有关**。 • 中央电视台的奥运会**频道**播出了这首**婉转**的歌曲。 • 用传统**民族乐器**演奏。 • 是一首**代表**中国文化的**歌曲**。
你为什么喜欢? Why do you like it?	喜欢的原因 (PPT Slide 2) • 我记得小时候在电视**频道**上听到过《北京欢迎你》,所以现在住在美国再次听到那**优美**的**旋律**,令我回忆起我的童年。 • 这首歌有很多名星一起**演唱**。 • 该**歌曲**抒发了我们中国人的爱国主义思想。 • 女生**细腻**的**嗓音**。 • **轻快**的**旋律**特别动人,**仿佛深入**我的**心灵**。
对社会有什么影响? What impact does the song make on the society?	对社会产生的影响 (PPT Slide 3) • 音乐视频里展示了许多北京的名胜古迹,比如说故宫、正阳门、国家体育场等等。这些名胜古迹象征着中国传同文化。 • 奥运会期间,这首歌曲**给**人们**留下了很深的印象**。 • 歌手们是来自中国、香港、台湾、日本、新加坡和韩国的名人,**象征**着中国跟亚洲**良好**的关系。 • 这首歌的视频也帮助来自外国旅游者更加了解中国的传统文化和**悠远**的历史。 • 音乐视频**细腻**的视觉效果使中国旅游业生意更好,因此提高了中国国内生产总值。

Source: Xu (2023)

(iii) the song was played with some traditional Chinese musical instruments; and (iv) it reflected Chinese culture. The students then provided five sentences on the second slide to explain why they liked the song. One team member first mentioned that the beautiful melody of the song reminded her/him of her/his childhood when s/he initially heard it from TV while young in China. Second, the song was sung by many well-known singers, some of whom were the students' favorite artists. Third, the song conveyed a sense of patriotism shared among Chinese people. Fourth, the singer's beautiful and soft voice left an unforgettable impression. Finally, the lighthearted melody was moving, touching one's heart. Regarding the impact of the song on society, students made five points, as shown on the third slide in Table 6.5. The song (i) symbolized Chinese culture through famous places of interest in Beijing such as the Forbidden City, (ii) left a deep impression related to the Beijing 2008 Olympic Games, (iii) created a good relationship between China and other Asian countries with Asian celebrities singing the song, (iv) helped foreign travelers understand Chinese culture and its long-lasting history and (v) promoted tourism and elevated China's gross domestic product (GDP).

The work on the PPT slides in Table 6.5 show that not only did the students fulfill project requirements/specifications by recommending a song, but they also adequately explained the reasons why they liked it and shared their thoughts about the impact that the song had made. It can be seen from the writing that the students employed accurate words and grammatical structures to convey their ideas, expressing themselves fluently and naturally. It is also interesting to note that some elements on the slides are colored in red or yellow by students according to the original work (I emboldened them in Table 6.5 to capture that feature). Examining these highlighted areas carefully, we can see that those elements were the important words and phrases that were either unfamiliar to students, hence requiring extra attention when presented, or taken from the list of language elements required to be used, as specified by the instructor. Given that students only had three days to prepare, their performance in written Chinese is successful.

The Music and Culture Project is a fully structured project in configuration (e.g., Stoller, 2006, 2012; Stoller & Myers, 2019), as the instructor designed and planned everything (e.g., assigning the project on Monday, laying out the language requirements, conducting class discussion with survey prompts, and assessing students' written work as well as oral presentations). Students did not have much time to prepare the project, while the instructor's expectations were high. Despite the challenges, students had freedom in forming their teams, selecting their preferred song to write about, and explaining the reasons for the selection and the impact of the song. Once the project was assigned, it was completely driven by students, who were immersed in the work of coordination, corroboration, discussion, and presentation. The short process contained crucial components for project work. Students should first of all form their own teams. They then needed to decide which survey questions in Table 6.4 to talk about. With the first two steps taken care of, students should then brainstorm to select a song, give reasons, and highlight the impact of the song. After that, students needed to draft a script and revise it. While the script was being finalized, students moved to create PPT slides by keying in Chinese and adding relevant images. Next, students divided the presentation work among themselves so as to ensure that each team member would speak during the presentation. When most of the collaborative work was completed, each member needed to work individually on memorizing the vocabulary and grammar items used in the PPT and practicing their lines time and again. Before the final presentation, students met again for rehearsal. It is clear that throughout the entire process, everyone on the team must work together with other peers so as to contribute to the success of the joint work.

This project, though mini in scale and short in duration, possesses primary characteristics of effective PBL, as postulated in Stoller (2006). That is, (i) students were directed to focus on both the process and product; (ii) they learned the Chinese language and cultural content simultaneously in order to express themselves; (iii) they worked both collaboratively and individually; (iv) they were held collectively responsible for their learning; and (v) they reflected on their work. For this project, the questions that the instructor developed and used in class as survey prompts served as effective scaffolding instruction to guide students to learn. It is also very important to note that the instructor informed students of her expectations regarding their use of the target language in both speaking and writing. To present Chinese music and culture in the target language is challenging to students, but it is relevant or fascinating to them and significant enough to hold their curiosity and desire to dive in. The requirements that each of the team members was responsible to participate in the final oral presentation in class and the follow-up class discussion are remarkable design features, as they promoted the project work to be a true student-centered task. In order to complete the project, students must collaborate for the common goal. Some of these characteristics were noted by students, as captured in a reflection from one student (Xu, 2023).

> *The projects helped me review the week's text as well as get to know my classmates! It also helped me practice my presentation skills. I liked working in a group because if one person didn't know the best term to use in a description, another group member could help out. It was beneficial and very collaborative.*

A few pedagogical features are noteworthy for Chinese-language curriculum reform. First, the instructor planned three mini projects and one large term-end project for the course in one semester, all requiring intensive team efforts as well as individual work, with the first three involving joint oral presentations and written scripts on PPT slides. All the projects required class discussion. The switch from traditional passive rote learning of linguistic elements to more collaborative interaction among peers fostered active social learning, which enabled students to co-construct knowledge and skills of the target language (e.g., Lantolf, 2012). Related to this shift is the increased weight of the percentage given to the project work for the course grade. Three mini projects plus other assignments amounted to 15% of the grade, while the large term-end project added another 15%, resulting in a total of 30% for the entire course grade, suggesting that the instructor placed an emphasis on the development of students' interpersonal and presentational skills in the target language. Replacing the final exam with the term-end project is another brave stride, which gave students more freedom to use the language creatively, an effective way to help retain acquired knowledge and skills as compared to a final paper-pencil exam, the content of which students tended to forget easily. Finally, the decision to involve students in additional project work, necessitating the teacher to design, plan, and facilitate outside class, indicates that the instructor appreciated the importance of peer learning through interaction and collaboration. Therefore, the instructor was ready to change her role, serving as designer, developer, organizer, and facilitator rather than an authoritative figure. All these changes, which contribute to a successful curriculum reform, assure the effectiveness of PBLL instruction.

6.4 Conclusion

In this chapter, I presented six best practices in PBL from other Chinese language educators in the K–12 and university settings. All exposed students to real-world issues no matter whether they were implemented in secondary schools or in universities. The projects designed with this kind of configuration commendably prepared students to be aware of the challenges that they will face in the near future and encouraged them to learn, for example, how to think critically, work collaboratively, communicate effectively, and make use of technology smartly to advance their learning. Such a skill set is expected of current students upon graduation from either high schools or universities so that they enter the workforce ready to survive and thrive. As students are learning a foreign language, it is ideal for instructors to put them in a PBLL classroom or, at least, integrate PBLL into their classroom instruction. In particular, when immersing students in research-oriented, team-based, and technology-supported PBLL joint projects for exploration and expression, instructors help students build and improve their 21st century skills as well as linguistic and cultural competence of the target language.

For these projects, students learned and built their products by means of technologies, visible or invisible. For example, the *Padlet* tool was applied for the students taking the calligraphy class to post their daily reflections for the calligraphy project. Other tools or apps were employed to create and edit videos on calligraphy. Likewise, *Google Site*, *Wix*, or *Weebly* was used to develop the survival guide website. As for the Music and Culture project, students were required to use PPT slides for presentations, which must be posted on *Canvas* (a course management tool) before a deadline. Clearly, the three cases show that the projects were heavily mediated or supported by some particular technological tools, without which the completion of either the video production or website development or PPT presentation would have been impossible. While no particular tools were highlighted for the three projects implemented in the K–12 setting, it is obvious that students and the instructors of middle and high schools must have accessed the internet for doing research or getting onto the *Google Classroom* to participate in discussion and communication or coordinating the project. Students must have also looked up online dictionaries while doing their work. One point is worth highlighting. Technology has advanced so rapidly that many instances of using technology, such as access of internet for doing research or getting on to *Blackboard*, *Canvas*, or *Google Classroom* to manage teaching materials, has now become part of the daily life of teachers and students. As both instructors and students are getting more comfortable with the use of technology for language teaching and learning, the presence of technology is becoming more commonplace, and we may sometimes fail to recognize it. This reflects the idea, as noted by Bax (2003, 2011), that more technology will be integrated into classroom instruction, which will eventually make the use of technology in language instruction more and more invisible or normalized. It seems that the COVID pandemic, which made everyone get online to teach or to learn, has definitely accelerated technology integration or normalization.

All the projects, when completed, were "shared" in a community, small or big. The high school students presented in class their interview results with Chinese native speakers about their experience in the USA. The university students who took the Intermediate Chinese course also presented in class their self-built website for prospective international Chinese-speaking students as did the university learners of the Advanced Heritage Chinese course, who shared their observations about Chinese music and culture inside a class. The students at a middle school posted their AAPI posters on the bulletin boards and the hallways of the entire building to attract students from the whole school. The high school students' presentation on Chinese and American sports culture educated and entertained the audience of the cultural contest. Finally, the calligraphy videos are available on the university website, benefiting the general public.

For the three projects implemented in university context that I focused on, I provided an analysis of project design, and students' end products in view of Stoller's

(2002, 2006) project configuration and conditions. Other than the dependence on technology to complete the project, there are three additional commonalities among the three projects. First are the instructors' explicit requirements (i.e., a video on Chinese calligraphy from interdisciplinary perspectives for the Calligraphy Project, a functional survival guide website for prospective Chinese-speaking students for the Website Development Project, and the spoken and written presentation of Chinese music and culture with PPT slides for the Music and Culture Project). These pedagogical and linguistic requirements urged students to work hard towards the project, resulting in quality products.

The second feature that they all shared is their remarkable scaffolding instruction, though in different formats. Prof. Kang Zhou highlighted both explicit and implicit teaching for his video project. Dr. Lee and associates required students to integrate a mandatory use of lexicon and grammar items in describing the four topics/menus for their website. Prof. Xu developed a class survey to provide prompts for guiding students. Instructors' coaching and guidance crucially facilitated students to prepare and complete the project successfully.

Another element that the three projects possess is their nature of being sustainable from both teaching and learning viewpoints. The video production project was initially launched by Prof. Kang Zhou at MIT in January 2018 for the inaugural Chinese calligraphy course. The project has been repeated over the past five years except the year of 2021 due to the pandemic (Zhou, 2023). With different cohorts doing the project for the Chinese calligraphy course, the assignment to create interesting videos on calligraphy has remained as a viable and enjoyable project among students. The project effectively fostered student learning of calligraphy, and some students have become lifelong learners. The Website Development Project that targeted prospective international Chinese-speaking students was designed and implemented by Dr. Chih-Jen Lee and two other colleagues at the University of Pennsylvania for the Intermediate Chinese course. The three Chinese language instructors initiated the experiment in Fall 2020 and have since continued the same project by modifying its design and implementation for more effective student learning. The Music and Culture Project, pioneered by Prof. Peisong Xu at Yale University in Spring 2023, was based on her trial with one course during the COVID-19 pandemic. Her advanced heritage learners of Chinese, apart from attending the regular class, were involved in additional project work, with both oral and written presentations and class discussion in the target language. Assigning students with more project work is part of Prof. Xu's curriculum reform, for which she experimented with incorporating as many as four projects in one semester, increased the weight of the percentage on the projects with regards to the course grade, and changed the role of the instructor from "teacher" to designer, planner, organizer, and facilitator, all these making the application of PBLL approach more effective for student learning.

To conclude, all the projects discussed in this chapter align with the DATEPBLL model that I proposed in Chapter 4. The technology-supported projects, which target real-world issues and aim at benefiting a community, help students learn actively and effectively.

References

American Council on the Teaching of Foreign Languages (ACTFL). (1996). *Standards for foreign language learning: Preparing for the 21st century*. ACTFL.

American Council on the Teaching of Foreign Languages (ACTFL). (2015). *World-readiness standards for learning languages*. ACTFL.

Bax, S. (2003). Call-past, present, and future. *System: An International Journal of Educational Technology and Applied Linguistics, 31*(1), 13–28. https://doi.org/10.1016/s0346-251x(02)00071-4

Bax, S. (2011). Normalisation revisited: The effective use of technology in language education. *International Journal of Computer Assisted Language Learning and Teaching, 1*(2), 1–15. https://doi.org/10.4018/ijcallt.2011040101

Chen, D., Meng, L., & Hegedus, M. (2016, November). *Applying project-based language learning in the Chinese classroom* [Panel presentation]. ACTFL.

Hegedus, M. (2016, November). *Using project feedback to guide learning and task completion in PBLL*, [Part of a panel presentation]. ACTFL.

Hegedus, M. (2019, May). *Increase cooperative learning and language proficiency through diverse instructions, activities and assessments* [Paper presentation]. The 17th New York International Conference on Teaching Chinese, New York, NY.

Hegedus, M. (2020a, August). Using project based learning in the Chinese classroom to tackle racial bias [如何在中文课堂上用项目学习模式来克服种族偏见]. Chinese Language Teachers Association of Greater New York (CLTA-GNY) Online Lecture, Zoom. www.youtube.com/watch?v=PqXdP3wJlaw&list=UUpGQZCfhbllRxRG3n3EehGg&index=11

Hegedus, M. (2020b, October). Promote the Chinese language project series to develop students' shining points and build a big stage for their dreams [推广中文项目系列之发掘学生闪 光点、搭 建梦想大舞台], CLASS FRONTLINE [热点谈] 23, 10/3/2020. Zoom Workshop. www.youtube.com/watch?v=ZIMLYyH2Tng

Lantolf, J. P. (2012). Sociocultural theory: A dialectical approach to L2 research. In S. M. Gass & A. Mackey (Eds.), *The Routledge handbook of second language acquisition* (pp. 57–72). Taylor & Francis Group.

Larmer, J., Mergendoller, J., & Boss, S. (2015). *Setting the standard for project based learning: A proven approach to rigorous classroom instruction*. ASCD.

Lee, C.-J., Zhang, X., & Fan, S. (2022, November). *Implementing Project-based Instructions in Intermediate CFL Classroom* [Panel presentation]. 2022 ACTFL Annual Conference, Boston, MA, United States.

Lee, C-J., Zhang, X., & Fan, S. (2023a). *CHIN0300 final project instructions*. University of Pennsylvania.

Lee, C-J., Zhang, X., & Fan, S. (2023b). *CHIN0300 final project grading rubrics*. University of Pennsylvania.

Meng, L. (2016, November). *Project-based language learning: Design, instructions and assessment* [Part of Panel presentation]. ACTFL Annual Meeting, Boston, MA.

Meng, L. (2022, February). *Multi-dimensional Use of PBL in Teaching Chinese*. Chinese Language Teachers Association of Greater New York (CLTA-GNY) Online Lecture, Zoom.

Morrison, K. A. (2008). Democratic classrooms: Promises and challenges of student voice and choice, part one. *Educational Horizons, 87*(1), 50–60. https://files.eric.ed.gov/fulltext/EJ815371.pdf

Qin, Y. (2023, May). *Exposure to AAPI activities in middle schools* [Panel presentation]. The 21st New York International Conference on Teaching Chinese: A New Chapter in Teaching Chinese, New York, NY.

Stoller, F. L. (2002). Project work: A means to promote language and content. In J. C. Richards & W. A. Renandya (Eds.), *Methodology in language teaching: An anthology of current practice* (pp. 107–119). Cambridge University Press.

Stoller, F. L. (2006). Establishing a theoretical foundation for project-based learning in second and foreign language contexts. In G. H. Beckett & P. C. Miller (Eds.), *Project-based second and foreign language education: Past, present, and future* (pp. 19–40). Information Age Publishing.

Stoller, F. L. (2012). Project-based learning: A viable option for second and foreign language classrooms. In *Perfect score: methodologies, technologies, & communities of practice* (pp. 37–47). Proceedings of the 20th Annual KOTESOL International Conference, Seoul, October 20–21, 2012.

Stoller, F. L., & Myers, C. C. (2019). A five-stage framework to guide language teachers. In A. Gras-Velázquez. (Ed.), *Project-based learning in second language acquisition: Building communities of practice in higher education* (pp. 24–47). Routledge. https://doi.org/10.4324/9780429457432-3

Xu, P. (2023, August). *Increasing language and intercultural competence—classroom practice* [Paper Presentation]. Chinese Language Teachers Summer Workshop, New Haven, CT.

Zhao, J. (2019). Bridging cross-cultural teaching practices with technology-enriched PBLL in Chinese as a foreign language education. In G. H. Beckett & T. Slater (Eds.), *Global perspectives on project-based language learning, teaching, and assessment: Key approaches, technology tools, and frameworks* (pp. 146–163). Routledge.

Zhao, J., & Beckett, G. H. (2014). Project-based Chinese as a foreign language instruction—A teacher research approach. *Journal of the Chinese Language Teachers Association, 49*(2), 45–73.

Zhou, K. (2023, May). *Designing a Chinese calligraphy curriculum to enhance cultural understanding* [Paper Presentation]. The 21st New York International Conference on Teaching Chinese: A New Chapter in Teaching Chinese, New York, NY.

7 DATEPBLL
From Here to Where?

7.1 Introduction

In Chapters 2 and 3, I discussed CALL and DH respectively. In Chapter 4, after introducing PBL and its evolution to PBLL, I proposed combining DH and CALL with PBLL for teaching Chinese as a foreign language (TCFL) to have a Digital Humanities–Augmented Technology-Enhanced Project-Based Language Learning (DATEPBLL) model, whereby DH serves as a pedagogical foundation, while CALL offers tools and "networks that facilitate and support social interaction and collaboration" (Thomas & Yamazaki, 2021, p. 7). With this DH-empowered and technology-supported PBLL, I then demonstrated, in Chapter 5, the application of the model by illustrating three projects that I designed and implemented in the light of the project framework (Stoller, 2006, 2012, Stoller & Myers, 2019). The first two projects were completed with second language learners of Chinese and the third one was with preservice Chinese language teachers. In Chapter 6, I introduced best practices from other teachers in the K–16 setting, with a focus on analyzing three projects implemented in the university context in terms of teachers' scaffolding instruction and students' end products.

In this chapter, I will explore the implications of this DATEPBLL model and discuss its future directions. Before I dive in, I must first discuss what seems to have become a household name, which people talk about either with curiosity, excitement, enthusiasm, or apprehension, cautiousness, and skepticism, depending on who they are. That is ChatGPT, whose emergence marked the start of an era of generative artificial intelligence (AI) technologies. Released by OpenAI in November 2022, ChatGPT is an example of large language models (LLMs) that use generative AI technologies to, among others, produce human-like text, answer questions, provide information, translate language, and write computing codes (OpenAI, 2022; MLA-CCCC, 2023; Marr, 2023). Because "artificial intelligence [is] designed to mimic human language," ChatGPT is included as a non-person in addition to ten other outstanding scientists by *Nature's 10* for its influence over the world of science in the year of 2023 (Nature, 2023). With "seismic shifts warranted by LLMs" (MLA-CCCC, 2023, p. 4), which affect education, it is imperative that we achieve a good understanding of AI technologies and their impact on language education. Therefore, after a brief introduction of ChatGPT and its relationship with LLMs and generative AI technologies, I will first provide some survey data about faculty and higher-ed officials' reactions to generative AI technologies with respect to risks and opportunities, followed by a review of the latest study of the use of ChatGPT in the Chinese classrooms. I will then examine the implications of the DATEPBLL model for TCFL. I will finally outline a few tasks as future directions for the application of the model in the context of a post-COVID technology-filled learning environment.

7.2 Generative AI Tools: Risks and Opportunities

Trained on massive, preprocessed text data for learning and reasoning, the system of ChatGPT works by predicting the next word in a sentence. Its free and basic version is capable of offering a myriad of functions, for example, making a content strategy, giving ideas, planning a trip, and recommending a dish. All can be done within a few seconds, though not free from errors (OpenAI, 2023). Due to the "versatility and human like quality of its responses" (Vogels, 2023), ChatGPT immediately created a worldwide sensation right after its public launch, much like the calculator did in the 1970s or the internet in the 1990s. It attracted 100 million users within two months of its release (Hu, 2023). Its potential to exceed human intelligence raised such serious concerns among top scientists that in March 2023, a call for a pause on "giant AI experiments" was made in an open letter, which has received over 30,000 signatures. The questions raised in the letter are as follows: "*Should* we let machines flood our information channels with propaganda and untruth? *Should* we automate away all the jobs, including the fulfilling ones? *Should* we develop nonhuman minds that might eventually outnumber, outsmart, obsolete and replace us? *Should* we risk loss of control of our civilization?" (Open Letter, 2023). Some signatories from the Institute of Electrical and Electronics Engineers (IEEE) "expressed a range of fears and apprehensions including about rampant growth of AI large-language models (LLMs) as well as of unchecked AI media hype" (Anderson, 2023). Despite these concerns, as many as ten products similar to ChatGPT have already been rolled out in less than one year (PCWorld, 2023), including *BARD* created by Google, *Bing Chart* by Microsoft, *LLaMA* by Meta, and *Ernie* by Baidu, suggesting that the competition for more robust AI technologies and tools has remained fierce. In addition, the rapid development of different LLMs products has made AI-enhanced language learning apps available. For example, *Duolingo*, one of the leading language learning programs, has already integrated ChatGPT technology to enrich personalized and interactive learning experiences. Running on both mobile and desktop platforms, this AI-powered app can serve as a conversation partner and offer immediate feedback to learners.

Following the release of ChatGPT on November 30, 2022, the Modern Language Association (MLA) and the Conference on College Composition and Communication (CCCC), a chartered conference of the National Council of Teachers of English, formed MLA-CCCC Joint Task Force on Writing and AI (TF) in December of 2022. The purpose of TF is to understand AI technologies and learn how language educators can tackle the challenges of using AI technologies as writing aids.

According to MLA-CCCC (2023), generative AI "refers to computer systems that can produce, or generate, various forms of traditionally human expression, in the form of digital content including language, images, video, and music. Large language models (LLMs) are a subset of generative AI used to deliver text-based formats like prose, poetry, or even programming code" (MLA-CCCC, p. 5). Standing for generative pre-trained transformer, GPT is a product that OpenAI created by connecting its own generative pre-trained models with Google's transformer architecture (OpenAI, 2022). ChatGPT "combines an easy-to-access browser interface with a chatbot style of interaction, whereby a user can enter a series of discursive prompts and engage with the outputs of the model in an ongoing dialogic stream" (MLA-CCCC, 2023, p. 6).

Not long after the formation of TF, the MLA-CCCC conducted a survey among 456 academia stakeholders about their perceptions of LLMs. Included in the working paper (MLA-CCCC, 2023) is the analysis of answers to the two questions about risks and opportunities that generative AI technologies may bring to classrooms, programs, and campuses. Regarding the question that solicits participants' rating of their concerns about the use of ChatGPT and other AI text generation technologies in teaching, the average score from the 456 respondents was 3.82, with 1 being the least concerned and 5 the most concerned, suggesting that these educators worried about the technologies. When asked what their biggest concerns were, the majority selected two categories: (i) plagiarism and integrity and the inability of instructors to detect the use of AI and (ii) worries about students' use of AI not for learning, in general, or in particular, for example, how to write or how to improve thinking skills. Regarding the question that solicits participants' rating about how significant they think opportunities of ChatGPT and other AI text generation technologies are, the average score from the 412 respondents was 3.24, with 1 being the least significant and 5 the most significant, suggesting that they saw promise in the technologies for classrooms and programs. These respondents identified the two most common opportunities by AI on writing: (i) AI tools could help students during the writing process at multiple stages and (ii) AI tools could help students learn how to improve their writing. However, there were many respondents who were either unsure of possible opportunities or did not see any opportunities, suggesting that they had either mixed perceptions about, or little understanding of, generative AI technologies (p. 14).

From June 19 to July 14, 2023, *The Chronicle of Higher Education* (TCHE) conducted a survey asking 404 higher-ed leaders to share their perspectives about generative AI on 20 questions (TCHE, 2023). Relevant to our interest under discussion are five questions. One asked for participants' opinions about (i) whether generative-AI tools pose a threat to how higher education educates, operates, and conducts research and (ii) whether generative-AI tools offer an opportunity for higher education to improve how it educates, operates, and conducts research. It turns out that 60% of leaders think AI poses a threat to higher education, while 78% of them think that AI offers new ways to improve higher education. As for the question whether their institution is worried about AI-powered cheating because students can use generative-AI tools to complete assignments and pass the work off as their own, most of them (i.e., 33% strongly agree and 51% agreed) believed so. When asked what their biggest concern is about AI technologies, 35% of the higher-ed officials worried about the misinformation or false information that AI technology would bring to students, and 28% of them worried about the students' weaker skills or insufficient content knowledge if AI technology is used. Only 27% regarded academic integrity as the biggest concern when it comes to the use of generative-AI tools by students. Of these respondents, almost all, or 98% (66% strongly agree and 32% agree), agree that generative-AI tools will require instructors to rethink how they assess students. Another interesting finding was that the majority of the higher-ed leaders identified teaching (57%) as the area of college operations that AI tools would have the most impact on in the next five years. Surprisingly, 69% of them think that the impact would be positive, while 60% think otherwise. These data suggest that like those as surveyed in MLA-CCCC (2023), higher-ed officials are also not very clear about possible consequences that generative AI technologies will bring to the field of education, though many had a mixed feeling of excitement and concern.

ChatGPT has some limitations, such as giving answers that may sound correct but are wrong, being sensitive to changes in prompts, providing too much information sometimes, guessing user intentions, and responding to harmful instructions or showing bias (OpenAI, 2023). MLA-CCCC (2023) identified some risks that generative AI technologies pose for students, teachers, and schools. For example, students (i) may not learn how to write, read, and think if they rely on AI for their work; (ii) they may not appreciate the value of studying language and writing if a machine can do the job for them; (iii) they may feel untrusted if detection software is used to ensure academic integrity; and (iv) they may experience linguistic injustice because LLMs promote standardized English (p. 7). As for the risks for teachers, there are also a few. Teachers may have to adopt new practices, may not receive enough support or training to understand LLMs, and will have to develop AI literacy about the nature, capacities, and risks of AI tools as well as how they might be used (p. 7). These risks are examined in view of potential costs related to the learning and teaching goals. Despite the risks, MLA-CCCC (2023) recognized many benefits of AI technologies for students and teachers as well, as shown in Tables 7.1 and 7.2.

As far as TCFL is concerned, Cai (2023) identified some weaknesses with respect to the use of ChatGPT in Chinese classrooms. For example, in addition to the academic integrity and ethical issues that others already noted, Cai pointed out that ChatGPT lacks affection and feeling. It is also difficult for learners to craft the right input (i.e., prompt) to get the best out of generative AI. Above all, ChatGPT makes mistakes on the number of strokes in terms of writing Chinese characters. However, Cai claimed that ChatGPT presents five features that aligned with ideal conditions for second language (L2) acquisition. First, ChatGPT's capability of retrieving information at an enormously fast speed creates rich comprehensive input. When properly prompted, the input can be tailored to L2 learners' proficiency. Second, the interactive engagement with ChatGPT enables L2 learners to have meaning negotiation, clarifications, and identification of discrepancies in between L1

Table 7.1 Selected Benefits of LLMs for Students

Categories	Benefits
Language instruction	• Language students can use LLMs to create translations that include explanations and wording options. • Language students can develop expertise even while using generative AI. Although it may be used to produce a rough draft of a translation, refining such translations will still require knowledge about language choices, especially with literary works. • Language students can ask LLMs questions about a text in another language.
Writing instruction	• Students can use LLMs to help stimulate thought and develop drafts that are still the student's own work and to overcome psychological obstacles to tackling invention and revision. When used in these ways, LLMs have the potential to act as literacy sponsors to emerging academic writers. • Students can use generative AI to produce creative materials when developing multimodal writing projects that communicate in modes other than written text, since generative AI can process data involving still images, sound, and moving images.

Source: MLA-CCCC (2023, pp. 8–9)

Table 7.2 Selected Benefits of LLMs for Teachers

- Teachers can use generative AI to quickly come up with examples. Teachers can use generative AI to quickly come up with examples. Teachers can integrate LLMs into the writing process and enhance students' rhetorical knowledge, critical thinking, and knowledge of conventions.
- Teachers can use LLMs to offer a practical demonstration of some key rhetorical concepts that have influenced writing and rhetoric studies, especially as related to questions of process, praxis, and the construction of meaning.
- Teachers can use LLMs to provide models of written prose that can be used to highlight differences in genre, tone, diction, literary style, and disciplinary focus.
- Teachers can use LLMs to offer new processes for students developing multimodal writing genres since LLMs have the capability to process multimodal inputs and outputs.
- Teachers can use LLMs to provide course content that bridges the gap between writing across disciplines.
- Teachers can use LLMs to quickly generate different models of response and stimulate discussion about various approaches to a writing prompt. These technologies allow instructors to "show" as well as "tell" what different writing strategies look like.
- Teachers and students can use LLMs to complement existing tools for English language learners—such as usage dictionaries, grammar checkers, language tutorials—to experience success more rapidly in their writing efforts.
- Writers who come from diverse and various linguistic and educational backgrounds may benefit from the more sophisticated grammar, style, and genre editing capabilities of LLMs by receiving access to the "language of power."

Source: MLA-CCCC (2023, pp. 9–10)

and L2. Third, ChatGPT's immediate feedback, explicit or corrective, facilitates learners to carry a meaningful exchange for language learning. Fourth, ChatGPT's ability to incorporate frequent use of target words or structures can draw learners' attention to those linguistic elements. Lastly, the interactive nature and fast feedback of ChatGPT makes an ideal environment for L2 learners to produce language. These five features of ChatGPT provide input, interaction, feedback, noticing, and output, all helpful for learners of a second language.

Li et al. (2023) incorporated the use of ChatGPT in three different university Chinese language classrooms: (i) Intermediate Low Chinese class; (ii) Intermediate High Chinese class; and (iii) Academic Chinese Writing class. It is found that for the Intermediate Low Chinese class, ChatGPT can assist students in learning grammar and carrying conversations about cultural insights covered in the text. For the Intermediate High Chinese class, ChatGPT can help students learn how to develop narrative short texts through comparing their initial drafts with ChatGPT's revised versions. For the Academic Writing class, ChatGPT can evaluate students' drafts based on grading criteria and offer revision recommendations. Li and colleagues found that ChatGPT's capability of being flexible, giving real-time responses, allowing access to a wealth of information, acting as a peer, and providing a reference point and a discussion platform engages L2 learners to improve in speaking and writing while also learning to think critically. They conclude that as a versatile peer-assisted instructional tool, ChatGPT can, when aligned with curricular goals, enhance student learning and contribute to effective language education.

In sum, generative AI text technologies pose risks as well as offer opportunities, as shown by the surveys that MLA-CCCC Joint Task Force and *The Chronicle of Higher Education* conducted respectively. Cai (2023) suggests that ChatGPT may bring benefits to learners of Chinese as it possesses some features that align with the critical elements for second language acquisition. Li et al.'s (2023) study on the use of ChatGPT in three different Chinese classrooms in the university context shows that students were benefited in both speaking and writing. The generative AI technologies represented by ChatGPT mark a milestone in the history of technology. Just as COVID-19 forced instructors to shift to online teaching abruptly in the spring of 2020, bringing in "both a crisis and an opportunity to reconsider language learning strategy" (Zhao, 2020) and many challenges (e.g., Thomas, 2021), it is clear that generative AI technologies that have arrived on campus will affect language education no matter whether one likes it or not (Anft, 2023). Testing out ChatGPT for teaching Chinese (e.g., Cai, 2023; Chen, 2023; Da, 2023; Li et al., 2023) or other world languages (Zamora, 2023) suggests that generative AI technologies are worth exploring for language education.

7.3 Implications of the DATEPBLL Approach

As we are entering the era of AI, generative AI technologies will be part of the new normal in the school setting. Although it is not very clear as to the role of the AI technologies, serving as "friend" or "foe" (Vista Higher Learning, 2023), "boom" or "burden," (Chandrasekar, 2023), higher-ed leaders see that the academic setting is inevitable to be affected or impacted by them (TCHE, 2023). More than half of college officials surveyed (63%) chose personalized educational experiences and assessment as the two top areas in which generative AI technologies will benefit students, according to the TCHE survey (p. 14). They believe that in face of the challenges, instructors must endeavor to redesign their curriculum and try innovative assessments. In light of the survey results about AI technologies (MLA-CCCC, 2023; TCHE, 2023) and the encouraging findings about benefits of ChatGPT (Cai, 2023; Li et al, 2023) for the study of Chinese by students with different levels of proficiency, the DATEPBLL approach would be an effective instructional model to consider for language education, in general, and TCFL, in particular. When applying technology-supported projects with DH teaching methods in the AI setting for second language classrooms, there are some implications to consider.

First, the DATEPBLL model brings DH and CALL together and adds its combination to PBLL, thereby enriching PBLL a great deal, as well enhancing DH and CALL. Beckett et al. (2019) identified four primary pillars that sustain PBLL: Dewey's education philosophy (Dewey & Dewey, 1915; Dewey, 1916); Vygotskian social constructivist learning theories (1978); Halliday's systemic functional language view (1975); and Schieffelin and Ochs' theory of language socialization (1986). They all highlight the significance of considering language as a dynamic and social phenomenon in sociocultural contexts. In Chapter 4, I argued that L2 acquisition theories such as Long's (1983, 1996) interaction hypothesis and Schmidt's (1990, 2001) noticing hypothesis also reinforce PBLL crucially. This is because during the process of doing a project, learners certainly encounter new linguistic phenomena, which they may pay attention to and endeavor to find out meanings and usages through interaction with other peers. Such a process helps learners internalize the language. I argue, here, that the hybrid DH and CALL, furthermore, empowers PBLL, making the latter much stronger, more solid, and more robust. With DH added, it brings in one more theoretical caliber to PBLL—its digital pedagogy that underlines the conception of openness, collaboration, play, practice, student agency, and identity (Davis et al., 2020). Specifically, digital pedagogy reinforces the characteristics of PBL (Stoller, 2006) by emphasizing individual work as well as collaboration with peers and by sharing end products in the form of openness within a community. Engaging students to play and practice collaboratively heightens their agency and identity, thereby adding extra pedagogical value to PBLL.

The call for augmenting PBLL with DH may be little heard let alone explored, though not unreasonable. In fact, the significance of linking DH to PBLL cannot be emphasized too much. As mentioned before, they both highlight the idea of learning by doing, collaborating, and sharing, hence greatly strengthening the nature of project work, a primary format of PBLL. DH has been enormously involved in the teaching of English literature, or literary studies, inspiring faculty and students for effective teaching and learning (e.g., Travis & DeSpain, 2018). The application of integrating DH into PBLL for L2 instruction should be examined as well. The case studies in Chapter 5 and best practices in Chapter 6 suggest that DH can be applied to language education through PBLL. Similar ideas of applying DH to L2 learning were explored by Cro (2020), who proposed taking the form of DHL2 methodology—an instruction that avails "digital advances to facilitate collaborative and cooperative modes of learning while considering reflectively the act of building and making in a digital frame" (p. 19). Unlike Cro's (2020) direct inflection of DH to L2, under the current DATEPBLL approach, the participation and contribution of DH is reconciled by PBLL, the latter being supported by CALL. DH can shed light on language instruction, guiding instructors in designing and implementing innovative projects to engage student learning.

While the beauty of linking DH to PBLL for TCFL and language in general is illustrated, there is some additional value of involving CALL into PBLL. In fact, much important work was completed, as demonstrated by the studies in Thomas and Yamazaki (2021) and by other scholars whose research is collected in Beckett et al. (2019). Technology in education is becoming more ubiquitous. The COVID-19 pandemic required "the wide scale adoption of web-based instruction within a matter of weeks" (Thomas & Yamazaki, 2021, p. 1). As a result, instructors and students are not only more comfortable and perceptive about the use of technology in classrooms but also much more ready and more skillful in using technology for teaching and learning. Naturally, the role of technology in PBLL will be further emphasized, and technology-enhanced PBLL will be a trend. In the era of generative AI technologies, it is most likely that more generative AI technologies will be applied to PBLL with emergence of the ChatGPT-empowered *Kahoot!* and the ChatGPT-enabled *Duolingo* app. In terms of the involvement of ChatGPT in L2 learning, Da (2023) made an interesting point. As ChatGPT is applied to language learning and instruction, it directly participates in the interaction with learners because of its "human-like" intelligence. As such, it shifts the role of CALL from assistant to participant, hence, Computer-Participated Language Learning (CPLL) rather than Computer-Assisted Language Learning (CALL). The issue raised is worth addressing but not in this chapter due to the restriction of space.

Combining both DH and CALL with PBLL and applying it for the teaching and learning of Chinese is significant. As two separate disciples, DH and CALL have been developing over the past six decades, both derived from computing technologies. While each has its own objectives and scope, both have their best to offer to language instructors and students, with DH contributing pedagogy, and CALL contributing technology and more. PBL/PBLL has established a solid framework (Stoller, 2006, 2012; Stoller & Myers, 2019), which has guided language instructors to implement numerous projects with their students. The potential synergies of DH and CALL, with each complementing the other, would greatly reinforce PBLL, driving for more effective L2 learning. It would inspire language instructors to design innovative learning projects to engage student learning with digital pedagogy and tools. In a word, with DH and CALL joining PBLL, their pedagogy and technology serve as additional wings, propelling PBLL to greater heights.

In so much as we have seen the contributions that the joint DH and CALL makes for PBLL, the DATEPBLL model also enhances DH and CALL individually. Pitman and Taylor (2017) addressed the relationship between the discipline of modern languages (ML) and DH. They proposed a "critical DHML" approach to "bring the critical cultural studies of ML into the DH fold" (para 26). They argued that by doing digital cultural production, the work "can help to strengthen DH's profile overall" (para. 28). According to Pitman and Taylor, while ML and DH are two separate disciplines, more interactions should be promoted to "ensure that ML is embedded in DH, and vice versa" (para. 43). Along with Pitman and Taylor's argument for the inter-participation between ML and DH, I highlight that the current research makes a strong case for the importance of using DH pedagogy for the teaching and learning of Chinese, suggesting DH's impact on language education. As for CALL, technology has been evolving rapidly and will continue to do so. What is innovative now may soon be outdated. Therefore, the key for educators as well as for students is not to focus just on learning one particular technology in order to achieve a full mastery of it but to be willing to learn new digital tools and experience the process of learning either through working with peers or on one's own. How can this process be ensured and guaranteed? A technology-enhanced project is the means to the end. When working on a project that involves technologies, students learn from and help each other, which creates a supportive learning environment for students to grow. With a bond tying everyone together, students build up social skills such as effective communication, empathy, and cooperation. They learn the target language and the subject matter simultaneously (Mohan, 1986; Beckett, 1999; Stoller, 2006; Beckett et al., 2019), as well as shape skills in technology (Thomas & Yamazaki, 2021).

Second, just as the DATEPBLL model enriches PBLL, DH, and CALL, it also corresponds with the needs of social advancement. In the current learning environment with the emergence of generative AI technologies, doing projects along the DATEPBLL approach will become a much more common practice. Based on the survey conducted by TCHE (2023), personalized education experiences and assessment are considered as the two top areas in which generative AI will benefit students. This suggests that more project work as postulated in the DATEPBLL model is needed to mobilize students to collaborate as they are learning. It is through project work, which requires participants to work together towards a joint goal, that students will learn how to resolve issues through communicating with each other and sharing their own thoughts and reflections. Without project work, some individual students would continue to hide themselves from others, buried among social media apps. Lenz (2018) pointed out that the current world is "project-based," because by 2025, 60% of people in the US will work as contract employees, shifting between projects for different clients (p. xi). Due to the changing nature of work in the real world or the influence of business and marketing models in the field of education, it is crucial to foster and enhance students' abilities in undertaking project work and prepare them to meet the job market during their stay in school.

Third, applying DATEPBLL will help address the language learning standards and requirements for 21st century skills. The standards of foreign language education as advanced in the US and Europe, along with the requirements of the essential 21st century skills, pose a real challenge for language teachers. What does it mean? A challenge that language teachers face is when teaching a target language, they must meet state and national standards as well as the expectations of the 21st century skills by implementing sound methods and techniques (Mikulec & Miller, 2011). As shown by the cases studies and those best practices in Chapters 5 and 6, the Digital Humanities–Augmented Technology-Enhanced PBLL approach can be used to address standards, in particular, communication skills, and cultivate 21st century skills in language education. These projects lend support to the claim that language instructors are able to address world-readiness standards and other skill sets through PBLL instruction, as proposed by Miller (2006), Mikulec and Miller (2011), and Gleason and Link (2019). The essential elements of the PBL method, as defined in Boss and Larmer (2018), and its characteristics and benefits, as captured in Stoller (2006), Stoller (2012), and Stoller and Myers (2019), along with the reported literature review of the research in Chapter 4, justify the candidacy of PBL/PBLL as an effective instrument to prepare students for today's society. As observed by Larmer et al. (2015), an "ideal graduate" from the K–12 system is someone who is a critical thinker and problem-solver, who is responsible, confident, and capable of working well with others and independently, managing time and work effectively, and communicating appropriately with people of different backgrounds (p. 1). These complex abilities and attributes are part of the valuable skill sets for the 21st century, which can hardly be taught through the traditional lecture-based instruction in the classroom. After entering colleges or universities, students should continue to develop these skill sets and harness the qualities so as to overcome challenges for academic learning and for their future careers. Thomas and Yamazaki (2021) noted that success of teaching in UK higher education, according to the government's Teaching Excellence Framework, is evaluated by how marketable or employable graduates are six months after the completion of their course of study. Language education is thus heavily influenced by the world of business and marketing (p. 3). Related to the 21st century skills is the so-called global competence (Boix Mansilla & Jackson, 2023), which contains capabilities in four dimensions. Namely, learners should be able to "(i) examine local, global, and intercultural issues; (ii) understand and appreciate the perspectives and worldviews of others; (iii) engage in open, appropriate, and effective interactions across cultures; and (iv) take action toward collective well-being and sustainable development" (pp. 23–24). As can be seen, the global competence standard is more comprehensive and concrete as compared to the 21st century skills because it outlines how learners are expected to think, reflect, and act towards the world. In her newly published article, "A New Framework for Mandarin Language Education in Prek–Grade 12 Schools in the United States," Wang (2023) argues that education must prepare students to develop their "global competence" (p. 2).

Fourth, CALL and DH were initiated and driven by computing technology. They have developed separately over the past 70 years. It is high time that language professionals make use of these two for more effective language teaching and learning. The current research is conducted in hopes that language professionals see the potential of the unity of CALL and DH. The projects presented in Chapters 5 and 6 show that CALL and DH can and should be combined as far as language teaching and learning is concerned. As they are complementary to each other, the joint approach of DH and CALL generates potential synergies. In particular, digital pedagogy offers methodological perspectives such as why projects should be conducted and how projects can be designed, planned, and implemented, while CALL provides versatile technologies and materializes the conception that technology can create a networked setting for communication, which assists language learning. Whether or not a project can be completed successfully and achieve desired learning outcomes depends on many separate factors, of which pedagogy and technology are the keys. Technology is a means, and pedagogy is a method to implement the means. Pedagogy guides and determines how technology is integrated into the classroom to meet the curricular goals. In the era of generative AI technologies, exploring and experimenting with the DATEPBLL approach is an effective way to support and advance student learning because it capitalizes on both pedagogy and technology.

7.4 Future Directions of the DATEPBLL Approach

The DATEPBLL approach has a long way to go. I will outline some directions with respect to the following three questions: What are learning outcomes under the DATEPBLL model? What can be done to promote the model to Chinese language teachers as well as teachers in the general? What are basic strategies to apply the DATEPBLL approach in language classrooms? These three questions will be examined one after another.

Regarding the first question about learning outcomes, more studies are needed. The most important research is on the question of whether the learning outcomes under this model are as good as or better than those from traditional non-PBLL classrooms in terms of linguistic competence of learners of Chinese. PBLL aims, through project work, to cultivate learners' holistic capabilities, including critical thinking, social skills, problem-solving skills, collaboration, communication, and skills of using the target language. Since linguistic structures are not the only focus under this type of learning model, it is necessary to evaluate learners' performance in terms of language fluency and language accuracy. To find out learners' language performance, some quantitative research should be conducted. A careful experimental design using empirical methods should be administered in order to achieve objective data on fluency and accuracy, which will provide helpful information about students' learning outcomes in listening, speaking, reading, and writing. Related to this question is what learners' perceptions are about PBLL. This is to examine learners' attitudes or preference towards the PBLL approach as compared with the traditional instructional approach not involving PBLL. Thus, qualitative research, or ethnographic study of learners' perceptions about the PBLL instruction should be conducted. Results of this kind of research will inform us whether and why students like or dislike the PBLL instructional approach. It would be more crucial to study the learners who do not like this learning approach and find out why they do not feel comfortable about it and what needs to be done in order to get them to like it. Likewise, it would also be useful to analyze the learners who like this learning approach and find out why they enjoy it and whether their experience can be applied to others. We may also need to design a measurement to evaluate learners taught through PBLL, trying to find whether there is a correlation between their good language performance and positive attitudes towards this kind of instructional research. Results from these studies will shed light regarding the application of the PBLL approach. Likewise, more research should be conducted with respect to teachers' perceptions about the PBLL approach along the lines of Zhao and Beckett (2014) and Zhao (2015, 2019). Some language teachers are used to the teaching mode, in which they can be in control. Under the DATEPBLL approach, instructors no longer teach by merely transmitting knowledge. Instead, they are expected to design and plan a project and then scaffold and facilitate students to learn through the project. Not all teachers may like to work in this kind of nontraditional instructional environment, in which they are no longer authoritative. Knowing their attitudes towards PBLL and challenges in applying PBLL will be insightful in helping teachers achieve a sound understanding of PBLL.

With respect to the question of promoting the DATEPBLL model, much work needs to be done. The priority is teacher training. Programs must be designed to upgrade teachers for professional development. To that end, first is the training on each component of the DATEPBLL model, or DH, CALL, and PBLL. Of the three, CALL might be the most familiar to language teachers, as this technology has been around for a long time. As the COVID pandemic has made the use of technology more "invisible" and "normalized" (Bax, 2003, 2011), teachers' technology skills as well as their readiness to integrate technology in classrooms may have been improved. However, as technology advances rapidly, in particular, as the impact of ChatGPT and other generative AI text tools are unavoidable to language learners, instructors need to develop literacy about generative AI technologies and learn how to handle the challenges that AI technologies bring to language teaching and learning. Second is the training on DH so that language teachers understand this discipline. In addition to reaching a good understanding of what DH is and what digital humanists do, language instructors should become familiar with the concepts of digital pedagogy. A training focusing on DH and its contributions to language education in terms of digital pedagogy shall help teachers attain a good mastery of fundamentals of the DATEPBLL model. Third is the training on PBL/PBLL. In this regard, language instructors need to learn to grasp the PBL basics, such as the seven fundamentals of PBL and seven project-based teaching practices (Larmer et. al., 2015; Boss & Larmer, 2018). In addition, it is crucial to help teachers understand project conditions, project configuration, and project framework in terms of language learning (Stoller, 2006, 2012; Stoller & Myers, 2019). Furthermore, teachers should be trained to distinguish in-class group work or cooperative learning from PBL, which some language professionals may equate, as noted by Stoller (2002). Like other group work, or cooperative learning, PBLL requires students to work together in or outside class and to collaborate with other team members. However, what makes PBLL unique is a series of characteristics such as orientating learning on both process and product, focusing on the simultaneous learning of content and other skills, emphasizing students' reflections about the project, and sharing the end products in a community. Another crucial factor for PBLL is the teacher's instrumental role of designing and planning before the assignment of the project and providing scaffolding instruction afterwards. More importantly, the teacher must reflect on the project throughout the process in order to achieve great success. The fourth kind of training is on the methodology and procedures of project design, planning, and implementation. Such training should not only cover theoretical underpinnings of PBLL and project framework (Larmer et. al., 2015; Boss & Larmer, 2018; Stoller, 2006, 2012; Stoller & Myers, 2019) but also practical steps or cycles during the entire process (Stoller & Myers, 2019). It is important for teachers to recognize that PBLL is not elaborate TBLT. PBLL and TBLT both focus on developing learners' higher-order critical and problem-solving skills instead of rote learning. However, PBLL has some traits that TBLT lacks. For example, PBLL has wider, larger, and cross-disciplinary objectives because it aims to produce L2 learners' holistic abilities with multiple skill sets while developing their linguistic and cultural competence. In addition, project work in PBLL usually needs longer time to complete, engaging learners' diverse range of skills, most of which are beyond language learning. There are some strategies with respect to how long a project should last. For example, as observed by Thomas and Yamazaki (2021), longer project durations may result in lower levels of learning anxiety and stress but higher-level engagement and creativity, if students are collaborative with peers. Gaining a sound understanding of PBLL vs. other group work, and PBLL vs. TBLT is very important.

Second, related to training is the organization of conferences, workshops, or roundtables to provide platforms for teachers to learn and improve in view of the application of DATEPBLL approach. Designing and planning an effective project is hard but implementing it in class is even more challenging. Thus, holding conferences or workshops for teachers to exchange ideas would be helpful because practitioners can discuss and address common and practical issues together. Inviting specialists to talk or conduct workshops or having experienced teachers showcase their good practices would be informative and inspiring for those who would like to try the new approach. It would also be very helpful if there will be an opportunity for those who are new to the approach to observe an experienced teacher's PBLL classroom so that they could learn by seeing how the teacher's scaffolding instruction is provided in class and how it is received by students, who are engaged to learn.

Third, to help teachers achieve skills in teaching Chinese language using the DATEPBLL approach, it would be beneficial to establish a website dedicated to this model. Such a website will serve as a resource center, which may contain teachers' reflections about teaching with the DATEPBLL approach or notes on project design, planning, and implementation, aligned with Stoller's (Stoller, 2006, 2012; Stoller & Myers, 2019) project framework. Having teachers who have experimented with the application of PBLL in their Chinese classrooms write down their own stories as to what works and what does not will be helpful to other new teachers because knowing others' failures as well as their successes is an effective way to learn. At least, the failures could be avoided. Reflections or notes like these, which document the journey of doing PBLL along with experience, strategies, advice, or even failures, would be valuable to others who want to try the PBLL teaching approach. These reflections along with the information such as conferences and workshops should be posted on the website, which will serve language educators interested in PBLL.

As for the third question about how to integrate the DATEPBLL into Chinese classrooms, there are some practical suggestions to consider. First, Chinese language teachers need to be open-minded towards the PBLL approach, studying it and endeavoring to apply what has been learned into practice. Second, trying a mini project to get some experience is a good starting point. If that succeeds, then try a second mini project. If not, reflect on the process and find out the reasons why it failed. With more experience accumulated gradually, start to integrate a large mid-term or term-end project. Any project, mini or large, requires the instructor's efforts in designing, planning, scaffolding, and reflecting. While learners are the ones to undertake projects, the quality of their end products and learning outcomes largely depends on the teacher's instruction and implementation, which involves a wide range of skills and numerous practices. Third, think about some strategies such as increasing the weight of the percentage of the project in terms of the total grade. Boosting the weight of the percentage in relation to the total course grade sends a clear message to learners that a diligent attitude and significant efforts towards project work are anticipated. When students are committed to working hard on an assigned project, their chances of generating quality products increases. Furthermore, with more weight allocated to the project in terms of the grade percentage, it enables students to invest more time and energy in the assignments. Another suggestion to increase the importance of project work is to replace a mid-term or a final exam with a project. Learning effects might be more desirable when students are given more freedom to learn and to create while being guided and scaffolded. Finally, it is worthwhile repeating a successful project with new cohorts at the same or different level of language proficiency. The repeated practice with various groups may benefit students since it has been tested, and the instructor has acquired more valuable lessons through reflections. For the students who have experienced doing a similar project before, they will feel more confident about the learning experience, and their skills will be further strengthened.

How should complex procedures of a project be sequenced so that students can handle and enjoy learning by doing rather than being stressed? How should the time be managed from the project assignment to completion? How should instructors motivate and assist the students who have difficulty or struggles with learning through a project? All these are real challenges in the application of the DATEPBLL approach. Can generative AI technologies help in this regard? ChatGPT is disrupting the world of technology in unprecedented ways. What will it do with the DATEPBLL model? What challenges will Chinese teachers face if ChatGPT or other generative AI tools are applied to the Chinese classroom to promote the DATEPBLL approach? For these questions, I do not have answers. However, as long as PBLL is pursued, conforming to DH pedagogy (Davis et al., 2020), and sticking to CALL technology, to support language learning, Chinese language instructors will be on the pathway to success with regard to the journey towards DATEPBLL.

References

Anderson, M. (2023). *'AI Pause' Open letter stokes fear and controversy: IEEE signatories say they worry about ultrasmart, amoral systems without guidance.* https://spectrum.ieee.org/ai-pause-letter-stokes-fear

Anft, M. (2023). AI on campus. *The Chronicle.* https://connect.chronicle.com/rs/931-EKA-218/images/TrendsSnapshot_CampusAI_Cisco.pdf

Bax, S. (2003). Call-past, present, and future. *System: An International Journal of Educational Technology and Applied Linguistics, 31*(1), 13–28. https://doi.org/10.1016/s0346-251x(02)00071-4

Bax, S. (2011). Normalisation revisited: The effective use of technology in language education. *International Journal of Computer Assisted Language Learning and Teaching, 1*(2), 1–15. https://doi.org/10.4018/ijcallt.2011040101

Beckett, G. H. (1999). *Project-based instruction in a Canadian secondary school's ESL classes: Goals and evaluations* [Unpublished Doctoral Dissertation]. University of British Columbia. https://open.library.ubc.ca/soa/cIRcle/collections/ubctheses/831/items/1.0078180

Beckett, G. H., Slater, T., & Mohan, B. A. (2019). Philosophical foundation, theoretical approaches and gaps in the literature. In G. H. Beckett & T. Slater (Eds.), *Global perspectives on project-based language learning, teaching and assessment: Key approaches, technology tools and frameworks* (pp. 3–22). Routledge. https://doi.org/10.4324/9780429435096-1

Boix Mansilla, V., & Jackson, A. W. (2022). Educating for global competence: Preparing our students to engage the world. ASCD. https://eric.ed.gov/?id=ED624535

Boss, S., & Larmer, J. (2018). *Project based teaching: How to create rigorous and engaging learning experiences.* ASCD.

Cai, W. (2023). ChatGPT 环境下的汉语学习与教学 [Learning and teaching Chinese in the ChatGPT context]. 语言教学与研究 [*Language Teaching and Research*], *222*(4), 13–23.

Chandrasekar, S. (2023). *One year of ChatGPT: A boon or burden in the generative AI era?* www.azoai.com/article/One-Year-of-ChatGPT-A-Boon-or-Burden-in-the-Generative-AI-Era.aspx

The Chronicle of Higher Education (TCHE, 2023). *Perspectives on generative AI college leaders assess the promise and the threat of a game-changing tool.* PerspectivesGenerativeAI_ResearchBrief.pdf (chronicle.com)

Chen, D. (2023, May). *ChatGPT: A potential assistant for teaching Chinese as a second language.* The 21st New York International Conference on Teaching Chinese: A New Chapter in Teaching Chinese, New York, NY.

Cro, M. A. (2020). *Integrating the digital humanities into the second language classroom: A Practical Guide.* Georgetown University Press. https://doi.org/10.2307/j.ctv19vbgjv

Da, J. (2023, February). *From assistant to participant: An initial exploration of the paradigm shift in using computers for second language learning and instruction.* A talk given at International Chinese Language Education Forum—Opportunities and Challenges Fueled by ChatGPT, Beijing, China. Zoom.

Davis, R. F., Gold, M. K., & Harris, K. D. (2020). Curating digital pedagogy in the humanities. In R. F. Davis, M. K. Gold, K. D. Harris, & J. Sayers (Eds.), *Digital pedagogy in the humanities: Concepts, models, and experiments.* Modern Language Association. https://digitalpedagogy.hcommons.org/introduction/

Dewey, J. (1916). *Democracy and education: An introduction to the philosophy of education.* The Macmillan Company.

Dewey, J., & Dewey, E. (1915). *Schools of tomorrow*. Dutton. www.gutenberg.org/ebooks/48906

Gleason, J., & Link, S. (2019). Using the knowledge framework and genre pedagogy for technology-enhanced form-function project-based language learning. In G. H. Beckett & T. Slater (Eds.), *Global perspectives on project-based language learning, teaching and assessment: Key approaches, technology tools and frameworks* (pp. 204–223). Routledge. https://doi.org/10.4324/9780429435096-1

Halliday, M. A. K. (1975). *Learning how to mean: Explorations in the development of language*. Hodder Arnold.

Hu, K. (2023). *ChatGPT sets record for fastest-growing user base—analyst note*. www.reuters.com/technology/chatgpt-sets-record-fastest-growing-user-base-analyst-note-2023-02-01/

Larmer, J., Mergendoller, J., & Boss, S. (2015). *Setting the standard for project based learning: A proven approach to rigorous classroom instruction*. ASCD.

Lenz, B. (2018). Foreword. In S. Boss & J. Larmer (Eds.), *Project based teaching: How to create rigorous and engaging learning experiences* (pp. xi–xvii). ASCD.

Li, J., Ren, X., Jiang, X., & Chen, C. H. (2023). Exploring the use of ChatGPT in Chinese language classrooms. *International Journal of Chinese Language Teaching*, *4*(3). https://doi.org/10.46451/ijclt.20230303

Long, M. H. (1983). Native speaker/non-native speaker conversation and the negotiation of comprehensible input. *Applied Linguistics*, *4*(2), 126–141.

Long, M. H. (1996). The role of the linguistic environment in second language acquisition. In W. Ritchie & T. Bhatia (Eds.), *Handbook of second language acquisition* (pp. 413–468). Academic Press.

Marr, B. (2023). *The best examples of what you can do with ChatGPT*. www.forbes.com/sites/bernardmarr/2023/03/01/the-best-examples-of-what-you-can-do-with-chatgpt/?sh=74e649ffdf11

Mikulec, E., & Miller, P. C. (2011). Using project-based instruction to meet foreign language standards. *The Clearing House: A Journal of Educational Strategies*, *84*(3), 81–86. https://doi.org/10.1080/00098655.2010.516779

Miller, P. C. (2006). Integrating second language standards into project-based instruction. In G. H. Beckett & P. C. Miller (Eds.), *Project-based second and foreign language education: Past, present, and future* (pp. 225–240). Information Age.

Modern Language Association—Conference on College Composition and Communication (MLA- CCCC) Joint Task Force on Writing and AI. (2023). *MLA-CCCC joint task force on writing and AI working paper: Overview of the issues, statement of principles, and recommendations*. https://hcommons.org/app/uploads/sites/1003160/2023/07/MLA-CCCC-Joint-Task-Force-on-Writing-and-AI-Working-Paper-1.pdf

Mohan, B. A. (1986). *Language and content*. Addison-Wesley.

Nature (2023, December 13). Nature's 10: Ten people (and one non-human) who helped shape science in 2023. *Nature*. www.nature.com/immersive/d41586-023-03919-1/index.html

OpenAI. (2022). *Introducing ChatGPT*. https://openai.com/blog/chatgpt

OpenAI. (2023). *Ask me anything*. https://openai.com/chatgpt

Open Letter (2023). *Pause giant AI experiment*. https://futureoflife.org/open-letter/pause-giant-ai-experiments/

PCWorld. (2023). *10 ChatGPT alternatives & competitors (free and paid): ChatGPT might be the best-known AI, but it's not the only one out there*. https://www.pcworld.com/article/2086819/chatgpt-alternatives.html

Pitman, T., & Taylor, C. (2017). Where's the ML in DH? And where's the DH in ML? The relationship between modern languages and digital humanities, and an argument for a critical DHML. *Digital Humanities Quarterly*, *11*(1). https://dhq-static.digitalhumanities.org/pdf/000287.pdf

Schieffelin, B. B., & Ochs, E. (Eds.). (1986). *Language socialization across cultures*. Cambridge University Press. https://doi.org/10.1017/cbo9780511620898

Schmidt, R. (1990). The role of consciousness in second language learning. *Applied Linguistics*, *11*(2), 129–158. https://doi.org/10.1093/applin/11.2.129

Schmidt, R. (2001). Attention. In P. Robinson (Ed.), *Cognition and second language instruction* (pp. 3–32). Cambridge University Press. https://doi.org/10.1017/cbo9781139524780.003

Stoller, F. L. (2002). Project work: A means to promote language and content. In J. C. Richards & W. A. Renandya (Eds.), *Methodology in language teaching: An anthology of current practice* (pp. 107–119). Cambridge University Press.

Stoller, F. L. (2006). Establishing a theoretical foundation for project-based learning in second and foreign language contexts. In G. H. Beckett & P. C. Miller (Eds.), *Project-based second and foreign language education: Past, present, and future* (pp. 19–40). Information Age Publishing.

Stoller, F. L. (2012). Project-based learning: A viable option for second and foreign language classrooms. In *Perfect score: methodologies, technologies, & communities of practice* (pp. 37–47). Proceedings of the 20th Annual KOTESOL International Conference, Seoul, October 20–21, 2012.

Stoller, F. L., & Myers, C. C. (2019). A five-stage framework to guide language teachers. In A. Gras-Velázquez. (Ed.), *Project-based learning in second language acquisition: Building communities of practice in higher education* (pp. 24–47). Routledge. https://doi.org/10.4324/9780429457432-3

Thomas, M. (2021). Epilogue: Critical project-based learning and moving forwards in the post-pandemic university. In M. Thomas & K. Yamazaki, K. (Eds.), *Project-based language learning and CALL: From virtual exchange to social justice* (pp. 263–273). Equinox Publishing Limited. https://api.equinoxpub.com/books/3034

Thomas, M., & Yamazaki, K. (2021). Introduction: Projects, pandemics and the re-positioning of digital language learning. In M. Thomas & K. Yamazaki (Eds.), *Project- based language learning and CALL: From virtual exchange to social justice* (pp. 1–18). Equinox Publishing Limited. https://api.equinoxpub.com/books/3034

Thomas, M., & Yamazaki, K. (Eds.). (2021). *Project-based language learning and CALL: From virtual exchange to social justice*. Equinox Publishing Limited. https://api.equinoxpub.com/books/3034

Travis, J., & DeSpain, J. (2018). *Teaching with digital humanities: Tools and methods for nineteenth-century American literature*. University of Illinois Press.

Vista Higher Learning. (2023, October). Vista higher learning professional development webinars on ChatGPT and AI in the world language classroom: Friend or foe?

Vogels, E. (2023). *A majority of Americans have heard of ChatGPT, but few have tried it themselves*. https://www.pewresearch.org/short-reads/2023/05/24/a-majority-of-americans-have-heard-of-chatgpt-but-few-have-tried-it-themselves/

Vygotsky, L. S. (1978). Interaction between learning and development. In M. Lopez-Morillas (Trans.) & M. Cole, V. John-Steiner, S. Scribner, & E. Souberman (Eds.), *Mind in society: The development of higher psychological processes* (pp. 79–91). Harvard University Press.

Wang, S. (2023). *A new framework for Mandarin language education in preK-grade 12 schools in the United States*. https://asiasociety.org/education/new-framework-mandarin-language-education-prek-grade-12-schools-united-states

Zamora, Z. (2023, October). *ChatGPT and AI use in the world language classroom*. Talk given at the vista higher learning professional development webinars on ChatGPT and AI in the world language classroom: Friend or foe? https://go.vistahigherlearning.com/rs/156-GRO-136/images/ai-webinar-2023.pdf

Zhao, J. (2015). Project-based instruction in teaching Chinese as a foreign language. In T. Hansson (Ed.), *Contemporary approaches to activity theory: Interdisciplinary perspectives on human behavior* (pp. 108–127). IGI Global.

Zhao, J. (2019). Bridging cross-cultural teaching practices with technology-enriched PBLL in Chinese as a foreign language education. In G. H. Beckett & T. Slater (Eds.), *Global perspectives on project-based language learning, teaching, and assessment: Key approaches, technology tools, and frameworks* (pp. 146–163). Routledge.

Zhao, J., & Beckett, G. H. (2014). Project-based Chinese as a foreign language instruction-A teacher research approach. *Journal of the Chinese Language Teachers Association, 49*(2), 45–73.

Zhao, Y. (2020). COVID-19 as a catalyst for educational change. *Prospects, 49*(1–2), 29–33. https://link.springer.com/article/10.1007/s11125-020-09477-y

Author Index

Alan, B. 75, 93–94, 133
Aljaafreh, A. 8
Ally, M. 6–7
Armstrong, T. 9

Bauerlein, M. 56
Bax, S. 27–29, 34, 161
Bećirović, S. 65
Beckett, G. H. 74–77, 79, 84–86, 94, 115, 171–172, 176
Bellanca, J. 83
Berlińska-Kopeć, M. 78, 83, 115
Blewett, C. 64–65
Boss, S. 72, 75, 174
Brandt, R. 83
Brumfit, C. 73
Burdick, A. 4, 46–47, 50, 115
Busa, R. 4, 5, 43–44, 50, 52

Cai, W. 168, 170
Chapelle, C. A. 3, 21–22, 35–36
Chen, D. 32, 120
Cheng, C. 24
Chik, A. 99
Chism, R. 133
Chomsky, N. 7
Cook, G. 99
Cro, M. A. 5, 85, 87, 172
Croxall, B. 62

Da, J. 3, 26, 172
Davies, G. 21, 28
Davis, R. F. 4, 48, 62–63, 65–66
DeFrancis, J. 100
DeSpain, J. 49–50, 66
Dewey, J. 71, 75, 171
Du, X. 79–80, 115
Ducate, L. 3, 21

Eyring, J. L. 76–77

Faidley, E. 133
Flinn, A. 44, 52
Fried-Booth, D. L 73

Gao, Y. 3, 26
Gardner, H. 9
Gass, S. 8, 35
Gibbs, F. 47
Gleason, J. 83, 86, 174
Glisan, E. W. 30
Godwin-Jones, R. 30, 34, 36, 98, 101
Gold, M. K. 57–58, 65
González-Lloret, M. 3, 11, 21
Gornall, A. 57
Grant, S. 78
Gras-Velázquez, A. 78
Greenier, V. T. 79, 133
Grusin, R. 65

Halliday, M. A. K. 75, 171
Harris, K. D. 62
Hasan, M. M. 109
Healey, D. 22, 27–30
Hedge, T. 73
Hegedus, M. 141–143
Hill, H. V. 49, 52–53
Hockey, S. M. 48, 51, 59
Holbah, W. A. 10
Hoon, T. B. 109
Hsieh, H. 25
Hubbard, P. 2, 21, 32, 36

Ke, C. 25
Kilpatrick, W. 71
Kirkebæk, M. J. 79
Kirschenbaum, M. G. 49, 55, 65
Klein, J. 109
Klein, L. F. 58, 65
Koh, A. 62

Krashen, S. 8, 73, 109
Kusyk, M. 36

Lado, R. 7
Lam, R. 133
Lan, Y. J. 36
Lantolf, J. P. 8
Larmer, J. 72, 75, 174
Laverick, E. K. 77
Lee, C.-J. 149–150, 155, 162
Lee, J. L. 98
Lenz, B. 83, 173
Levy, M. 1, 2, 21–22, 36
Li, J. 170
Link, S. 83, 86, 174
Liu, A. 65
Liu, S. 3, 26
Lomicka, L. 109
Long, M. 8, 76, 171
Lord, G. 109

McCarty, W. 47, 50, 55
McTighe, J. 33
Meng, L. 133, 141–142
Mikulec, E. 174
Miller, P. C. 60, 77, 83, 174
Mohan, B. A. 74
Moretti, F. 44, 51
Myers, C. C. 93, 96, 133, 174

Navarre, A. 26

Ortega, L. 11
Oskoz, A. 1, 5, 21, 29, 64, 66, 85, 87, 107
Otto, S. E. 21
Oxford, R. 6, 9, 35

Phillips, B. 108, 116
Pitman, T. 5, 172
Pitura, J. 78, 83, 115
Potter, L. E. 107, 115
Prensky, M. 98, 129

Qin, J. 143–144

Ramsay, S. 46, 51
Reinders, H. 33, 36
Reinhardt, J. 1, 21, 29, 97
Richards, J. 9
Rockwell, G. 59
Rodgers, T. 9

Salaberry, M. R. 34–35
Sanders, R. 21–22
Schreibman, S. 3
Schwartz, B. D. 7

Sevensson, P. 44
Shei, C. 25
Sheppard, K. 94
Shi, L. 7, 26, 29
Shrum, J. L. 30
Siemens, G. 7
Sinclair, S. 59
Slater, T. 77, 86, 94
Stickler, U. 7, 26, 29
Stoller, F. 75, 80, 93–96, 118, 133, 144, 147, 154, 159, 161, 174, 176–177
Stommel, J. 63, 66
Sula, C. A. 49, 52–53, 55, 57
Sundqvist, P. 98
Svensson, P. 46
Swain, M. 8, 73, 109
Sykes, J. M. 97–98
Sylvén, L. K. 98

Tavares, J. F. 107, 115
Taylor, C. 5, 173
Terras, M. 46–47, 49, 55, 62
Thomas, M. 10, 27, 29, 33, 37, 77–78, 86–87, 109, 172, 174, 177
Travis, J. 49–50, 66
Tseng, M. 3, 26
Tseng, S.-S. 86

Unsworth, J. 45–46

Vanhoutte, E. 45, 47, 52–53
Vygotsky, L. S. 8, 75

Wang, F. 19, 24
Wang, S. 78
Wang, S. C. 174
Warschauer, M. 22, 27–30
Whitton, N. 103
Wiggins, G. 33
Willis, J. 109
Wisbey, R. A. 52–53
World-Class Instruction, Design, and Assessment Consortium (WIDA) 83

Xie, T. 25–26, 29
Xu, D. B. 24, 26, 29
Xu, P. 156, 157, 162

Yamazaki, K. 78–79, 86–87, 172, 174, 177
Yao, T. C. 25–26
Yeh, H.-C. 86

Zhang, Z. 3, 11, 25–26, 31–34
Zhao, J. 79, 115, 176
Zhou, K. 144–145, 147, 149, 162

Subject Index

Note: Page numbers in *italics* indicate a figure and page numbers in **bold** indicate a table on the corresponding page.

3 digital literacy skills 82
4Cs 82
5Cs 83
5-cycle framework 133; *see also* PBL Five-Stage Framework
5 life skills 82
21st century skills 12, 71, 81–84, 87, 108, 116–117, 161, 173–174
2005 Humanities Computing Conference 49

accomplishments of DH 58; *see also* DH's contributions
Alliance of Digital Humanities Organization (ADHO) 53–54
American Council on the Teaching of Foreign Languages (ACTFL) 81, 117, 141
analytical learners 9
Asian Americans and Pacific Islanders (AAPI) 141, 144, 161
Association for Computers and the Humanities (ACH) 53–54
Association for Literary and Linguistic Computing (ALLC) 53–54
audio-lingualism 10, 21, 24
average words per sentence 59–60, **61**

Baidu 166
BARD 166
behavioristic 27
behaviorist theory 6
benefits of CALL 20, 29–30
benefits of LLMs for students **169**
benefits of LLMs for teachers **169**
Big Tent Digital Humanities 46

Bing Chart 166
Blackboard 23, **24**, 29, 105, 110–113, 161
Buck Institute for Education (BIE) 71
building 2, 4, 10, 12, 30, 46, 51, 62, 74, 83–84, 87, 100–102, 105, 109, 111, 120–122, **125**, 128, 130, 132, 150, 153–155, 161, 172
Busa, R. 4, 5, 43–44, 50, 52
Busa project 50; *see also* Busa, R.

CALL development 20–24, 26–28, 34
calligraphy project 144, 149, 161
Canvas 23, 156, 161
CCSS and WIDA Standards for Grade 3 83
Center for New Media and History 55
characteristics of PBL 171
ChatGPT 165–168, 170–172, 176, 178; ChatGPT-empowered *Kahoot!* 172; ChatGPT-enabled *Duolingo* app 172
Chinese CALL 20, 24–26, 29, 32
Chinese calligraphy 141, 144, 145, 147, 162
Chinese Computerized Adaptive Listening Comprehension Test 25
Chinese Language Association of Secondary-Elementary Schools (CLASS) 142
Chinese Language Teachers Association (CLTA) 142
Chinese Language Teachers Association of Greater New York (CLTA-GNY) 142–143
Chinese Writing Master 25
The Chronicle of Higher Education (TCHE) 167, 170–171, 173
Clavis Sinica 25

186 Subject Index

Click to Look Inside! 51
cognitivist 6–8
cognitivist theory 6
collaboration 4, 11, 27, 33, 49–50, 55–56, 63, 71, 74, 76–77, 80–82, 92, 117, 148, 155–156, 160, 165, 171, 175
committee 117
Common Core State Standards (CCSS) 81, 83
Common European Framework of Reference (CEFR) 82
communication 2–3, 7, 10, 23, 27–28, 30, 32, 35, 45–46, 49, 54, 56, 71, 74–76, 78–82, 93, 110, 115–117, 144, 148, 149, 156, 161, 166, 173–175
Communicative CALL 27–29
communicative competence 10
Communicative Language Teaching (CLT) approach 10, 11, 22, 24, **24**, 27–28, 97
communicatively competent language learners 10
Competency-Based Language Teaching (CBLT) 11
comprehensible input hypothesis 8, 73
Computer-Adaptive Test for Reading Chinese 25
Computer-Assisted Language Instruction Consortium (CALICO) 21–22
Computer-Assisted Language Learning (CALL) 1–3, 5–7, 10–14, 20–37, 52, 60, 66, 71, 78, 84–85, 86–87, 165, 171–176
The Computer in Literary and Linguistic Research 53
computer mediated communication (CMC) 23, 27, 33, 35–36, 93
computer and mobile-assisted language learning (C/MALL) 10
Computers and the Humanities (*CHum*) 49, 53
Computers in Humanistic Research: Readings and Perspectives 53
computing humanities 44–45, 54
concordance / concordancing 22, 25, 43–44, 46, 48, 50–52
concrete-sequential learners 9
Conference on College Composition and Communication (CCCC) 166–168, 170
connectivism theory 6
constructivism 6, 7, 35–36
constructivist / constructivist theory 6–7, 27, 75, 171
Content and Language Integrated Learning (CLIL) 11, 24

content and performance standards for foreign language education 82
Content-Based Instruction (CBI) 11, 24, 74
cooperative learning 6, 11, 176
Core Curriculum for Modern Languages 82
Council for Accreditation of Educator Preparation State Partnerships and Content Areas 117
Council of Europe 82
COVID-19 pandemic 23, 29, 37, 113, 132, 156, 161–162, 166, 170, 172, 176
creativity 80–82, 98, 116, 177
Critical DHML 5, 173
critical thinking 8, 27, 33, 57, 74–75, 77, 81–82, 120, 131, 149, **169**, 175

data mining 44, 47–48, 51
DATEPBLL / DATEPBLL practices 6, 13–14, 71, 85, 86, 87, 92, 107–108, 131, 144, 162, 165–166, 170–173, 175, 176–179
Debates in the Digital Humanities 57
Defining Digital Humanities: A Reader 3, 47
Department of Asian Studies 19
Department of East Asian Languages and Civilizations 149
Department of East Asian Languages and Literatures 156
Department of Global Languages 144
developing curriculum 56
Dewey's education philosophy 75, 171
DH-Augmented Technology-Enhanced Project-Based Language Learning (PBLL) approach 70, 85–87, *86*, 144, 174
DH minor program 57
DH pedagogy 13, 50, 87, 110, 173, 179; *see also* digital pedagogy
DH programs 55, 57
DH's contributions 58
digital humanists 45, 48, 58–59, 65, 176
Digital Humanities (DH) 1, 3–6, 12–14, 37, 44–60, **61**, 62–66, 71, 84–85, 87, 92, 110, 114, 144, 165, 171–176, 179
Digital Humanities–Augmented Technology-Enhanced Project-Based Language Learning (DATEPBLL) approach 6, 92, 165
The Digital Humanities Manifesto 2.0 46, 48
Digital Humanities Quarterly (*DHQ*) 54
digital natives 9, 101, 129

Subject Index 187

digital pedagogy 1, 4–5, 58, 60, 62–66, 84–85, 87, 171–172, 175–176; *see also* DH pedagogy
Digital pedagogy in the humanities 62–63
Digital Scholarship in the Humanities (DSH) 54
distant reading 43–44, 48, 50–51, 59–60
Duolingo 166, 172

Electronic Numerical Integrator and Computer (ENIAC) 19
English as a foreign language (EFL) 73, 78, 80, 113
e-portfolio project 117, 119, 122, 128–129, 132
Ernie 166
eStroke 25
eTandem English-Chinese exchange 93
European Association of Computer Assisted Language Learning (EUROCALL) 22
European Association for Digital Humanities (EADH) 53
Exemplary Projects in K-12 Settings 141
Exemplary Projects in University Contexts 144
eXtensible Markup Language (XML) 58–59

Facebook 9
FaceTime 9, 112, 131, **131**
feeling-oriented learners 9
five Cs 81; *see also* 5Cs
future directions of the DATEPBLL approach 175

gaming project 97, 100, 104, 107–108, 131
Generation Z 9
generative artificial intelligence (AI) 13, 165
Geographic Information System (GIS) 46
global competence 174
Google 23, 64, 166–167
Google Classroom 23, 161
Google Ngram Viewer 51
Google Site 150, 161
Google Translate 9
grading rubric **152**
grammar-translation 10, 21
Gutter, Pinchas 50

Halliday's systemic functional language view 75, 171
holistic capabilities 176

Hot Potatoes 23, **24**, 32
humanities computing, 4, 5, 44–49, 52–56, 59, 62
Hybrid Pedagogy: The Journal of Critical Digital Pedagogy 62–63

implications of the DATEPBLL approach 13, 170
Independent Activity Period (IAP) class 144–145
The Index of Digital Humanities Conferences 53
Index Thomisticus 4, 43, 50
individual differences 6, 9, 35
individual differences theory 6, 35
information and communication technology (ICT) skills 82
information display cycle **97**, 106, 113, 123, 133
information gathering cycle **97**, 105, 111–112, 121–122, 133
information processing cycle **97**, 105, 112, 122–123, 133
innatist 7
Instagram 9
Institutionalizing DH Education 54
Integrated CALL 25, 28–29
Integrated Chinese Level 1 Part 1 92, 104, 132
Integrative CALL 27–29
interaction hypothesis 8, 76, 171
International Conference and Workshops on Technology and Chinese Language Teaching (TCLT) 26
intuitive learners 9
ISO (International Organization for Standardization) standards 58

The Journal of Interactive Technology and Pedagogy (JITP) 54, 62
Journal of Technology and Chinese Language Teaching (JTCLT) 26
Juegos Comunicativos 22

Kahoot! 23, 107, 132, 172

large language models (LLMs) 165–168, **169**
learners' perceptions about PBLL 175
learning through doing 71
Linkit 25, 26
Literary and Linguistic Computing (LLC) 49, 53–54
Literary and Linguistic Computing Centre (LLCC) 52–53

LLaMA 166
logical problem 7
Long's interaction hypothesis 76, 171

Maryland Institute for Technology in the Humanities 55
Massachusetts Institute of Technology (MIT) 22, 144–145, 148, 162
matching game 100–103, 103, 104–106, 107, 131, **131**, 132
Matching Game Template 102
Meta 166
Microsoft 166
Middle States Commission on Higher Education 129
Miles, Josephine 43, 44, 49
millennials 9
Modern Language Association (MLA) 62–63, 166
Modern Language Association–Conference on College Composition and Communication (MLA-CCCC) 165–168, 170
Moodle 7, 29
multiple intelligences 9
Music and Culture Project 156, 159, 161–162

National Council for Accreditation of Teacher Education 118
nature 2, 9, 12, 25, 33, 81, 84, 94–95, 101, 129, 162, 170–171, 173
negotiation for meaning 8, 76
no tent approach 46
Novice-to-Expert Paradigm 6

Omeka 59
OpenAI 165, 167
Open CALL 28

Partnership for 21st Century Learning 82
PBL curriculum 73
PBL Five-Stage Framework **97**
PhD in DH 56
podcast project 108, 111
post-COVID in-person class 156
Poughkeepsie Principles 58
preparation cycle **97**, 104, 110, 121–122
preservice teachers 13, 92, 117–124, **125**, **126**, 127, **127**, 128–131, **131**, 132–133, 142
primary pillars 75, 171
Program Logic for Automated Teaching Operation (PLATO) 20–21, 24, **24**, 25, 29

program standards for the preparation of foreign language teachers 117
PROJECT 142, **142**
Project-Based Instruction (PBI) 76–77, 79, 83
Project-Based Language Learning (PBLL) 1, 72, 75, 77, 83, 85– 87, 92, 141
Project-based language learning and CALL: From virtual exchange to social justice 78
Project-based language learning with technology: Learner collaboration in an EFL classroom in Japan 77
Project-Based Learning (PBL) 12, 24, 48, 71–74, 76–77, 79–80, 83–86, 92–94, 96, **97**, 115, 118, 141–142, **142**, 144, 147, 155, 160, 165, 171, 174, 176
Project-based learning in second language acquisition: Building communities of practice in higher education 77–78
Project-based second and foreign language education: Past, present, and future 77
project framework 93, 96, 133, 165, 176–177; *see also* PBL Five-Stage Framework
project method 80

Quizlet 23, 107, 132, 143

readability index 59–60, **61**
reflections cycle 106, 124
A la rencontre de Philippe 22
Restricted CALL 28

scaffolding instruction 105, 117, 122, 132, 143, 159, 162, 165, 177
Schieffelin and Ochs' theory of language socialization 75, 171
Schmidt's noticing hypothesis 76, 171
second language acquisition (SLA) 1, 6–7, 27, 35–37, 76, 84, 109, 121, 170
Second Life 23, **24**
Seton Hall University 19, 29
seven fundamentals of PBL 176
six key concepts 63
Skype 7, 9, 24, **24**, 64, 93, 112, 131, **131**
Skype-based Computer-Mediated Communication (CMC) project 93
Social CALL 27, 29, 33
sociocultural 7–8, 23, 36, 75–76, 171
Spion 22
Standard 5 (TESOL, 2008) 83

Subject Index   189

Standard Generalized Markup Language (SGML) 58–59
Standards for Foreign Language Learning and 21st Century Skills 71, 81
Structural CALL 27, 29
Survival Guide for Studying Abroad at Penn 151–152

Task-Based Language Teaching (TBLT) 11, 22, 24, **24**, 30, 74, 79, 177
teaching Chinese as a foreign language (TCFL) 1, 3, 12–14, 24, 29, 34, 77, 79–80, 100, 104, 122, 141, 165, 168, 171–172
Teams 9, 23, 131, **131**
technology-enabled PBLL 87
technology-mediated PBLL 144
telecollaboration 7, 36, 64, 78
ten conditions for effective project-based learning 93
TESOL Tech Goal 3 83
text analysis 1, 4, 46, 48, 50–51, 58–60, 65
Text Encoding Initiative (TEI) 52, 58–59
thinking-oriented learners 9
Thomas Aquinas' texts 4, 43–44
Time-Shared Interactive Computer Controlled Information Television (TICCIT) 20–21, **24**
Twitter 9, 55

Unity 102, 104–105, 131, **131**
University of Pennsylvania 20, 149–150, 162

video production 6, 92, 145–147, 161–162
visualization 46, 48, 51, 58–60
vocabulary density 59–60, **61**
VoiceThread 23
Voyant Tools 58–60, **61**
Vygotskian social constructivist learning theories 171

Website Development Project 149, 162
WeChat 7
Weebly 133, 150, 161
Wenlin 25
Wix 150, 161
WordCruncher 49
WordPress 118, 122, 129–131, **131**
world-readiness standards 81, 174

xml encoding 46

Yale University 53, 156, 162
YouTube 9, 23, **24**, 64

zone of proximal development (ZPD) 8
Zoom 9, 23
Zotero 59

For Product Safety Concerns and Information please contact our EU representative GPSR@taylorandfrancis.com
Taylor & Francis Verlag GmbH, Kaufingerstraße 24, 80331 München, Germany

www.ingramcontent.com/pod-product-compliance
Lightning Source LLC
Chambersburg PA
CBHW061348300426
44116CB00011B/2039